BEING HUMANS

Good news for the next 100 years on Planet Earth

A channeled guide to humanity and its growing place in the Universe

Aralamb & Melissa Gates-Perry

Paperback ISBN: 978-1-66785-792-3
eBook ISBN: 978-1-66785-793-0

This book is dedicated first to my sister Stephanie. She and I rode the lightening together. We always will. I adore her for agreeing to this lifetime with me. I also dedicate this book to my husband Isaac Charles Perry and my son Hunter Michael Carney. Without the support of these two amazing souls, I would be no more than a rudderless ship in the vast universe. I love you all three, so much.

"Each and every beautiful dream, belief, emotion, joy, and thrilling visionary idea that you hoped to be true when you were a child, and were still *OF* The Creation and not yet fully integrated into Earth's society and The Forgetting is, was, and will always be true."

Aralamb

"There are only two kinds of people in the end: those who say to God, 'Thy will be done,' and those to whom God says, in the end, "Thy will be done."

C.S. Lewis
1945

CONTENTS

PREFACE

Melissa

PREFACE

If I have learned anything in my life thus far, it is that there are truly no complete monsters, nor are there complete victims. In every situation, when looked upon at a deep level, the monstrous perpetrator would have been the victim to someone or something before becoming the monster, and the victim would have knowingly or unknowingly been the perpetrator at some time in this lifetime or another. I have been both monster and victim, I am sure, in someone else's story, knowingly or unwittingly. The only action, I think, that any of us can take is to accept this and grow from that knowledge. Knowing that each of us can and will be on both sides of this coin in our lifetimes leaves us only forgiveness of ourselves and others to begin to heal. Try to avoid being the monster or the victim.

This book is filled with stories from Aralamb, and stories from my own life. I want to be clear that although there are some obvious "baddies" within my life stories, I do not hold any of them as monsters. I know through Aralamb that they were simply other souls who came in to struggle with me in some very, very difficult situations. I prefer to think of us all as souls within creation, equally responsible for our experiences and our truths.

When I first met Aralamb in my early 20s, he spoke about writing this book in the future. He told me that I had agreed to write it. At that time, I had no idea exactly what its form would be, or when I was to work with Aralamb to write it. Over the years I would ask Aralamb if it was time, and he would simply say no. Some 30 years on, when it was time to write, I had stopped asking him and suddenly the time was now. You see, all the information in this book about the "Laws of the Universe," "The Creation," even the "science," are concepts that I have been working with in readings with clients that Aralamb and I have met with over the years. To me, these concepts have been at play in my life the whole time. To me, this book is just who I have grown to be within my relationship with Aralamb. Most of this information is to me now just second nature.

This book was not created in order to proselytize or convert you in any way. As persons here on the planet, you need, and I would say it is your responsibility to work out your relationship to your soul or conversely not work it out as you see fit. This book is a project that, in Aralamb's own words, is meant to "possibly change your paradigm of who you are, as well as what you are capable of in this Universe." I would also like to clear up a misconception before you read any further into the chapters.

Aralamb refers to *The Creator/God* throughout this book. Aralamb will tell you that The Creator/God is not female, male, or anything in between. Gender has no specific meaning in the use of the name The Creator/God. The only caveat is that Aralamb insists that The Creator/God is the singular creation emanation space that all others come from. That's it really. In this book, God is not a man, God is not a woman, God is just everything and all things from which everything ***other*** comes.

In human history there has been a need for some kind of ***name*** to use when talking about the hugely vast notion of the energy force which created the whole of our Universe. So, Aralamb uses the term The Creator/ God.

As an end to this very short preface, I wanted to just reiterate that I have come to a place in my life where I do not hold any grievance or anger toward any person or persons in my past, and actually I give the people in my past stories all of the love I can send them because without them, and their agreeing to dance life with me in some of the most difficult learning situations, I would not be sitting here with you now. For that and so many other reasons, I want you to just keep an open mind, and above all else, just bathe in the amazing crackle and beauty of all the souls around you in your life! We are on an amazing journey together. Give it a read, and if at the end, you just want to go for a walk with your dog and use this book as a door stop, or campfire kindling so be it! But enjoy yourself and your life either way!

Melissa Gates-Perry

INTRODUCTION

Melissa

Introduction

Some of the history within this book is mine. Aralamb has used some of my history to impart specific knowledge about how we should be functioning, uplifted, working human souls on Planet Earth in the next 100 years. Earth is changing, humanity is evolving, and the whole Universe is shifting upward in one symphonic energetic movement. This book is not actually "about" me at all, but some of my history makes great examples for Aralamb's lessons. We are souls, spirits, bodies living in a vibrating fabric of energy. We are all energetic beings vibrating at different frequencies in order to have this experience of "life." We need a venue, a field, a court, a stage on which to learn life lessons. This is it, people! This is your stage. This is your life; this is your time. If you have not already, get in there and swing for the bleachers!

I am a regular human. I can be a total pain in the ass, and I can be like a friggin' saint. Just like you! Just like you I have had amazing life experiences and horrific ones. Aralamb tells me that one of the largest roadblocks to healing and expanding is that we all feel alone in our pain and in our joy. This is the exact opposite of the truth. Below I am listing just some of the experiences I have had, both wonderful and horrible. You could probably add to both lists with situations that I could not even touch upon. I openly share these lists with you to show you that no one is truly alone. Ever. No one gets a perfect life. We are all in this together.

The following is a list of many of the difficult issues that I have personally and/or closely and emotionally dealt with in my lifetime so far. I share them because I am not special, and I am not immune to all of life's rollercoaster rides!

Deaths of a loved ones, tooth extraction, lying, cocaine, infidelity, abuse, cancer, dying while bleeding out (obviously survived it), abortion, alcoholism, religious fanaticism, domestic abuse, crushing debt, getting fired, hurting others, kidnapping victim, child abuse, one-night stands, bad choices, running from problems, multiple weird surgeries, avoiding conflict, people-pleasing, body odor, sugar addiction, cigarettes, depression, being a victim (because it was easier than taking responsibility for myself already!), rolling three times in a vehicle, selfishness, uncontrollable gas, judgment, road rage, painful family dynamics, semi homelessness, toilet paper theft, being judged by others, swearing uncontrollably, and I am sure 1,000 more items that could and will be pointed out at some time in my life as not the best choices or situations to have put myself in.

The following are a list of many of the amazing and wonderful situations and blessings I or those close to me have personally experienced within this same lifetime:

The birth of my son, soul-filling love, friendships with huge people, amazing luck, synchronicity, Aralamb showing up in my life, helping people when they have needed it, getting support from amazing people at just the right times, forgiveness, an amazing soul mate, so many sunsets, music, family, the ability to write, sharing, secret gifting, travel, the ability to sing, all of the times I have survived, lessons learned, full moons, chocolate, my dad's guitars, tasting the ocean, dog love, forgiving, wind on my face, unconditional acceptance, great luck, letting go of love without hate or judgment, release, amazing blessed family dynamics, physical healing, true learning, and understanding that we are all just humans with souls grappling to move forward. The ability to heal and grow.

I share all of these things as a kind of full disclosure because I want to share very openly my own life experiences in a way that lets you see and know that you are not alone, that we all have hardship, bad decisions, less than stellar pasts, and so much blessing, and a knowing that life is not meant to be all black and white. You will also notice that many life situations could be listed in both places.

Some of our most beautiful days come out of our darkest nights and some of our worst days show up on the most glorious sunny mornings. It's all life, it's all existence, and it's all a big fat harry amazing lesson to be worked on to the best of your ability throughout your whole huge lifetime! At this very moment here on our planet, we are meant to begin living our lives as if we are steering the boat, and not at the mercy of the wind and water.

We can be participants in the how, where, what, and the why of our direction. I hope that my stories and Aralamb's insights help YOU. That is truly the aim of this book. Let this book be a grand synchronicity for you, a blessing to you, a time when you stop and decide how your soul wants to travel now, right now, in this lifetime. How do you want to view your life, the planet, the galaxy, the Universe? **It really is up to you** and that realization can be the greatest and scariest realization you will ever come to. So, come on! Hop on! Saddle up, Cowboys, let's ride.

Melissa

CHAPTER 1
Aralamb-Who I Am

Aralamb:

Humanity is changing. The DNA by which humanity is connected to The Creator/God is changing. This change is the normal evolution of things. Souls are born into this Universe in order to grow, stretch, take on—the qualities that are needed to progress. There is no set timeline for each *individual* soul to make this continual transition toward The Creation. Although there is no set timeline for each individual soul, there is a larger energetic structure in place at the same time. This structure is meant to keep the "whole" of the Universe moving forward in an evolutionary, geological, spiritual, and physical manner. Within this system, there are not only physical aspects of growth but also energetic measures of growth and movement. Humanity on Earth is now fully involved in this evolution forward/upward in an energetic and spiritual sense.

Although "truth," as humans record it, is relative, some Universal truths are constant. The truth of the Universe in which you reside is exactly as you may secretly hope and recognize within your deepest places. There is an energetic order to the existence of everything you see with your eyes, and everything that is there but not seen with human eyes or by human inventions. There is a governing Creator energy/God which oversees in the least constraining way possible the forward movement of the Universe which it created. There is a connection (soul) within every living thing that will always bring it back to the Creation force.

This connection cannot be taken from you, it cannot be stolen from you, it cannot be removed from you. Your belief in (soul) is irrelevant, and not necessary. Believe what you will, free will was given to you at the time you were brought into being. The energy which resides in your soul will and has returned you to the Creation force many times. In this book, I will be referring to The Creator/God throughout. These words are not meant to indicate any gender specific norm. I am literally just using words that you might understand within your realm of reality at this time on your planet. You as humans have no real capacity for understanding The Creator/God in its entirety. I make that distinction in order for you to not get, as Melissa would say, "hung up" on the vernacular.

Your soul is in fact an unbreakable bond which will always return to The Creator/God. All the human behaviors and "mess," as Melissa would call it, is simply a tool for each soul to hopefully learn, grow, and continue to raise up along the paths to Creation. What you DO matters in your life. What you LEAVE BEHIND for others in the form of emotions and feeling memories matters in life. How you FEEL matters in the end. How you have MADE OTHERS FEEL matters in the end even more. What you BELIEVE is powerful. What you believe your life to be is what it will be. This is factual in the Universe. Simple and yet so powerful and dangerous. Please go back and re-read this paragraph. This is the whole point of incarnating.

I am Aralamb. I am not mythological. I am not a religious belief. I am not a religious doctrine. I am not an "alien" in the respect that you might determine from your entertainment industry or your "black" governmental programs. I am not a figment of the imagination. Who I am is not meant to be cryptic, imaginary, or shrouded in any mystical unintelligible parable.

I am a real entity, guide, teacher, living on the 89th energetic level of the Creation Field that is your Universe. I am not at this time "flesh and blood" as you the reader are. I am, however, made up of the very same sub-atomic energies, particles, and fields that you are as you read this. I am at this time much more a being made from light and sound frequency. The reason for this is that I am at a much higher sound, frequency, and vibration level than Earth. My personal soul history is not important for this book; however, some of that history will be used as it is supportive of the teachings.

My history with the soul Melissa is one of four distinct lifetimes on Earth, only one of which she remembers with any specificity. That lifetime was in the area of Earth that is now Wales, and I was a priest in a Druidic Society in which I taught the life path of Bard-ship. That lifetime took place approximately 1,953 years ago in the Earth timeframe. I was Melissa's spiritual teacher in that lifetime. Within this lifetime, I agreed to be her teacher/ guide in order to work on the changing shift that is imminent upon your planet and this Universe at this given time.

I made the agreement with Melissa prior to her birth. Certain aspects of this lifetime were predetermined as "possible goals," and my relationship with Melissa, and disseminating the teachings in this book, was one of those possible goal sets for her.

I am no longer incarnate as a physical body. At my level of what Melissa calls "The Lobby" (heaven, next level of being, where your soul goes at death), there is no real need for organic, corporal bodies. All of the souls passing to and from "The Lobby" are in their pure energetic soul form. This fact is constant regardless of where in the Universe the soul is coming from or departing toward. No matter which planet or species you are coming from, upon birth you will receive some sort of corporal body if it is deemed necessary for that lifetime, and upon the death of that body/vehicle, you will return to The Lobby in pure soul or energy form for your review.

I am in the "department" of communication. I am literally a guide/ teacher whose sole purpose is that of communication, so that souls/ humans on Earth will begin to see the reality of where they are living and the system that The Creator/God has in place. There are many levels of energetic teachers and guides "above me," whom I work, take counsel, and confer with. The energetic bodies above me are part of the infinite network of support which The Creator/God has in place for the advancement of souls. I suppose you would liken it to a hierarchy of management within an endless, albeit very functional governmental system.

I reside as an energetic being here. There are an uncountable number of other teacher/guides in this area of The Lobby. Each of those teacher/ guides works with an incarnate soul on any number in the millions of planets in your Universe. I am but one of those teacher/guides working with my student, Melissa, in this timeline on Earth. Due to the fact that I have no need of a physical corporal body here, Melissa has attached her last memory of what my physical body looked like in that Druidic life incarnation that we shared.

This ability of the human mind to "see" is very useful in the connection process, particularly early on in a teacher/guide relationship. So, for the purposes of this book and the information herein, I look a bit like a white-haired, bearded male human. To Melissa, I appear tall and slender. I have light blue eyes, which I had in that last lifetime and an easy smile. I believe she would see me to be about 80+ years old on your Earth plane. Although I feel as though I have retained a humorous soul, Melissa often feels that I have quite a dry sense of humor and am a bit "stern". My soul, like all others, retains the most fundamental elements from lifetime to lifetime as I learned more and more lessons. Souls do not, however, retain any of the negative elements. Negative lessons learned incarnate are to be overcome and released.

Universal Soul Guide/Teacher Covenant

I am, in my role as Melissa's guide/teacher, always to reside within the Universal Laws of the soul guide/teacher covenant. Every soul who is born into any kind of organic body in this Universe is given a soul guide/teacher. The range of souls incarnate at any given time who are even remotely aware of their guide/teacher on Earth has been sitting at 21 percent of the living population. This very low percentage of souls who can connect with their guides has been very stable and unchanging for many thousands of years on your planet. In the mid-section of the last Century A.D., that number of sensitive souls began to rise and sits now at this time at 38 percent. The evolution of humans is meant to bring this number up to 62 percent in the next 100 Earth years, which will tip the populations energetic imprint in the Universe and shift the planet "up" in frequency, thereby creating a new reality, a new direction, and a new paradigm for the human species. I use the phrases "up," "down," "forward," and other directional indications only so that you, the reader, will have a "plane" upon which to imagine the workings of energy. In a literal sense, these descriptive words do not fully explain the nature of sound, energy, frequency, and gravity, but for now, these words will suffice.

The Universal Soul/Guide Covenant is the agreement set in place upon the inception of this Universe by The Creator/God at the first point of creation. At that time, I am told, there were no souls incarnating yet, but the Covenant was in place. The Covenant is there in order to uphold "free will" which is The Creator's most highly lauded and held Law. All souls have free will and a teacher/guide must always adhere to that law for the student. As Melissa's teacher/guide, I CANNOT do, say, impart, or force any knowledge or decision upon her that would in any way impinge upon her free will. This law is absolute. For example, in the beginning of this book, Melissa listed many, many life situations that she chose to experience. You may ask, "Well, what good is a teacher/guide if he can't step in and stop the student from *doing*, as Melissa would say, "Stupid shit?"

The Covenant and the free will rule does not allow me to stop my student from doing, saying, being, believing, accepting, or choosing anything. My sole job is to hopefully, protect, mitigate, support, and generally be that voice deep inside that says, "Are you sure this is a good idea?" I think that all of you reading, no matter where in your life you are, have had that moment or many moments. Those moments when you think, "I remember that day, I knew in my gut that I should not date that person, or that time when I missed that off ramp, but I knew it was fine and found out later that there was a huge wreck that I missed." I could go on forever with the "if only I had listened to my gut," that situation would or would not have happened conversation. The main point to understand, and I cannot state if firmly enough, is *free will is paramount for every soul. There is no flexibility in this law. There are no caveats to this law. The law of free will/ Covenant is primal and was set in motion prior to what humans would call "the big bang" moment for this Universe. It is law.*

Very often when sitting with clients, Melissa will ask me a question about the clients' future, and I am NOT given the directive to answer, simply because a "direction" given from me could very well impinge upon their free will. Your lessons as a soul are your own, to be lived out by your own choice. Your guide's job is to assist you, possibly warn you, and very, very benevolently give you the inclination to "do the right thing." Nothing more is allowed. Melissa has often spent days trying to get me to give her some concrete answer to some question, which I cannot give. Ultimately her decisions are her own.

I am residing at this 89th level of the entrance to The Lobby. I do not constantly watch Melissa, she showers alone! That is often the kind of worry that a soul might have about their own guide. "Is my guide watching me constantly?" "What if I don't want a guide?" "I don't like the idea of there being a guide with me all of the time." "I like my privacy."

As a guide/teacher to Melissa, and as is the rule of all guides, I do not watch her all the time as I have many of my own responsibilities here at The Lobby, and on higher levels than this entry level. I do, however, have an integral energy connection to Melissa in this lifetime. I liken it to having a bell, or I suppose you might say a cell phone by which Melissa is the only number or contact saved in it. I do not hold it in my hand as you might imagine in your *Star Trek* movies, but we are linked energetically. I often will leave Melissa's side to attend to other responsibilities here, but should she focus her sudden attention on me, or should she be in a situation, or in proximity to a person or persons who could use the input from The Lobby, I am instantly present for her. There are times when my responsibilities here will give me need to attend a very far-reaching area of the Universal Energy Field. In that case, I will alert Melissa to the fact that I may "feel" absent to her for a few Earth days. I am, however, even at these times fully able to instantly be back at her side, should she have need of me.

In the beginning, Melissa tested this "proximity alarm," as she would call it, and called me back with no real emergency to see if what I was saying was true. Melissa no longer feels the need to test this connection. Over time, our connection has grown in such a way that there is no reason to "work hard" or "take some time to adjust the energy field." Melissa has, at this point, just learned to have, as she would say, "one foot in each energetic state pretty much all the time," which took some time to accomplish. All humans are completely able to do this, but most are just now beginning to feel the ability awaken. There is an innate ability for every human to have a direct contact with The Creator/God. Although through religious dogmas and other spiritual formats, many humans use symbols in order to connect, it is not necessary, but it is completely accepted as a road to connection with Creation as well. We will speak on religious frameworks in a later chapter but suffice to say that humanity is beginning to awaken to its own connection to The Lobby, Creation, and The Creator/God.

Here in The Lobby, my soul energy core is in full control of my "being-ness." This is the truth for all souls at the entry level of The Lobby all the way to The Creation level. There is no need to retain any kind of organic vessel, as all movement on these levels is motivated by a marriage of mental, energetic, and sonic threads which intertwine automatically. There is a constant pulsing oval of thermal magnetic waves and protons which coalesce to manifest a space in which my personal soul, personality, and visual energy can reside for Melissa to have kind of thought/sight of me. I could just as easily exist as a perfectly "clean" sound or color wave, but for the purposes of my connection with Melissa and her life's work, it is helpful for me to utilize the thermal sonic magnetic vessel.

The thermal sonic magnetic vessel is like a "bubble" if you will. It is an energy/sound field which allows me to keep all of my soul vibrations in one place for creating a semi-solid form. When I say "semi-solid," I do not mean this to indicate "organic" in any way. Semi-solid would maybe look like what you would call diaphanous. My soul is of the non-corporal nature at this point. For now, I do not need any kind of organic body to further my incarnation levels. I no longer need to incarnate into organic vessels/bodies in order to engage my soul lessons. I now have the ability to move freely through my lessons without the constraints of time, space, or organic vehicle (a body of any kind).

Time for me has no meaning whatsoever. Once the entry level/Lobby of the Creation is entered, time, as a human would describe it, no longer exists. At the higher energy levels of creation, everything that is, just IS. There is no timeline of any kind pushing events forward, backward, or in any direction, unless a soul or energy body wished to have that experience.

If you can imagine a space in your life that was so fulfilling and joyful, that time for you either seemed to "stand still," or "fly by," that would be how time might feel from the upper levels of creation. I was in my last incarnation on Earth as a druid/bard leader and teacher. Since that time on Earth, I have resided here at The Lobby level working in those same areas that I found so enjoyable and enlightening on Earth. Here, I can "do," "be," involve my soul and mind energy in anything that gives my soul pleasure. Here I am involved in communications with many other soul/guides. My group is involved with the evolution of study, sound vibration, music, communications, and energy shifting. Other groups of evolved guides can be in other areas of expertise, building, creation of planets, geology, prayer for species, evolution of species, evolution of galaxies, evolution of art, telepathy, law, evolution of physics in a galaxy, medical evolution, galaxy growth, internal evolution of groups, beliefs, knowledge, healing, music, etc. The list goes on and on.

To simplify, it would be likened to the idea that on Earth, people may be involved in sports teams, hobbies, political endeavors, philanthropy, education, learning, art, any study of positive issues. Upon a soul's entry into the upper levels of creation where an organic body is no longer needed, that soul may become involved in a timeless endeavor of their natural talents or leanings. The one caveat is that there is no negative inducement or gain at this level. The ability to "create" and "grow" here is unlimited, but is lacking in any kind of negative outcome, greed, need for competition, or other stimuli besides the growth and deepening of the soul's direction.

For example, if you were a human who loved nothing more than to bake beautiful cakes and sell them at your own cake shop on Earth, then when you arrive at The Lobby after death you may decide to spend hundreds of Earth years simply having *that* perfected experience with and for your loved ones here in The Lobby. You would not do this because of any "gain" in the Earthly sense. You would be experiencing this ability in order to feel the pure joy of doing and giving that talent to others. Your cakes would be perfection as everything around you would be as well.

After some time, you may want to use this gift to assist souls who are still incarnating onto Earth. You could become a guide to someone who shares your gifts of creating beautiful culinary experiences. You could be a part of the group called "evolution of consumption." This group is involved with the art, sustainability, and social ramifications of "how" species who "still" choose to deal with food and the evolutionary move forward. You would not be forced to become a teacher/guide, but you could. Or, without any judgment at all, you could literally enjoy your own skills and experience that joy *forever.* In this way, time is not relevant to us here at these higher levels.

Melissa will often ask me "how much time" will an event or situation take to unfold for her. From my perspective, all the possibilities for her are happening at once. There is no timeline at all. Time for humans is a construct that was built by their organic minds to push forward the physical agendas that they keep. It goes without saying that any human can actually "decide" at any "moment in time" what they are experiencing. They can experience as I am, "out of any kind of timeline." So, the timeline of any event or situation to unfold is for all intents and purposes the decision of the observer on Earth.

Here at The Lobby, Melissa and my connection to her is my priority for the time she will be on the planet. I do, however, have other responsibilities that I must attend to. As I said, I am in the communications/study/evolution/music group here. Often, I am called away to be involved in what we loosely call a group evolution/intervention. Hundreds of planets in the Milky Way Galaxy alone are shifting in evolutionary vibrations currently. Some of the planets are younger than Earth's evolution, and some are far in front of Earth's. While a planet is making a transition or if a planet gets into any kind of difficulty during these growth periods, my specialty group may be called to that planet's energy field to do group energy work.

Put very simply, I will be alerted through the fabric of magnetic dark matter that I am needed in some corner of the Galaxy. My energetic "hearing/sensing" of this call will immediately *hone* my energy field to the gathering field of others in my specialty. I then alert Melissa that I have been called away to do work, and that I am simply within a sent thought from her if she has need for me. I can usually also let her know how many Earth days or hours I may be away from her physical bodily senses.

I then allow my energy to connect more fully to my specialty group and I am immediately transported to the group. Once with the group, "we" will all combine our energy and intent upon whatever the issue is for the planet, species, or situation that we were called upon to assist. During this time of group intention for the healing, enlightenment, or change that we assist with, I never lose the core of my own soul energy. No matter how large the grouping of teacher guides that is called from my specialty, we do not combine into one soul or personality. We retain our personal soul boundaries. We simply combine our *intention* fully for the positive outcome that we were instructed by The Creation to employ. As a group of 10 or 10 million, we will all determine exactly what the intention for the situation might be. For example: *"Evolve this species' ability to have language to 12 degrees higher in order that they avert war-like behaviors."* Once the intent is decided upon, usually by the predetermined lead for that working, we all intend that energetic shift to "**BE**." We do not intend for "it to happen." We do not intend that "it will happen." We intend as one that "**it is**." Intention is the framework of what your scientists call "dark matter." Dark matter responds to the intention of "it is." This is the simple way to explain how we manifest and intend the Creator's assistance within the Universe. Again, I remind you that as a soul coming back into The Lobby, you are not pressed into any working group, but it is very common after a long rest and rejuvenation that souls decide to add their positive intention energy to a group of like energy souls. The work is very gratifying.

We may be called to a planet or species to avert a disaster; we may be called to heal a planet or species after a disaster has already happened. My group, as I said, is specialized in evolution/study/communication/music, so my group would be called forth for assistance if a planet or species needed to raise or evolve its speaking, communication, musical vibration, or ability to focus on learning/study, speaking with each other, and sometime telepathic communication skills. The group to which I belong is very specifically deemed for these issues within Galaxial evolution. My group would not be called in during the initial terra forming of a new planet. There would be a group who specialized in that area of energy manifestation.

You can see then why I am working with Melissa. In this life, through speech, writing, and music she is all about communication/telepathy/

evolution/music. This is how guides will become linked with students. Guides will be paired with an organic species that has natural leanings in the area in which their guide is proficient.

My soul/body is constantly awash with waves of cleansing energy/ frequency from the higher levels of creation. There is no need for my energy to ever become depleted or in need of rest. The Creation is the "food" upon which I reside at this level. All souls and beings above the 89ᵗʰ level of creational vibration exist in this state, and as a soul moves up the levels, the vibration and knowledge of "all" becomes more and more clear. The very fact that I am working with Melissa in this lifetime is also allowing me to learn and grow as a soul here in the Lobby. It is through my teaching with her that I am learning and growing as a soul at my level as well. The process of souls growing, and evolving is placed in a completely symbiotic system which constantly allows the teacher and student to grow. I am a student to souls much higher up the vibrational growth levels and yet I am a teacher to Melissa below me on the levels of vibration in Creation. Again, I must stress, however, that every soul has the right and free will to embrace the growth or not in that soul's own time with no repercussion. I spent many lifetimes incarnating upon the Earth plane before I decided to take the next steps to the guide levels of Creation.

If I wanted to, I could incarnate back to the Earth plane after my employment as Melissa's teacher is completed. I have the freedom to make that choice if I should deem it necessary. The beauty of The Creator's system is that all souls are gently given choices and free will throughout eons to hopefully move forward in positive growth through trial and error in many incarnate situations of their own free will.

As a being, I do not need rest or sleep in the sense that a human would. I am no longer dependent upon an organic existence so sleeping, eating, resting, and moving an organic body around in no longer necessary. I simply "am" and require no respite from "being." When I first returned from my last Earth plane incarnation, I spent a long while in a resting state, as I had been through a particularly difficult end and required a rest period to assimilate all of my lessons from that lifetime. This is normal for very many returning souls from Earth and all of the other planets and energy levels of this Universe. It took me what I believe would be 172 approximate Earth years to regroup, remember why I incarnated, who I truly am, and then begin to assimilate the positive and difficult lessons for which I incarnated to the Earth plane. Because I was a bard in that previous lifetime and had been in many prior to that, when I first returned here to the 89th level of the lobby, I sat in a beautiful garden and played and wrote music and spoken word. Time for me was irrelevant. My soul chose to sit in a beautiful sunny meadow near a lake. My soul family and fellow travelers would visit me often to talk with me about my journey and my last lifetime on Earth as well as listen to my playing and reciting. I needed nothing and simply "was." This is what I did to assimilate that last lifetime. At some point, my guide and partner Frenzlar came to me and suggested that I might want to move to the next level and have my meeting with the teaching group of souls who might help me to determine if or when I might decide to move to teaching.

I believe that I had been in my healing rest mode in that meadow for about 50 Earth years when Frenzlar first approached me; you must understand that it was as if we had just spoken, and no time had passed because in the upper levels of creation there literally is "no time." Love and positive movement simply "is." A soul can create a state that mimics "time," but it truly has no power in the same sense as on Earth.

After the 172nd year or so, I moved to the 89th level of The Lobby where teachers and guides can take up the work that they decide to engage in, or they can simply congregate and create beauty and new horizons and learn for their own engagement of the joy of it. I went to my meeting with the five teacher/guides who had been with me for many lifetimes and accepted the position of teacher guide with the communications group. They had been in contact with Melissa's soul upon her last return to The Lobby while I had been in rest, and she agreed that if I would accept the position, she would like me to be her teacher guide for the lifetime that she is in presently upon Earth. I agreed. At this time, she was prepared to be born. She had made agreements with those other souls who wished to travel a lesson path with her, and she with them.

I met her at the engagement point, we spoke and agreed upon possible contact points in her life, and walked with her to the departure "hall" in The Lobby. Wished her well and bid her Creator's speed at remembering why she was incarnating back to Earth and what her lessons were to be. Melissa then bonded with her pod souls that she was leaving behind this time, and engaged her energy core back to the field of Earth and the re-entry waiting period for the human baby yet to be born into which she would incarnate.

After Melissa left The Lobby, I then studied the basic lesson plan for what she and I were to accomplish for not only her but the common good of the Earth plane at this time in its history. The main theme of the lesson plan is to enlarge the paradigm and communication skills both theoretically, energetically, and organically on Earth. There are many guides in my skill group who are doing the same with souls now on Earth who deemed it critical that they be involved in the shift that is happening. After studying the general life plan for her, I was free to continue my own studies and move about with my family souls and teachers. Melissa incarnated onto the planet, survived the moment of soul implantation and birth, and I awaited her contact request.

It is important to note here that Melissa had no memory of me, The Lobby, her lesson plans, or any of the conversations we had before her birth. This is free will in action. The whole meaning of incarnating without memory is that the soul must gain strength through trial and error and decide to grow in positive ways. A teacher/guide such as myself cannot intervene in any real way with my student until, or unless, I am directly called upon for assistance. At the very point that an incarnated soul calls out or requests the assistance of its guide, the guide/soul connection is completed across the energetic chasm between Earth and The Lobby. If Melissa had never called out to me for assistance, I would not under any circumstances been able to intervene or contact her for any reason. I would have assessed her throughout her lifetime and simply met her when she traveled back over at her death. At that point, she would have remembered our connection and the fact that she never contacted me, and that those lessons and directives were not met. There are no repercussions for not remembering who you are in a lifetime. You will simply carry lessons still to be learned.

So, in our case, Melissa did indeed make the connection with me, and I was alerted to her engagement to her lesson plan. From that time to now, I have been teaching and guiding Melissa to this point where we are writing this book for you the readers. Melissa has had free will during the whole endeavor and could stop at any time and simply live out her lifetime. She could change her stance and never speak to me again with no repercussions from The Creator, myself, or The Lobby. She would continue to have the love and support of The Creator but would not fulfill those lessons that her soul found to be of the highest endeavor for this lifetime. The decisions to evolve, learn, and grow, or not to grow, are hers and hers alone.

That is a very general sense for you of who I am. What my existence is. What my role is. In further chapters of this book, it may be that your understanding of me increases when you more fully embrace the sonic and electromagnetic nature of the Universe in which we all reside.

CHAPTER 2

The Connection

The Connection/The Painful Bridge to Cross

Melissa

From the first day Aralamb showed up, he has never judged me in any way. Lately, he has told me to lose some weight if I want to avoid some nasty future health issues and be around for a long time to share this information! Ha! I have to get a guide who will tell me to "step away from the doughnut, Melissa!" Really? No lottery ticket numbers? No stock market advice? Come on! He also does very little in the way of "forecasting the future in any way," he says that free will always rules, and although there are always two to seven very likely outcomes or "possibility currents" of any situation or life direction, free will makes "prophesizing" against the rules as they are for him.

Everyone born has a guide. Right now, on this planet, humans are supposed to be waking up to what the Universe is really about. We are supposed to begin to trust our intuition and trust our inner guidance. Oooh, good time to bring this up; your guide will NEVER: ask you to hurt another human; steal; rape; pillage; or do any harm at all to any other being on the planet here or living on another planet in this Universe. PERIOD. The rule "DO UNTO OTHERS AS YOU WOULD HAVE THEM DO UNTO YOU" is a really BIG DEAL on this planet and every other planet and energetic realm within The Creator's known Universe. Period. This rule also covers pretty much every living thing. If you wouldn't want to be kicked, then don't kick a tree. If you determine to do any of these things at all, your guide will not physically stop you but will keep planting thoughts, things, people in your way to get you to STOP the negative behaviors. Free will always remains yours, but again I urge you to understand that no soul's guide will ever condone or assist in any negative activity. It is just not their job. They are there specifically to try to get you, with guidance, to be a much BIGGER, BRIGHTER soul! So, short story is that if your guide is giving you advice to do any negative shit, it's NOT your guide, it's not the word of The Creator/God, it's YOUR SHIT. Might be a great time to get into therapy and deal with yourself. Okay, spiritual disclaimer made.

Your guide was given to you in order to help you stay on your life's lesson path, even when you absolutely refuse to, in the most benevolent ways possible. I can tell you that in the 35 years that Aralamb has been in my life, I have tested him in every way possible to see if he was really "walking his talk." He has never failed me. I also want to take this time to explain that Aralamb has never professed to be anything but a humble servant of The Creator/God. When I have needed in my life to pray to God/The Creator, Aralamb and everyone around him, steps aside, they all look upward toward the light of Creation and my prayers flow up and away into an endless loving "light space," The Creator/God.

Aralamb and I Connect
Melissa

In the winter of 1987–88, I had moved back to my small hometown in New England. I was a 22-year-old single mom. I was working at a lumberyard, setting sticks. Setting sticks is where you take small 4x2 inch sticks and lay them along freshly cut lumber in stacks as they come off a sorting machine after they are cut to length and width. It was New England, and I can tell you it was friggin' cold that winter, amazingly cold. The cavernous main building which was the sawmill was open on both sides along the kiln wall, so that fork lifts could come and go, constantly bringing in green lumber for "sticking" and taking dried lumber from the kiln out to the yard to be stacked on pallets.

I had been hired as a yard worker, by a longtime friend of my family, who would eventually become my first husband. Ted was 10 years older than me, married to another family friend, and had two young children. I was 22 at that time. Ted's best friend also worked at the lumberyard as a manager. Les was 28 and the absolute opposite in nature and energy from Ted. Ted was a brilliant guy who knew about the lumber business, had grown up on a farm. Ted came from a well-known family in town, and really was all about having fun and just making life a party. He was one of those guys who was a friend to everyone who ever met him. "Give you the shirt off his back" kind of guy.

I was a single mom, living in a trailer, young, stupid for all intents and purposes, and was doing my best to pay for another tank of heating oil to make it through the winter. Trailers in those days always came with a big ugly oil tank attached somewhere on the backside. I'm sure the older trailers in circulation still do. The trailer I was renting was a big sturdy 1967 model, two bedrooms, one bath, kitchen and living area combined. As with all trailer homes from that era, all of that was arranged in a 60x14 (line) shape. So, if you needed to pee, you would walk down the long 54 feet to the tiny bathroom. It was like living in an "I". The whole of the interior was wood paneling. A weird red shade of wood that I painted all stark white so that it ended up looking like some kind of retro space capsule. That trailer was white on the outside, and aluminum, and like so many of its time, had a large aqua blue band painted all the way around the outside. It was warm though, and close to the lumberyard. I had my son Hunter with me who was two at the time. We had literally left Arizona just a couple of months before like two refugees in the night with nothing but a few packed bags. My Dad had given me a 1977 Chevy pickup, which my Grandfather Gordon had built a solid oak flatbed on. That truck was super cool. It was a four-speed shift on the floor with four-wheel drive. I wish I had it now. It was a standard and was like a tank in snow.

Ted, Les, and I became quick friends and began to have drinks after work on most Thursdays and Fridays, which was super innocent at first. The thing is, at some point, I began to realize that I was thinking a lot of Ted in a way that was, looking back on it, just plain wrong and not within the "do unto others" rule of life. Ted had a really nice wife named Sue. She was also a friend of my mother's. Ted and Sue were in that wide, wide circle of partying friends that Sally, my mom, had acquired throughout the years. Les was, for reasons I would glean later, not a part of my mother's entourage of partygoers, but his wife Ronnie was and had been. I know now, looking back at the situation, it was really all me. I was just young, stupid, and fully the person who looked at Ted and selfishly thought that no one else mattered but me. I am not proud of admitting that, but I know it's the truth. I do not believe that Ted and Sue were having a great marriage or that they would have stayed together in the end, but that young, stupid decision on my part was wrong and I know it now. I have, with Aralamb's input, gone back and at least taken responsibility for that time and that decision with both Sue and Ted. I was young, and to be honest just mad in love with Ted. No other way to put it really. I was at that time literally a "home-wrecker." Not proud of it, but it is the truth.

Where Ted was a come and go lucky kind of guy, always smiling, hard worker, great talker and fine friend who was ready to party, Les was darker and more brooding. A super intelligent guy, and the kind who would watch everyone in a crowd to figure them out. Les was the first person to bring ESP, extra sensory perception and energy to my attention. I can admit that I was a bit frightened of Les at first because he was very, very intense. I never feared that he would hurt me, but he was very quiet, and his energy was intense. I could sense something kind of strong about him from the first, but I could also sense that he was very closed off energetically and would block me if I reached out to him in my mind to figure out what he was thinking.

Before I met Aralamb, I did not understand that humans do this reaching out all of the time, they just don't understand what they are doing, and often just ignore the "intuitive" feelings they have as "stupid" or "imagined." The first time that Les brought sensory perception up to me was at work. I was standing in the lumberyard at the sticking station. It was so, so cold. I was standing in front of a huge stacking machine, 15 feet away from a fully open-ended building, with the roof being the only thing between me and a blizzard blowing outside. It was about 5 degrees, and the wind was blowing in gusts of 10–20 miles per hour. Every few minutes the wind would shift direction, and the snow and blizzard would blow into our faces as we stood there—brutal.

It was a Tuesday, and just about 2:30 in the afternoon and it had been blowing snow all day. The sky was so gray that just past the end of the open building, you could literally see nothing. I was standing next to a guy who I had gone to high school with whose name was Bryan and we would throw those dividing sticks between the layers of lumber being stacked in front of us. He kept a lit cigarette in his mouth the whole time, in a never-ending chain of smokes. I could never figure out how he did that. The machinery was so loud that talking was not really an option. We would throw those sticks in over and over every 10 seconds or so. I had on snow pants, winter parka, gloves, the whole deal, and it was still bone crushingly cold. You might be asking why I was doing that job instead of something more "girl"-oriented. Well, I don't know, except to say that in my life I have had some diverse employment, and in every situation, I have met a person or persons who moved me forward to this moment right now. So, it all was as it was meant to be, even the hard stuff. Aralamb tells me this all the time.

As we were robotically throwing those stickers into the lumber stack, I suddenly "heard" Les call my name, like right behind me. I spun and looked, and no one was there. I thought it was weird and kept throwing those stickers into the pallet of lumber. I could not stop because the one thing you didn't want to do was screw up and make them have to stop the stacker. I knew that break time and a hot cup of coffee was coming in about 15 minutes and I could hardly feel my hands anymore. Bend down, pick up sticks, lay them in, again, I hear Les call my name. "Melissa, come here!" This time louder, I threw my stickers in the pallet and yelled at the controller, "I gotta pee." Honestly, I knew that I had *heard* Les. The wind was blowing, and the snow was everywhere, but I knew that I had *heard* Les, even though he was nowhere to be seen in the warehouse. The span of the open warehouse was maybe 220 feet from where the stacker machine was, to the other end which opened out onto the yard where all the pallets were stacked for transport. I walked the long span and stepped out into the blowing snow, turned right, and there, 40 feet away, leaning on a pallet, smoking a cigarette in the blowing snow was Les. Smiling at me like a Cheshire Cat. I walked up to him through waves of blowing snow, and he looked right at me and yelled, "I knew you would hear me." "I have been watching you, and I knew you could hear me, right in here," and he reached out and tapped the side of my temple lightly with his index finger. "Also, stop fucking trying to press your mind into me. If I wanted you in my head, I would invite you!" He laughed and walked into the office across the yard.

At first, I was a bit freaked out because I was not even sure "how" I had heard him, but I knew that I had, and *he* knew that I had. I was so stunned really that I just stood there freezing for a few minutes, watching him walk away. That was how he began to teach me a bit about astral travel, energy transferring, and generally how I could assist him in his mission....

Later that day, Les asked if he could stop by my trailer after work to talk with me a bit. I said, "Sure," and immediately after felt a little like a lamb inviting a wolf to my house.

Over the next month or so, Les started coming over and bringing with him a deck of tarot cards. Up to this point in my life, at 22, I had not met anyone who seemed to have a connection to this other way of being, thinking, or feeling as I did psychically. It was as if "the teacher had appeared." Less taught me how to use the tarot deck, and often in that winter, had me read his cards for him as he said, "If I keep reading cards for myself, the results can be tilted. If I have you pull the cards for me, then they will be clearer." At this point, I was so new and ignorant of anything spiritual or occult-like that he would read the cards I would lay for him. I didn't even know how to do that at that point. I would shuffle, and I would lay out the cards for him in an elongated cross shape like he had shown me. Often, he would not even tell me what they were signifying, but instead tell me what cards meant when I would shuffle and randomly pull them out of the deck. He was teaching me the meaning of the cards.

In the meantime, Ted and I had been seeing each other more and more over that winter sort of secretly. Even writing the truth in the situation makes me feel like a piece of crap. I know better than to hold on to those feelings, but I am sure that when I get back to The Lobby after this life, I will have to look at this time in my life in my meeting. What would become very clear within the year or two to follow was that this time would be one of the most painful and pivotal times in the lives of all three of us, Ted, Les, and me. Les continued to teach me the meanings of the tarot cards and at some point, he started having me pull cards for him every other day or so, and the same cards kept coming up. I was pulling the Kings and Queens of Pentacles and the death card a lot. Les stopped talking to me about what the cards meant, and we would move on to astral travel. When I think back on that time now, so many random pieces and conversations fall into place. I was so young and so naive.

As the winter droned on, Les began to share with me that he had been involved with a group of "magical individuals" from one of the coastal towns in New Hampshire about 200 miles away. When I say magical, I don't mean "rabbit in hat" magician, I literally mean a coven or group of people who practice what might be called black magic. There is a huge swath of the population on Earth who think that this subject is not real, imaginary, or possibly delusional, but let me stress here, for every coin there are two sides, and humans wielding energy is **very powerful**, which is one of the biggest reasons for this book with Aralamb. Aralamb has always imprinted on my thought process the huge responsibility "energy work" carries and the idea that what you put out into the Universe energetically comes back at you much larger than you sent it out. So, it stands to reason that belonging to a coven or circle of black magicians might be a sobering and frightening situation to be in or try to get out of.

Les slowly unfolded for me a story in which he had been living on the coast in New Hampshire and was involved with such a group, a large one, that was "in the business" with all kinds of nefarious behavior, that is, drugs, money laundering, violence, and generally ruling over a sort of dark arts stranglehold on that city with energetic magical workings and violence for sale. You may be saying, "What??? Is this some kind of joke? A movie script?" Nope, it's true. You should know also that there are many groups similar to this one at work on our planet right now as you read these words. He also went on to tell me that this particular group was the kind that, not unlike the Mafia, was impossible to leave with your skin intact once you made the commitment to them. At some point, he had decided to get out, sort of leave on bad terms, and cut the ties that bound him to them. Just to add a little more danger, he took some books which he said were not only their sort of magical group meeting notes but also tons of contacts, names, and money information. He literally left in the night with some of their shit! Turns out that he was a very trusted person in their circle, so that pissed them off even more.

During the afternoon of one particularly massive snowstorm on a Monday in April, Ted let everyone out of work at noon from the lumberyard. He had to go home to plow his place and get his kids. I headed up Crow Hill in Chester to pick up my two-year-old son Hunter at Gramma Joanie's house from his day care. I drove up there in that flatbed pickup and had every intention of staying warm and dry back in town, in that cozy trailer for the rest of the day and into the night while the storm blew outside. Ted was coming later with some groceries and to plow the driveway. I was so happy to not be working in that cold warehouse on that afternoon. If a lumberyard shuts down due to weather, in *Vermont*, then snow is gonna be deep and it's gonna be bad. Vermonters, including me, pride themselves on being able to traverse any kind of weather with bald tires, no heat, no wipers, and no hat! No problem!

After picking up Hunter and getting safely down Crow Hill, we were snow covered, but warm in the trailer. I could crank that heating system up. There was no thermostat, it was either on at 90 or off, it kind of smelled a bit like kerosene, but it was so warm. It was so warm in fact that every window in that old trailer would steam up on the inside. We were cozy. I put Hunter down for his nap at 2:00 in the afternoon. He was a monster sleeper. He would sleep from 2:00 p.m. to 4:30 p.m. completely gone to the world when he was a toddler. Sometimes I would have to wake him up at 5:00 p.m. so he would go back to bed before 10:00 p.m. About 15 minutes after I got Hunter down, a car pulled in through the two feet of newly blown snow into our driveway. It was Les. He came in without knocking, which was not so strange, Les was not a big "stand on niceties kind of guy." He had two packs of cigarettes, Camels, a big box of doughnuts, and an unopened half gallon of Wild Turkey (this was 1988, back when doughnuts, liquor, and cigarettes were still considered a staple in any home, and a great hostess gift).

Les sat down on my couch. I will never forget that that Dwight Yoakam cassette was playing on my hobbled together stereo. Les cracked open that Wild Turkey, and said, "We gotta talk." The conversation that ensued was basically Les informing me that "I" was going to be his energetic partner in trying to bring the magical ring/group that he had fled from down. I sat there listening to his plans, "You're really fast learner," and he knew that together he and I could destroy this group before they even knew what had hit them. He explained that he had gotten word that they were "looking for him," and he believed that they had found him in our town.

Les seemed a bit desperate and said he had built up a blocking spell around the lumberyard, his home, his wife, his kids, family, and generally the area of our town, but he could not keep it going himself, it had grown too big. He told me that for a few years he had been looking for someone, preferably female, to assist him in "holding" this energy field in place for the protection of his family and friends. He said that I was the one who was going to help him and that my "real training would need to begin right away."

While he was talking, he had opened the Wild Turkey and was drinking it off and on straight from the bottle. I had eaten two doughnuts already and smoked a cigarette without saying anything. Before I responded at all, he handed me the bottle and I took a big, long pull from it. I had never had Wild Turkey before, and immediately understood that taking such a big long pull from that bottle would leave my throat and guts burning for hours afterward.

I have wished so many times in my life that I had been older or wiser, or just more knowledgeable about reincarnation, energy, astral travel, blocking energy, or any other tool that can be used energetically. But I was completely ignorant. I was ignorant, young, and because of that my response was young and immature and frankly selfish. I listened to what he was asking me. I was listening to what he was saying, but I could not wrap my mind around the idea that he was actually speaking "literally" to me. He was being literal and factual about the events that had happened.

Although I felt a real connection with Les, I didn't really believe him. I should have, but I just didn't. In the same situation today, I would have 100 ways to be of help to him, but then I didn't trust myself, I just didn't believe him…. What he was telling me seemed so outlandish and so crazy that I just thought he was literally messing with me for whatever reason. I just didn't believe him. I was thinking, as I am sure you are thinking right now, a movie script, or a fictional tale, he is crazy. I would come to understand later that it was none of those things, but the actual truth.

We spent a couple of hours with him explaining to me that "I" was a natural at this work, and I could help him put a new coven together. A "coven" is a specific group of people, who all agree to gather, work, and do ritual energetic magic in order to further a group cause. Covens can be small, as few as two people, or huge with no real number limit. Often, covens are in groups of 12 or 13 and female only. Some, like the large group Les had belonged to, were both men and women. The group was large, he said, consisting of about 40 members. Les believed that I could help him to put this group, who he was convinced was coming for him, away. He wanted to do it energetically. He said that he had connections and that we could put together a magical group that would be bigger, better, and, most of all, "more powerful" than the group on the coast who was threatening him. After a lot of trying to convince me, a bunch more cigarettes, and a few more sips of the Wild Turkey, I just said, "No." He became kind of desperate and said, "Please, please, let me teach you, I need your help." I again said "No. You know, Les, it's getting to be dinnertime, Hunter will be awake soon, Ted is coming with food, and I can't help you. You have to go." "Please Melissa, just let me explain how important this is, I need your help. We can stop them together." Looking at him then, I understood that he was serious, which scared me even more because I really thought he had lost his goddammed mind. I sat back on that big velour couch I had, lit my 20th cigarette in three hours, and just said, "No, and I don't want to talk about this anymore. I'm not your girl." I blew that menthol smoke out in a long arcing blue exhale that didn't stop until it was across the room hitting the kitchen curtains with the snow still coming down hard outside. There was a long, long silence. Then Les smiled a really broken kind of smile and took another long hit from the Wild Turkey.

I would think of this moment years later and still do today, and I will never forget the look on his face. In retrospect, I understand the look was some kind of understanding or resignation of having turned some corner. His face was so, so sad. I know now and I can see that the smile he gave me was so sad too. A broken and resigned smile. At the time, on that snowy afternoon, I didn't see what kind of sadness it was, but traveling back there, to that day, I wish I could have been more able to *see*....

At that very moment, a car pulled in. It was Les's wife. She had been worried about him in the storm and headed out to search for him. She came through the front door, without knocking, and without looking at me, said "Les, let's go, now, we gotta pick up the kids and get home before the stove goes out." He got up and walked out without his Wild Turkey, without looking at me at all. I felt weird and so sad myself, although I could not have told you why at that time. I was also just happy that he was gone. I felt like something important had just happened, but I could not put my finger on what or why I felt so amazingly shitty for not agreeing to help him. After the car pulled away, I put the Wild Turkey on top of my refrigerator where it lived for many years after that untouched but travelled with me through many moves after that trailer.

Ted pulled in about 10 minutes later, wet, smelling like snow with a big bag of groceries and I didn't mention that Les had even been at the trailer. That was Monday afternoon. In the next few days, life went on like usual. I did not see Les as much on Tuesday or Wednesday at the kiln but didn't think a lot about our conversation. He seemed a bit aloof but not angry with me in any way, and the huge snowstorm had left everyone scrambling to clean up the yard, move pallets around, and make up for the missed work.

One of my jobs at the lumberyard was to go in and do moisture readings on the lumber stacked in the kilns. It was dark and warm inside the kilns, and there were fans blowing all the time. The lumber was held at very specific temperatures so that the cut lumber would dry evenly, slowly, and without "checking." If the lumber dried too fast, it would have weird little spots and splits in it, which made it worth less at sale, so monitoring the kilns was important. On Wednesday that week, I was in the kiln with Les, following him and taking down the moisture measurements that he was getting. Ted was on a two-day trip to the home office in Maine, and so Les was in charge of the lumberyard for a couple of days.

I was following Les around in the kiln and picking my way around the various pallets of lumber which all had the small stickers in them to let the warm air circulate. It was so warm in there and smelled so lovely like freshly cut wood. I always associated that smell with my dad, as he was a full-time house builder and smelled like that all the time. When we were finished getting the readings, Les turned to go and I spun behind him to leave. He had not said anything at all to me; we had just walked around in the kiln taking readings. Normally, this would have made me really uncomfortable. I would have been chirping away, talking, and or asking him if he was pissed at me for "not" helping him, but on that day, his energy was just calm and not angry at all. So, we had done the whole inspection in a comfortable silence. I felt like offering him up a friendly hug, kind of an "I'm sorry," but didn't.

As I turned to leave the kiln, I walked at full speed right into a 2x6 piece of lumber that was jutting out from a pallet. I can sort of remember looking down in the dim light to step over a support strut that was on the ground, and when I looked back up, my face, more specifically the bridge of my nose, smacked the 2x6 in full force and with a forward motion. I felt the most pain in my face I can ever remember feeling. I fell backward, saw stars, and felt like throwing up all at once. Les leaned down to help me to my feet, and that's when the blood started streaming out of both sides of my nose. Les helped me to the yard office, grabbed a t-shirt off a hook, and placed it over my now swelling nose. My face was quickly doubling in size and my eyes were swelling shut. He told everyone he was taking me to the ER in Springfield which was about 15 miles away and we got in his car. I was in so much pain, that I just kept moaning. My nose was steadily bleeding. Les took the back way to Springfield, up over Crow Hill, which, looking back now, seems kind of odd as it was all up through the woods rather than just the main road. He was very sweet and kept telling me to just hold pressure on my nose which, he said, "was fucking broken as bad as he had ever seen!"

When we arrived at the emergency department, they took me right into an examination room. Most likely because I was dripping blood all over the floor in the lobby. I was laid out on a table with my heavy parka still on. It was so covered with blood that the nurse looked at me, then at Les, and said accusingly, "Did he do this to you, honey?" Les quickly let her know that it was going to be a work comp issue and generally what had happened. By this time, I was barely able to speak with the whole front of my head blowing up with swelling. This was 1988 and still a cell phone-free time. The nurse called my dad on a black wall phone from the ER cubicle where I laid. He was on his way to come get me. About that time a nice nurse came and gave me a shot of something in my butt cheek that made all the pain go away and made me nice and warm.

The doctor came in, removed the bloody t-shirt from my face, and I heard and saw Les take in a huge hissing breath, "jeeeeeeezzzzuzzz! Ssssssssssss." Due to the pain-killing shot, it made me laugh, which made blood spurt out my broken nose even more. The doctor took two long cylindrical, white-padded post-looking pieces of gauze out, grabbed both sides of my face, told Les to grab my hand, and literally jerked my broken semblance of a nose back into place. Les gave out another gasp, laughed, and the deed was done. The doctor pushed those two cylindrical pieces up into my nostrils, taped up my whole head, and said, "Okay, I am going to give you a prescription for the pain, but over the next two days your eyes will likely swell shut and it's gonna hurt like hell for a week or so. You will need to take it easy till next week anyway. No lifting or straining and I'd lay off any drinking or partying." He smiled and walked out of the room.

Les was looking pale, which made me think I must have looked pretty bad because not much got to Les. I couldn't talk at that point because my face was wrapped up like some Civil War casualty victim that you would see in reenactment photos. Les stood up, let go of my hand, and said, "Listen, I have something for you, but I don't want you to open it now. It's just insurance. If anything happens to me, open it." I started to shake my head, he was being weird, but the pain stopped me. He said, "I just want you to keep this and don't worry about anything." He leaned over, kissed my forehead, and said, "Your dad will be here soon. I will see you in a couple of days." He smiled, squeezed my hand, pulled an envelope out of his jacket, pressed it into my hand, smiled at me again, a really beautiful smile, which made me feel like a total piece of shit for some reason, and turned to go. He stopped one more time, looked at me with that happy, sad, loving sort of way, and something inside me wanted to rear up and say "No, don't go, I will help you, I love you, I'm sorry." I felt like I was letting my brother down even though we weren't related.

I didn't say any of those things; I was also really shocked that I wanted to say them. "I love you?" Jesus, what the hell was wrong with me? I figured it was the painkiller shot I had gotten but watching him go made my stomach burn. I didn't say anything at all. I gave him a thumbs-up. I felt like I should do more, something, I don't know. A thumbs-up? It felt hollow for some reason. I know better now, when I have that kind of an intuition, feeling, prompting from my soul to tell a person the truth, a true feeling, I do it. I do it when it's not easy. I do it when it's awkward. I do it when it's not the right time or place. I do it even if it's going to make me look idiotic. I do it because intuition is our connection to The Creator/God. It is our one true tool, and we avoid listening to it because half the dumbass shit we do in our lives, we would have avoided if we had just listened to our gut, our intuition, and worst of all, we know that and still choose badly.

My dad showed up just moments after Les left. He was a brilliant guy, my dad. He was also a maintenance alcoholic without one mean bone in his body, so he kind of smelled a bit like Picardy 151, but he came and took me home, went and picked up Hunter, dropped him off with my mom for a couple of days while I laid on my couch with my entire head throbbing like a bomb had gone off in my brain. I had put Les's envelope in the pocket of my big work parka in the ER, and due to the massive pain meds, I was on,

I totally forgot it was there. Ted came back to town on Thursday morning and brought me groceries and took one look at my nose and said, "Shit, that IS bad!" By that time, my face was purple, green, and black with dried blood where I could not wash it yet.

Ted had pulled up in a new car he had picked up. It was a gold tone 1968 Malibu or something like it. It was an old muscle car. It was loud, and it looked cool, and my dad said it would "go like a raped ape." Probably not such a politically correct phrase to use today but in 1988 it was fitting for Ted's new car. I stood in the window of my trailer, my giant swollen face throbbing, and waived as Ted pulled away in that car.

The next afternoon, Ted came by the trailer. He was checking in on me as I was not supposed to return to work until Monday. He checked out my face and said the words that often came out of his mouth followed by a whistle, "Jesus H Christ! That must hurt something fierce." We both laughed hard but that hurt even more, so I just waived him off. He said, "Hey, Les and I are going to go out on Saturday afternoon. Take my new ride out and hit some back roads. Maybe go for some food and a drink. You wanna ride along?" That was two days away, and I figured getting out of the house would be great. Plus, the weather had turned, and the Spring blizzard that had blown through earlier in the week was melting and it was supposed to be a beautiful weekend. "Sure, let me know what time." He kissed my forehead and left with a smile. The three of us, Ted, me, and Les, had gotten into the habit of cruising to various friends' houses to party so this request was not out of the ordinary. He had also left two bags of groceries, a 30-pack of Pampers and two packs of Newport Menthols on the counter. You might be thinking that is the most "white trash" things I have ever heard. I suppose it was. You know, in 1988, in small towns all over our country, there were people living just this way, and still are. Working, trying to keep warm, and take care of their kids. I would not trade the struggles for anything looking back. Like Aralamb always says, "All of the hardest things in our lives give us the opportunity for the biggest growth and change as souls." I have lived many ways, with money, without money, and every way in between. All of that has taught me that every soul is really the same.

By Saturday morning, my face was pretty green, but the pain was much less and my giant "nose strap" had been reduced to just a sturdy piece of tape running sideways across my face, making me look like a football player. My eyes were not so swollen; my whole face was just really bruised. I was ready to get out of the trailer and do something. I was getting dressed to go to my mom's and pick up Hunter, when my phone rang. Funny, how certain things in your past get stuck in your mind as kind of visceral high-definition slide show. That big avocado-colored wall phone was one of those things. It was hung on the wall right where the long trailer hall started. It had a 20-foot cord on it that was always tangled. Looking back on it, I guess the cord was 20 feet long so that if you were folding laundry onto your bed at one far end, you could stretch it all the way down the hall and cradle it between your chin and neck while folding laundry and talking. On the other side, you could stand at the kitchen sink end, doing dishes, talking with it cradled between you neck and shoulder. In either direction, you would have that cord stretched to its limits. I can only marvel at the fact that some "trailer park rocket scientist" figured out that to place it just to the right of the picture window in the living room would do the trick in either direction. Everything you needed, including the "crapper," was within reach of that cord. I bring this memory of the phone up because the ringing of that phone twice in the four days that were to come would be pivotal moments in my life. Aralamb tells me that sometimes the Universe will give "lucid color to certain moments in our lives in order that we remember and fully understand how that moment changes/changed us." It's as if the moment is to be imprinted upon our soul.

On that afternoon, when that phone rang, I was still healing up from my broken nose, and my voice sounded muffled and strange like I was breathing through a big gob of whipped cream. That phone was loud too, as the volume knob on the bottom was broken. If I was outside when it rang, my neighbor would often yell from her kitchen, "Melissa! Your phone is ringing." I think she did this just to be passive-aggressive, as I am not sure that she approved of my "comings and goings," as my Gramma Patty would say. I ran into the trailer to grab the phone and the voice on the other end was a total surprise.

Barry had been my high school sweetheart and first love. He would also go on to become my second husband. He had joined the Navy and moved to California. He was married out there, and I had not heard from him in three years or so. He didn't recognize my voice at first, as I was talking through a mound of swollen whipped cream of bandages and asked, "Is Melissa there?" I immediately recognized his voice, and if I am honest, prayed that he was calling me from California because I was mortified about having to see him with my face in the condition it was. Turns out that he was in town just for the weekend, for his Gramma's funeral and wanted to have dinner with me on Saturday evening. I agreed, even before I thought of anything else. I was young, having a kind of secret relationship with an older and still married man, I had made plans with Ted and Les for Saturday already, but I knew that if Barry was in town, I would have to see him. It was a no-brainer. We made plans that he would pick me up on Saturday afternoon. We would take a ride around some of our old haunts and then go get dinner. He kept telling me he was married, so I eventually said, "Hey, let's just get together as friends. I'm just so glad to be able to see you." It was so strange to me that he just appeared into my weekend after he and I had been so out of touch, but I was thrilled to see him.

Ted called me from the lumberyard the very next morning and asked what time he and Les should pick me up that afternoon. I told him that an old friend had come to town and that I was going to have to "rain check" them for next time. I was secretly glad that he didn't ask me "what old friend," or he would have most likely been upset. He told me that he and Les were going to be up at the lumberyard for a few hours catching up on some inventory lists. The inventory was a constant and massive undertaking at the lumberyard. Millions of feet of green lumber being brought in, stacked, dried, and then, hopefully, the same number of feet going out to buyers, without much loss. The numbers were checked and rechecked constantly. As we hung up, I asked him where they were going, and he said, "Probably Springfield, not totally sure yet. Give me a call here at the kiln if you change your mind!" I told him I would and that I would get with him on Sunday sometime. We hung up.

Later that day, Barry showed up to get me and we hugged, but it was a really long hug, which was also totally platonic. In a way it was like hugging a long-lost family member. I think Barry and I have always felt that way. Like family. We went for a drive, and we talked and talked about all that had happened to each of us over the last three years. As it turns out, he was married to a woman who he actually loved quite a bit, but she was kind of a "hell raiser" and liked to get drunk and "beat on him a bit." I laughed and said, "How the hell do you get beat on just a bit?" I was happy that he just came right out and told me all about his marriage in that way, as if I was his sister. There was comfort in that. After dinner, we went and had a drink at the local bar, and then back to my place to drop me off.

He wanted to come in, and it was late. I wasn't sure exactly if that was a good idea, and he said, listen, "I haven't seen you in a while, and I just want to talk more and just hang out. I don't want to go back to my mom's house tonight, I leave super early in the morning, and I would just like to stay here." So, he came in, and we just laid down on my bed, with all of our clothes on and talked for hours and hours till about 2:00 a.m. Totally in the dark. We lay side by side on the bed, on our backs, holding hands like two 10-year-olds at summer camp. Like brother and sister. We talked and talked.

Looking back on that time, I know that the Universe sent Barry into my life for one 24-hour period in order to "hold my space." Literally to hold me in a space. Barry woke up at 4:00 a.m., hugged me, and left. I would not see him again for 10 years. I would, however, be grateful every day that he came to lay on my bed that night and talk till dawn. Had he not done that, I believe that the writing of this book would not have been. After he left, I went back and crawled into my bed for a good long sleep. It was still dark, after I heard Barry's car leave my driveway, I thought I heard him walking back up to my door. I sat up, thinking he had left something, but he was not there. No one was there. I knew that I had heard someone. I was exhausted and my nose was throbbing, so I just let it go and went back to bed. I fell asleep hard.

I came awake at 7:45 a.m. to the sound of that big avocado green phone ringing, ringing, ringing so loud. The phone was down the long hall, but I could see it from where I lay when my eyes popped open. I can't remember what I was thinking when I jerked out of bed, but I can remember having that sensation in the front of my face which was not unlike that fainting sensation that accompanies acute pain. I hurried down the hall because it was so early for the phone to be ringing and I knew it was probably waking up my neighbor. She would be so pissed if it woke her kids up.

"Hello." "Melissa, it's Moana, have your heard what happened last night? "No, what?" I answered with a bit of annoyance because my face was throbbing, it was early, and I figured it was some kind of gossip that could most likely wait till later in the day. I was going to dinner later at my mom's house, and Moana would be there along with all the other menagerie of my mom's party friends.

Hunter had been at my mom's since Wednesday when I broke my nose. The doctor had told me that I should not pick him up at all or do any lifting, as the pressure would not only cause massive pain in my face but also dislodge his setting job. Hunter was still a little guy, and I was picking him up 100 times a day at least. So, I was headed over there that afternoon to have dinner, go to the soiree, and pick up Hunter.

"What, Moana?" I lit a cigarette and sat on the arm of my sofa. Her next words to me are a bit blurry because honestly, I think that my mind went into some kind of tunnel vision. "Ted and Les were in a wreck last night, and Les was killed. They went off the road up near Putney and a huge tree limb came in the front of the car all the way to Ted's side and it killed

Les. The ambulance got there about 30 minutes later, but he was gone. Ted was there with him, and he just died in his arms."

All the blood began draining from my face and I thought I might puke. I can't tell you what all I was thinking; it was more like a feeling. I was numb and on fire all at the same time. "Moana, I gotta go, I will talk with you later." I slammed that phone on the hook and slid down the wall into a fetal position. What, what, what, what, what? Tears started coming from my eyes, but I can't remember crying. I stood up, immediately ran to the bathroom, and puked. Puking made my face scream in pain, and I threw up again. I walked to the living room and sat down on the sofa, crying and crying but not making any noise. I lit up another cigarette and my mind was whirling in that kind of spiral that happens when someone you care about is gone. There is no sense, there is no time, you just go kind of blank while tears roll down your face. I took a huge inhale from that cigarette and across the room, my eyes rested on the coat rack and all my winter clothes hanging there. My eyes finally landed on my work parka, which still had some dried blood on it from going to the ER, and the realization hit me slowly that in the pocket of that jacket was the sealed note that Les left me.

Moving from the couch to the coat rack, that phone started ringing again, but I ignored it. I grabbed into the pocket for the envelope. Somewhere in my mind I thought that it must have been a dream, he had not really handed me this just three days ago and told me to "hold it in case anything happens to me. Just keep it somewhere safe." He could not have said those words to me just on Wednesday....

I jammed my hand into my deep parka pockets, hoping that I would find nothing. Instead, my hand wrapped around a white letter-sized envelope with my name on it. I walked back to the couch with it, thinking I might throw up again. I tore it open and saw a two-page letter typed on what looked to me to be a manual typewriter. I began to read, with so many tears running down my face that I kept having to wipe my eyes in order to see. For years later, that letter had the stains of those tears on it. It read like this:

Melissa,

I am writing this to you to explain some things. I am afraid that if you are reading this then something has happened to me. I want you to know some things. A lot of this is really important, and you have to do exactly what I say. I want you to know that you and I had a lifetime before this one a long time ago. We have known each other before, more than once.

I don't want you to feel bad about not helping me. I did not have enough time to teach you. It's okay. I told you that the group that I had been working for on the Coast were looking for me and that they wanted to hurt me. They have been reaching out to me for some time now with spell-casting. I have felt them getting closer. I am afraid that they have found me. I have never told them about you, but I am afraid that they may be looking for you also now. They know I was looking for help and had found someone. If something has happened to me, I need you to listen to me now. Do not go to my funeral. Do not go to any memorials for me. Do not go to any parties that are thrown in my honor. Do not go to my graveside and visit or leave flowers. Never go to my gravesite. I know I talked with you about these things already, and you didn't want to talk about it, but I mean it. I don't want you going to any services or memorials for me. I don't want you to ask any questions or go looking for them. I was going to leave you the items that I took from them, but I have hidden them instead. I did not want to leave them with you or my family. I want you to lay low and stay out of sight. These people will come to my funeral as old friends. They will show up as my friends, they will be watching. They will be looking for anyone that they think I might have talked to about them or made friends with. Please do this for me. Don't feel bad, it's okay. I was too late finding you. It's not your fault.

Love Les

I don't know when the phone stopped ringing, I can't remember when my tears stopped flowing that morning. I don't know how long I sat there with that letter in my hand, hunched like a child against the wall of that trailer. I don't know. I only know that reading his letter made me suddenly understand, without even having any details about the accident, that the world was not as I had understood it. The Universe was not what I had been led to believe. Fear. Cold, sorrowful, out-of-control raging fear gripped me. I thought of Les's wife and small children and a rage grew in me, and a fear grew in me that I didn't recognize at all. Can this be a real thing? Can this kind of energy really be true? Am I having some kind of actual mental breakdown? Did the hit to the front of my face leave me brain damaged? I could not make my thoughts stop swirling around in a circle. It was clearly an accident, just a terrible accident, but the letter in my hand pointed at something else entirely. Was the letter in my hand some piece of proof about horrible coincidence? Was it just a weird fluke of timing, nature, and the complete non-specificity of life events? What the fuck was happening. My mind kept on going in circles while I sat there crying. I would learn later in my life that energy, the kind that Einstein wrote about, is and can be used as a tool, but on that early morning I could not make sense of what had happened, and I was so very afraid of how the world was tilting on its side.

At some point, that big green phone had stopped ringing, and started up again and this time it did not stop. I stood up and grabbed the receiver. It was my dad. He was crying and said, "Oh my god! You're okay. I didn't know where you were last night, and I thought you might have been with them. Your grandmother just called me out of her mind with worry." "I'm okay, Dad," I said. He asked me if I knew what happened and I told him I did not, only that Ted and Les had been in a wreck and Les had been killed. I was talking to him in that kind of voice where you hear it coming out of your face, and you also know that it's not in any way connected with what is going on emotionally in your body, mind, or heart. He said he was going to my mom's later for dinner and he would see me there. I said, "Okay, Dad, I love you. Don't worry, I met a friend last night, I was not with them."

We hung up, and then it hit me again, Les was gone, and I had not been with them. I was not in the middle seat front of that big old car. I had not been a witness or victim of that horrible event. The next few days will always live in my mind as a tunnel of just dark, frightening feelings, interspersed with taking care of Hunter, going to work, and generally trying to piece together what had happened to Ted and Les on that night.

I was still trying to be in complete denial about the accident and the letter from Les which had been given to me just days before. I had not talked to Ted. Ted had gone home after the accident and was holed up with his family, which was the exact right thing to do. Ted did not know about the letter at this point, and I had no idea how I would have explained it to him anyway. He had been in a horrible accident, come out with no injuries that were physical at least, and had lost his best friend in the package. I could not reach out to him, and I could not stop thinking about him and the pain he must be in. I could not stop thinking of Les's wife and family. I also could not stop reading the letter....

In the weeks to follow, I laid very low. I did not go to the funeral. I did not go to the wake afterward. I did not attend the party at the P-House held in Les's honor. My mother, I think, was surprised, but I have no idea if anyone else even noticed that I did not go. I just told people that I was sick. That I had come down with a horrible cold and that my nose was still hurting a lot. I just worked and went home with Hunter. I felt so much guilt for not attending the services and so much fear about Les's warnings not to attend anything. The day after Les's funeral, I was at home in the evening. I still had not seen or spoken to Ted, and I knew that he was dealing with the fallout of the wreck and trying to sort it all out. I did not reach out to him. I knew he would get a hold of me when he felt like it was time.

In the days after the services for Les, I had phone calls from my mother and my dad telling me that some of Les's friends had stayed in town for a bit and was I coming to the bar later that night for drinks as a band was playing. I declined. I did not want to meet any of Les's old buddies, and as a matter of fact had been warned against it by his letter. The bar that my dad was referring to was the main watering hole at that time for the whole town. It was literally two city blocks from my house, just out of sight, but just a stone's throw away.

That night, I was getting ready for bed and my phone rang again. I grabbed it quick so as not to wake Hunter and it was Shelly. Shelly was a friend from work and was calling from the P-House to get me to come over. "It's packed in here tonight! There are tons of people from out of town, you're single, get your ass over here!" Getting a call from the P-House was not a strange event for anyone who was within my mom's party circle and by birth, I was in that circle. "Oh, no, Shelly, I'm done, I have Hunter here and I'm just gonna hit the sack." "Come ON," she said. "Don't be a pain in the ass! Come over for one drink." "No, I will talk to you Monday," I told her, feeling a heavy bad prickly sensation crawl up the back of my neck. I could hear the crowd and music in the background. The P-House had its own large goldenrod-colored phone with a long stretched out cord hanging off the wall, which patrons used all the time in their efforts to get more of their favorite party buddies to "come on down!"

"Fine then, be a shit! I will see you on Monday." I told her to be safe on the way home and hung up the phone. I realized right then that I had been having a coiling, creeping, growing fear deep in my belly. The fear had been growing and rising up day after day without me really knowing it was happening. I left the kitchen light on, headed down the hall, checked in on Hunter who was fully sleeping and climbed on my bed. I became suddenly very aware that I was in a trailer full of windows whose curtains were all open and I was like a big, dumb, goldfish in a well-lit bowl. Anyone could be outside looking at me and I would not know it. I turned off my bedroom light and started to yank all the curtains shut. I ran down the hall and literally slid my hand around the corner to turn off the kitchen light. I was in the dark now but could still see the streetlight flooding into the main rooms of the trailer from Depot Street.

I ran around yanking all those curtains close too. The trailer was dark except for the glow of the streetlights through the white curtains. At least I was not such a fish in a bowl. I stopped myself, what was my fucking problem? Nothing was happening, no one was watching me, but I could not shake the feeling of being watched or searched out or stalked in a way. I was so scared. I thought about crawling into bed with Hunter, but that only seemed more desperate and paranoid, so I ran down the hall and climbed under my covers and laid there in the dark. My alarm clock showed 10:30 p.m. It was not even late. I would get out of here tomorrow. I would go shopping and take Hunter with me. In the daylight, this stupid fear would go away. At some point, I fell into sleep.

I don't remember dreaming anything, and I don't remember hearing anything per se, but I came fully awake in the dark of my room very abruptly. The head of my bed was along the wall where the hall was, so without moving, I could see the whole length of the trailer all the way to the end where the kitchen was, one long open space lit softly by the streetlight at the end of the circular drive. As my eyes came open, something in me said, "Stay still." I did not move a muscle. It was as if I was still sleeping, but my eyes were open. At the far end of the long hall, at the front door of the kitchen, I could just make out a moving shape. At first I thought it might have been Ted, he had a key, he could have come in quietly so as not to wake Hunter. He had done so many times, but there was no sound, just a dark shape. A kind of dark quasi human form moving very deliberately, and it/they seemed to be kind of searching around. I had a bird's eye view of the whole event as if it were a movie. I was wide awake, and I knew that I was. I could feel my body break out in a prickly sweat under the blankets. I was watching a dark shadowy human-ish shaped energy moving around my kitchen and living room sort of looking around and into things. Seemingly peering into cupboards, boxes, drawers…. I had fear knotting in my body that was like something atomic which was at the number 5 of a 20-second countdown to detonation. The only part of me moving was my eyes and they were wide open.

Again, I heard in my mind, "Be still." At that very moment, the dark shape seemed to be moving toward me down the hall, passing Hunter's bedroom door. As the shape passed the halfway point of the hall, the smell of roses filled my head, my face, and the whole trailer. Again, I hear, "Be still." I know the smell of roses filled the whole trailer because it lingered in reality for days afterward. As the smell filled the air, I lay there literally frozen in my bed as just 15 feet away, the dark shape paused, paused again, turned away from me, paused again, turned back and came three feet closer to me, and as suddenly as it was there, moved back down the hall and out "through" the front door and was gone. My pillow was wet. I had not realized that tears, fear, and sweat had been rolling out of my body the whole time I lay there "being still."

I cried openly then, sat up on the edge of my bed, and went to check on Hunter. The smell of roses was heavy but so safe feeling somehow, and Hunter was asleep and fine. I crept silently with my back against the trailer wall down the long hall and out to the living room, peeking out past the curtains. No one in the yard. No cars, no people walking by. I could see the glowing lights from the P-House. It was 1:30 a.m. on the kitchen clock so the bar would be closing up soon. I have never been so dazedly scared ever in my life as I was at that point, and I had no one at all to talk to about it. I had witnessed something, someone, something inspect my house while I laid there paralyzed and watched, and I was done. I was so scared that I could not feel my body anymore.

I ran back to my bed, rolled up in my blankets, peered down the hall, and I started praying to God....

When I say praying, I mean praying to GOD with a capitol G.... I prayed to my God, I prayed to your God, I prayed to Buddha's God, to Allah's God, I prayed to Jewish God, I prayed to Hindu God, I prayed to Jesus and all the Saints, I prayed to Catholic God, I prayed to who the fuck ever was the maker of THE UNIVERSE, I apologized for it in advance if I was in any way picking the wrong path to GOD, but I kept on praying to every God that any human has every prayed to. I prayed to whatever GOD was the GOD who created everything. My prayer was simple, it went like this. I still say this prayer to this day. I will never forget it. **"God, you made me this way, you made me sensitive, you gave me the ability to see things, to hear things that others don't seem to hear. Please send me help. If you made me sensitive, then I want to do YOUR work. I want you to send me help so that I can do what it is YOU put me here to do. Please send me help, I need you to let me know what it is YOU want me to do for YOU with my life. Please send me help."** I prayed, and prayed, and repeated that prayer, and kept smelling the roses, and cried. Then I prayed some more until I fell asleep at some point.

I came awake at 7:00 a.m. with Hunter crawling up into bed with me. He climbed under the blankets and said, "Momma, I'm hungry." The smell of roses was everywhere. Hunter has always been my fellow traveler in this world, and he has always been my rock. I could even smell roses on him. Once I had him on the couch, under a blanket with a big bowl of Fruit Loops and some Pop Tarts, cartoons blaring (don't judge, it was a different time), I sat with my coffee thinking about the night before and the dark presence that had so physically been in the trailer. The trailer felt light now, sunshine was pouring in all the windows, and the smell of roses was still hanging in the air. I know that it sounds completely unreal, but it is true. I was still really scared, but something had shifted, and I could feel it right to my bones.

Rather than bore you with all of my mundane chores of that Sunday, I want to go right to when Aralamb showed up in my life, which was later that evening. It was that evening after I went to bed that my Aunt Ruthie showed up.

My Great Aunt Ruthie had died when I was about eight years old. Ruthie and Herbie Fostman lived in Rutland, Vermont. They were a childless couple and seemed to put all of the love they had into their huge Victorian house in the old part of Rutland. The house was huge and white with multiple porches and turret annexes. The entry to that house had a huge polished elegant stairway leading up and away into the upper floors. Handmade doilies were everywhere like snowflakes on every surface. As a little girl, my grandmother would take my sister and I to Aunt Ruthie's house on weekends. She was a tiny, white-haired woman who always smelled like roses. She had huge rose gardens in the back yard of her house, and in the summer she had over large white vases of them inside her house, which was magical to me as a child. I can remember that they were beautiful, velvety, pink, and white ones mostly.

The summer air there would be filled with the smell of roses so strong that it was literally intoxicating. Aunt Ruthie was like one of those magical fairy godmother types, or maybe Mrs. Santa Claus, or Good Witch Glinda when she finally got old. She always wore a long dark skirt and a pressed white blouse with a beautiful broach at her neck. Ruthie had a soft stark white puff of hair and clear skin. She had a beautiful smile and would set up elaborate tea parties in that rose garden for us with sandwiches and 10 kinds of star anise cookies, glaze dripping from them. She wore bright pink lipstick and her huge kitchen always shined and smelled like wax paper and cinnamon. I loved her dearly when I was a very young child. She was just one of those special people that you recognize immediately as one of a kind, just special.

That night in my trailer years after her death, Ruthie came to me in a dream. She sat on the edge of my bed and stroked my head. She said,

"Melissa, help is coming. I am going to stay with you always, but your help is coming. Don't worry, little girl, help is coming. Aralamb is his name. He is your teacher, your guide. His energy is very big and it may take you some time to get used to it, but your prayer has been heard, your help is coming. I will stay with you and when you wake up in the morning, Aralamb will be here too. Don't be afraid, he is going to teach you." I do not remember any more dreams that night, but I will always remember that one.

When the alarm went off in the morning before work, I awoke to the smell of roses and the presence of Aralamb in my life. I was not afraid, I was overwhelmed because the presence of Aralamb was huge, big, and filled the space like a beautiful clearing or meadow you find on a trek in the woods when you don't know it existed. From the most terrifying time of my life came a safe place. I can't tell you how, but I could FEEL Aralamb there, at my side, with me, but my journey began then.

I could not speak directly with him back then, but I would often get impressions of his opinions on things. As time went by, I began to be able to hear him, and respond in kind. For many years now, I have been able to have conversations with him as if he is standing next to me in the room. That time was a huge transition for me. I understand now that bringing one's guide into one's life need not be that dramatic or frightening, but for me this was that moment.

CHAPTER 3

The Lobby
(Heaven, the other side)

The Lobby

(also known as Heaven, Nirvana, The Afterlife, Shambala, The Other Side, The Great White Way)

Aralamb

I have allowed Melissa to continually use the term "The Lobby" as a descriptive name for the energy plane strata from where I reside. It is a universal human ideology and mental picture that is most correctly and universally used to engage the visual imagination of the human mind for the work that we do. You will hear me refer to "The lobby" many times throughout this work, and it is to be used as a literal example of the "time/space/frequency area," of the comings and goings of souls or the actual (place) where souls are born from, and where the soul returns at the time of the body's death. In many Earth texts this plane is known as Heaven, Shambala, The Great White Way, Nirvana.

As I said in the chapter before this, the initial entry plane of The Lobby is at level 86 of the Universal Creation Field. The 86th through 88th energetic levels are what humans have described as the tunnel of light or archway that they may see when their organic body dies and the soul travels back to my plane of existence. These levels are simply the entry and exit point where the soul's energetic signature realigns itself with The Lobby after an incarnated lifetime or conversely within the soul's birth into a new lifetime. I reside at approximately the 89th level, where all of the working, teaching, and counseling guides reside. There are many levels of entities above me and below me who are working on the immediate re-entry and exit of souls who are incarnating into bodies and energy pods at all the many levels of energetic strata in this Universe at any given time.

From an Earth life perspective, "The Lobby" has been depicted as a fully mythological ideation which is not what most humans would describe as real. This could not be further from the truth. The Lobby is actually a time/space/frequency area of this Universe, and is the only time/space/frequency area where The Creator/God is in direct contact with the evolutionary forward movement of the "said created Universe." Each Universe has its own time/space/frequency arena in which the souls from that Universe can incarnate and reincarnate through many hundreds of lives while working up the "ladder" of energetic lessons and soul evolution.

On Earth, The Lobby, as Melissa calls it, is called by many names. Heaven in the Judeo-Christian religious doctrine, Shambala, Nirvana, The Great Walkabout, The Great White Way, the other side of the veil. All and every one of these descriptions point to the same energetic destination. These descriptive names are referring to where I and an uncountable number of my fellow teachers reside. The Lobby. I believe that Melissa originally began to refer to the time/space/frequency Universal Creation Arena as The Lobby because in her teachings with me, I have shown her through the comings and goings of souls what the energetic realm would look like visually to her. Melisa sees something that might be akin to a sort of roofless, huge, sun-filled, beautiful, bright, marbled train station in which travelers were coming and going while being met by loved ones and old friends. Minus the trains, of course. As her connection to me grew, she was able to see further into the arrival area and could see ornate seating areas, library wings of the Akashic records, and the unending garden spaces beyond. With all of these images she decided to call it a grand kind of lobby where traveling souls were coming and going. If this image were very far from the truth, I would have corrected her, but in fact most humans who cross to and from this area at birth and death experience something quite closely akin to what Melissa does, and thus, the name "The Lobby" has remained.

I also believe that having a sort of mental picture of the time/space/frequency Creation Arena in this way will help you, the reader, to experience what that might be like. I do offer this caveat, however: each soul who at death passes back over to the lobby will have an experience that is within "their" beliefs about a connection to The Creator/God. This is a very important piece in understanding The Lobby.

If, for instance, you have spent a whole lifetime on Earth as a devout Catholic, you would most likely not come back to The Lobby through the entrance of a soul who was a devout Buddhist. When souls travel back to the Creator upon death of a physical body, usually their memory of The Lobby and their last life is forgotten, and they are heavily imprinted with the energetic signature that was the present lifetime being left behind. Due to this, the soul is greeted by its guides or waiting family soul members in a way that will be the least jarring for that soul. Thus, they will be entering in such a way that the belief system from that lifetime is not initially shocking to that soul. The whole mission for the soul from our perspective is to live a life, return easily back to the time/space/frequency Creation Arena, and assimilate those lessons in the most loving and seamless way possible. As the returning soul begins to "remember" where they have come from and where they had been, The Lobby becomes more closely resembling what Melissa sees. As she is seeing The Lobby from the perspective of a living human soul, she is not being veiled from it in any way. When she moves back over, she will most likely see it exactly as she sees it now, as well as those soul family members that have already passed back in this lifetime.

If you are a soul on Earth who, for instance, is within the Buddhist religious tradition, you would most likely pass back and arrive in a beautiful temple setting and be met by your soul family. At the point in your experience of arrival where you become comfortable with the fact that you have returned to the time/space/frequency Creation Arena, and that you had passed from your last Earth life, you would be able to then move freely toward the main levels of the Arena/Lobby for your guide meetings and assimilation of lessons. The point I am making is that the initial entry levels of The Lobby are going to be whatever that soul returning from Earth believes or needs to "see" in order to return in a loving and non-threatening manner.

Many times, a soul returning to The Lobby will be arriving from a particularly difficult life experience. In the case where there was much physical pain or trauma around the transition, the incoming soul's family and guides will create a kind of rest place or cocoon for that soul. In a later chapter, Melissa will share just such an experience that she witnessed with her mother's return to The Lobby. Transition back to The Lobby is very different with each soul, no matter which plane of existence, planet, or Universal strata that soul is returning from. The most important piece to a soul returning to The Lobby is the comfort and "holding" of that soul until it is by its own will calm, rested, and ready to begin the learning process again. Should the soul pass over in a freely moving manner, or even better with full knowledge of the return to The Lobby with no fear, then that soul will pass directly to The Lobby and meet friends and loved ones with no holding pattern whatsoever.

The Lobby is the actual energetic time/space/frequency area that was created in the very beginning of this known Universe by The Creator/God. Each Universe is given an upper level by which all souls living within that Universe can traverse, learn, and evolve through layer upon layer of experience all designed to create more enlightened, instructed, talented, and loving members of that Universe. This process literally marches on over eons of time which the human mind and, to be honest, my mind cannot fully comprehend. There are an uncountable number of souls living within The Lobby at my level and the levels above all the way up to and including The Creator/God. At my level, and the levels above me, most of the souls no longer incarnate into organic life forms but exist as energy life forms. There are, however, at levels much closer to The Creator/God, souls who will incarnate upon planets and planes of being as spiritual leaders, messianic persons, and seeded species incarnates who are specifically meant to change the direction of whole species of incarnated souls at certain times during that species evolution.

This is known as species seeding and it occurs not only on the Earth but on many planets and energetic species planes across the Universe. It is important to understand that within this structure of movement, free will is the constant which allows souls to always "choose." No soul can be compelled to any action or belief. The Creator/God gave this irrevocable gift to every soul upon inception of this Universe. The law of free will cannot be taken from you, even by The Creator/God.

The Lobby is the time/space/frequency plane from which souls are born into lives and return after those lives in order to continue to evolve and grow. The Earth plane is only one destination for souls being incarnated into lesson plan lives. Earth is a very new destination for souls in this Universe to incarnate, as in Universal timelines it is very young and the human species on Earth is very new and has not yet evolved enough to harness its true potential on the Universal plane. Here at The Lobby, there are approximately, 40,000 teacher/guides working with souls incarnated to the Earth plane. Within those souls, there are groups of communicators (Melissa and I are within this group), geo-engineering specialists, energetic evolutionary specialists, space travel specialists, and more abundantly energetic creation specialists, as well as others. These groups, including our own, are working in unison to facilitate the full evolution of the Earth planet and its energetic plane to the next level of knowledge and paradigm reality.

Understand that at any given time, there are uncountable numbers of teacher/guides and souls working on millions of planets and energy plane from The Lobby. There is a system in place within the structure of the Lobby and its whole purpose is to assist in souls growing and moving more closely to the energy of the Creator. As I have said, there is no "time" as humans would know it, and so any soul who wishes to "rest" instead of "learn" for any amount of space time is fully capable of choosing to do so. Should a soul returning to The Lobby from the Earth plane decide to spend an eon in a beautiful valley growing apple trees and enjoying the company of other souls, that is what will be. There is no right or wrong here as you would know it from Earth standards. I do not mean that low-level energies are accepted or allowed to be experienced here. That is not permitted. Should a soul want to be in the experience of pain, suffering, abusive behaviors of all kinds, loss, fear, anger, that soul would need to seek out that lesson within another incarnation to a planet or space time similar to Earth's in order to experience those feelings and lessons. The Lobby is a place for the soul to experience the beauty and grandeur of Creation. The incarnations are specifically tailored by the soul to have the lessons that display the often-painful realization of exclusion and separation from the beauty and grandeur of Creation. Souls take as long as they need to see and feel this separation and learn from them at their own pace and in their own timeline.

There are souls residing at all points in the Universe at The Lobby level of Creation who will not incarnate again, and there are some souls residing here that will incarnate again and again to many energetic planes, planets, and existences. There is no judgment in The Lobby except the judgment of the soul itself.

The 40,000 or so souls from Earth who are in connection with the working groups here all have the opportunity to connect with The Lobby in the way that Melissa does, although many will not choose to do so. Many of the souls will have connections that are more similar to "the muse," "intuition," "automatic writing," "faith-based," or "inspirational input" from their teacher/guides. Melissa hears and sees me due to the fact that we are in communications, so it is very important that she have a very visceral and definite connection with me. This is why Melissa has such a clear vision of The Lobby in a very factual way.

The Lobby operates most literally as you might picture a large company or organization. The Lobby is, however, completely without any of the negative energies or trappings that an Earth soul might attach to such organizations. The Lobby has levels rising above the entry levels to about 2,400, which is where the levels begin to coalesce into simply an energy field which blends with The Creator/God plane. As souls rise through lesson paths, they become more closely aligned with The Creator/God energies. There is no "ceiling" here, as Melissa calls it. When she gazes upward toward what she might call the "sky" of The Lobby, she sees an unending spiral of light levels which reach eventually up to a brilliant, white, never-ending space. It is almost too brilliant for her to look at even through the filter of the space/time/frequency bridge which she is using to "see" it. There is no stop at the uppermost level. I do not have access to the uppermost levels at this time in my journey but am simply imparting the knowledge that The Lobby exists and what The Creator/God has given souls traveling through it is the fact that there is a benevolent, all-powerful Creation Source in place in the Universe, and it is a paradigm change that it is Earth's time to understand. It is simply evolution on a much more grand and brilliant scale than simple organics can contain or explain.

When Melissa first began working with me and experiencing the entry levels of The Lobby, it was to begin working with souls who had travelled back over from Earth at death and wished for many different reasons to contact those loved ones they had left behind. As you might understand, when souls began to share that I had a student who was being able to straddle both planes and be a verbal "channel" for communication, there were many, many visitors here at The Lobby who wanted to contact their loved ones on the Earth plane to let them know that they were okay and doing fine. This was very overwhelming for Melissa. As Melissa grew in her connection to The Lobby, she began to understand that she could literally build herself a small annex to the entry halls here which had a door, so that she could close it when she needed to rest her organic body, mind, and "not do the work."

The Lobby allows for constant growth and there is no constraint on what is possible here. That is the point of The Lobby. Souls are home here and actually not "at home" when they are incarnate. When souls are here in The Lobby, they can literally recreate some of the very best and most loved experiences from their incarnations. So, Melissa created a comfortable, small annex or what you would call an office with a huge, white, ornate door to The Lobby Hall which she can open or close at her will. Her office creation has huge windows that look out over the gardens of The Lobby and sky. Many of her pets who have passed over visit this area when she is working as do souls who have had lifetimes with her previously. As she sits and takes this information from me, her soul literally has a piece of itself sitting in her sun-filled annex connected to one of The Lobby's never-ending hallways beyond. Her door is open and often souls passing back and forth on their own business will pass by her door. I stand in the doorway to keep friendly visitors from interrupting the work. It is in a way not unlike any working community except that it is the realm of Creation and, there-fore, missing any of the difficult lessons of incarnation.

Should Melissa become fatigued, she can and often does request that the door be shut so that she can be more fully and energetically on the Earth's energetic plane to live her life. She is in complete control of her con-tact with me and The Lobby. Melissa often requests to be able to stretch her soul's energy signature through her door out into the hallways and learn-ing spaces of The Lobby. I can only allow her to peer out into the spaces that surround her doorway, as to travel too far into The Lobby's energy signature would pull too much of her soul from the Earth plane. She must remain at most a 60/40 distribution of her soul's energy signature between the Lobby and Earth in order to remain in the incarnation in which she resides at this time. To be clearer, she needs to be rooted in the present Earth incarnation energetically at a minimum of 60 percent or she would risk "literally" leaving the incarnation. So, I guide her in the ways of how much she can traverse her intention and attention upon The Lobby and keep the ratio to 60/40.

Keep in mind that a belief in a "life after death" is in no way needed to return to The Lobby after each incarnation. A belief in a soul, a belief in a creator is also unnecessary in order for your soul to travel back to the Lobby after a lifetime is completed. Every soul returns of its own volition to The Lobby. Should you return to The Lobby from a lifetime that was of an atheist nature, your soul will still return to The Lobby, and will simply be given the opportunity to "remember" that lifetime and the soul's connection with Creation. There is no judgment other than the soul's own judgment of itself in the face of complete truth. We will speak of this more in a later chapter.

The Lobby is, as Melissa calls it, a great and endless area where souls come and go being born and born again. Melissa likens it to a grand college where souls can learn at their own pace and without any obstacles.

CHAPTER 4
Birth, Death, and Rebirth

Aralamb

The birth into an incarnation, death, and rebirth is the tool by which The Creator/God put into motion the energetic offspring of its own light. To be born, live, exist, die, and return to The Lobby is the facilitation of the growth of the souls that were seeded into existence at the creation of the Universe in which they reside. Experiences of every unimaginable facet of emotion, action, energetic magnetism, and feeling are a growth pattern which is undertaken upon the birth of every soul upon its entry into an organic or fully energetic vessel. This system of being born, living, experiencing, growing, evolving, dying, and returning to The Creation and The Lobby *is* the reason. It *is* The Creator/God's directive for each individual soul.

This process, which humans call reincarnation is the actual "reason" for souls to be. The Creator/God wanted to fill our Universe with "children" who, through lessons and lifetimes, will become more closely resonant to his/her own energy signature. As a guide here in The Lobby level of Creation, I do not have direct access to The Creator/God's level of energetic signature. Souls may live and experience thousands of lifetimes within a Universal time period to eventually achieve these highest levels. A soul must begin to "know" the full truth about any situation and its actions extrapolated out to the 23rd move in order to begin to "know" the mind of The Creator/God. I do not suggest that I am anywhere even near that level of "beingness." I have, however, graduated past the need to return to any kind of physical body unless I wanted to for the sake of experience and have a good, solid knowledge of the reincarnative system.

The soul that you have was given to you at the inception of this Universe. You may not have incarnated into any body, energy signature, or light body for eons of Universal time since the beginning, and the life you are living at this moment may be your third lifetime, it may be your 500th. In the case of souls such as Jesus, Buddha, or other very sophisticated and emotionally intelligent souls, Einstein, Plato, etc., you may have had thousands of lifetimes and be sent to a planet like Earth at pivotal times of change for the organic species living there. These souls are at the very highest echelons of the Creation. Please know The Creator/God does not judge or give favor to souls who are "higher" on the learning spectrum. The whole of the Universe is structured as a schooling system just as you would find a school on your planet might be structured. The Creator/God has no judgment for his children. Judgment is all in the eye of the soul.

When a soul deems itself ready to begin traversing the life schools, that soul as a very new arrival to The Lobby will be given a guide, not unlike myself, in order to get the general instruction on how the life school works on the many given planets and strata of the entry levels of learning.

Prior to the new soul arriving at The Lobby to begin entry into the life schools, that soul would have been in a sort of timeless beautiful sleep within the Creation strata of the Universe. The exact timing of when to wake up and begin to access the life school is totally up to that individual soul. In this kind of "sleep," a soul is literally a kind of spectator. It would be as if a two-year-old child were being held by its mother while a 4th of July parade was marching by. That two-year-old might be afraid, might grip its mother harder, but at the same time be exhilarated by the parade and at some point, would probably want to be put down to go and join in the fun. This is a very good example of how a young soul is held within The Creator/God's protection until such a time comes when that soul decides to "join in the parade of life." At that point, the soul will immediately arrive (or be) on the entry platform of The Lobby. That soul's guide will meet him or her and the process of awakening will begin. Before a soul is ready to start choosing a lesson plan or lifetimes to inhabit, that soul must spend what would be approximately 150 years of Earth time to acclimate itself to The Lobby and its energies. The Lobby is, as I stated in the previous chapter, a coming and going area for souls coming into and out of lives on many levels of organic and non-organic lifetimes and strata in the Universe. Time does not exist here in The Lobby, but on Earth the time between arrival of the new soul, and acclimation to The Lobby would be approximately 150 years.

Once the new soul is fully acclimated, that soul has complete free will to determine how and when it begins to traverse lives. The new soul will, just as in Earth schools, begins to group into similar energies and make friends so to speak with other new arrivals. In this way, soul pods are formed very early in a soul's entry to the life schools. This is a very integral part of the process from The Creator's/God's perspective because these new souls may stay together trading places in lives for thousands of life cycles. By the time so many lives have been traversed, there is a distinct connection and "soul memory" for these groups. The love bonds run very strong and, in this way, one member will do or be in a lifetime whatever the others need to accumulate the lessons necessary to move forward and upward in the process.

At some points within a soul's life lesson plan, a soul will request and migrate to a different soul pod in order to have an experience that they cannot accrue through their own group. Again, I would like to stress that all of these groupings are totally the choices of the souls within them. Free will always reigns. Every decision about groupings or the decision by a soul to leave a grouping is the free will of that soul.

For example, when I met Melissa, in our first lifetime together, which was approximately 18,000 Earth years ago prior to your last ice age, she had requested to be allowed into the pod that I travel with and have traveled with for many millennia. My pod had a kind of vote on the issue after a short meeting with Melissa's soul to see if that would be a good fit for us. If this sounds very civilized and business-like, it is. At The Lobby level, all souls are devoid of any kind of malice, deceit, hatred, self-aggrandizement, or machinations. Every soul has complete knowledge of the central "being-ness" of every other soul. The need to "hide" becomes unnecessary at the soul level. These groups are formed much in the way that a great artist might blend colors. If a group of souls is primarily blue on the color spectrum of the emotional and intellectual arc, they may decide that a bit of orange or green would round out the possibility of learning for the whole group in lifetimes shared.

When Melissa joined my soul grouping, we were heavily intellectual, egalitarian, and what Melissa would describe as "dry." We were heavily maroon, violet, and navy in shades of energy. Melissa's soul energy was going to bring the emotional experiences of leaf green and sky blue to our energetic lessons, she also brought a sense of levity to our otherwise serious group. We determined that to bring her in would, as a human might say, "open a window and bring in some fresh air." In her first 50 or 60 lifetimes within our group, part of her entry to our pod was that she wanted to expedite her intellectual pursuits, and we needed a cosmic kind of aid, sidekick, scribe, assistant, etc. I do not mean to say that she was less than any of us, but souls have a decided upon the parameter of give and take. As I was the deciding vote to bring her into our group, it was determined that I would be the one who was sharing lives with her for many, many lifetimes, with Melissa as my apprentice as it were. My group of souls even at that time had been in the life school for many thousands of Earth years.

The soul that is Melissa in this lifetime travelled with me through many lifetimes as my student, scribe, bard, and assistant. Melissa chose those positions pre-birth and wanted to engage in the lessons that those lives would afford her.

Being Born

At the point that a soul would be born to a human family group, there would have been a meeting of the extended grouping prior to the pre-entry period. There are uncountable numbers of planets in your galaxy alone upon which souls incarnate into organic and non-organic light bodies for lifetimes, but for this description we will be working with only your planet, Earth.

As you will foresee in your thinking, in your time period upon Earth, a human lifetime spans from 0 to possible 110 years for each incarnation. Due to this, soul groups will often rotate in and out of lives and lifetimes, taking up the mantles of "actors" if you will within that 100-year scope. Before you were born into the life you have now, you would have been meeting at a high soul level with those souls in your extended pod/family who would be your parents, your siblings, your loves, and they with you. In this way, you would all have agreed upon which parts they and you would play for each other in the subsequent life to be lived. Now, in this way, the soul who was your grandmother or great grandmother in one life will likely come back into your present life as the soul of your child or grandchild. There is a constant rotation of the soul pod in and out of the lives of each other, constantly playing different roles in order to facilitate the forward movement of learning for *each other*.

As an example, if your mother in this lifetime struggled with depression, you might very well have agreed to be her child in this lifetime and try to hold a safe place for her and her soul to work through this painful issue once and for all. It may be that in a past lifetime, or a future one, you and she will have or will change roles in order to allow the other to grow and overcome certain lessons about depression. The system is set up in this way so that every soul can truly "walk in another's shoes" or "do unto others as they would do unto themselves." There is a perfect balance within the system that not only allows for "choice" at every moment but free will as well.

As an incarnated soul, it is your "choice" at every moment as to how you want to navigate amazing experiences as well as the most difficult with your fellow souls. Within every lifetime, the magic in the choice is that it only takes one member of a group within a lifetime to "change its mind," and address a difficult issue differently, in order to raise up the whole family group within that lifetime. Levels of learning can be traversed very quickly within soul groups when this law becomes evident. As an example, if a family soul group has traversed many lifetimes and soul generations of sexual abuse in the family, it only takes the one soul to stand up, speak out, and refuse to live in fear and/or continue the behavior. Once this decision is made, the behavior, which may have invested itself in many generations of a family, is at once transmuted out of the soul group's experience. It just takes one soul to uplift and remove the souls coming after it, from that painful lesson.

After the soul pod meeting takes place in The Lobby, facilitator souls, not unlike myself, will then begin to assist the soul who is being born onto the Earth plane to the area of the "forgetting." The area of the forgetting is a kind of cocoon, and it is the closest area of The Lobby to the Earth plane in terms of energy levels. The energetic signature of this area, although much higher than Earth's, is still at a much slower rate of vibration than The Lobby levels above it. This area is where the incoming soul is held and cared for during the phases of being slowed down and introduced to its host mother's body. The soon-to-arrive soul is held in a kind of concentration area which is very much like the holding area that souls abide in before they determine to begin the learning process. There is what a human would call a warm, loving cocoon feeling to this area and it is constantly overseen by guides, teachers, and facilitators until such time that the soul is released to the energetic signature of its mother host in the lifetime that it is entering into. It is very important for the soul to have the time to be coalesced into that lower energy signature which vibrates much slower than in The Lobby. For a soul to be resided in a new human body, it must align its own energy signature initially with that of its chosen mother. The soul will be "seated" in this waiting platform area until the chosen mother is in her soul's timing, ready to accept the new soul of the incoming child. This time for the soon-to-be-born soul is also where past lives, The Lobby, and former agreements are forgotten.

The Forgetting is a two-pronged and integral part of the reincarnation process, as it serves two distinct purposes. The Forgetting is meant to 1) facilitate virgin experience of choice, free will, and living; 2) allow growth from the soul level without any knowledge of consequences that are not chosen by the soul. Choice equals reaction equals experience.

The Forgetting Part (1)

The incoming soul begins the process quickly of forgetting The Lobby and the pre-decided points of experience or decisions that would have been chosen by that incoming soul and those other souls who would have agreed upon those experiences and lessons. When that new soul is born to a mother and begins life, free will and that soul's connection to The Creator is the same one that it carries throughout time. Free will is, as I have stated, the one overriding character of the soul and its connection to The Creator/ God. Simplified, the whole purpose of the forgetting on Earth over the many eons of time is to facilitate difficult challenges within a lifetime and the ability to either learn and grow through them or the choice to repeat those same difficult lessons over and over in infinite time spans. Up until this point in your planet's history, the forgetting was in full force in order to support the idea that human evolution would require it in order to make full free will choices.

For example, if you live many lifetimes in the role of a victim to those around you, you will have chosen that stance in those lifetimes. Even in the most dire and difficult situations within a lifetime, the choice to remain in that situation is your own. Emotionally, physically, intellectually, and spiritually there is always a choice to be made. It is important for you to understand that the forgetting is what will slowly awaken you to the reality of the Universe.

Earth is now at the precipice of the evolutionary change that will allow some of the forgetting veil to be lifted from human incarnates. This evolutionary process is what will allow a soul within a human body to understand that all of the choices made in this lifetime will be felt and realized over and over again until the lesson is learned, engaged, and eclipsed by the soul and there is no need to relive that particular lesson. At this point in Earth's history, very few souls were allowed to incarnate without The Forgetting because at the very immature level of the bulk of humanity, there would has been a completely hedonistic rush to do, say, and imperil the free will of others within the system of incarnation. Even with The Forgetting, civilizations upon Earth have risen and fallen on the backs of slavery, which is the most heinous kind of free will and its negative uses. The point I make here is that without The Forgetting, immature souls would and could choose to never move forward on the evolutionary path and determine that the stagnation of their soul's journey was of no consequence and just keep repeating the same vile lives again and again, by choice. This is not within The Creator's/God's directive for the growth cycle of the soul.

In the past and at the dawn of your present evolutionary state, when you were last seeded by the pre-Sumerian species which inhabited Earth for some time, you were touched by this very incidence. The pre-Sumerian species who seeded humanity into this its present form were and are species who evolved past The Forgetting and chose to ignore the directive of positive growth. These species chose to embrace a fully technological path and chose to continue within lifetimes without growing their souls past the need for aggression, violence, and slavery. Due to this free will choice, there are at this very time several species who will not be rising up in vibrational reality within the impending Universal shift upward. These species will find themselves in a Universe which has taken many of its inhabitants and risen above what is accessible to them in the future. There will also be a marked lack of ability for these species to procreate into the future of this Universe. At a time in the future when the last of these species finally dies out over eons, their fully recovered souls will return to The Creation for a period of rest. This is one of the reasons that The Forgetting is slowly being peeled back on your planet at this time. The Creator/God is preparing the consciousness of all humanity that chooses to shift up within the structure of the coming change or at least have enough knowledge to make that choice using their free will.

The Forgetting Part (2): Choice, Reaction, and Experience

The second piece of The Forgetting upon being born is that every emotion, experience, and second of your life is imbued with an action experience, reaction, or choice. All of these choices, reactions, and emotions add up to your full life experience. Because of the vast level of complicated relationships and life situations that can and will occur, it is very often that souls will need many, many experiences of the same life situations from many angles to truly find the highest and most positive lessons from those situations. If The Forgetting were not employed within many lifetimes, souls would possibly never learn some lessons, as they would be fully avoided due to a fear of experiencing pain, loss, perceived separation, and so many more fundamental emotional experiences. By the same token, a soul might decide to spend multiples of lifetimes in complete self-absorption, not taking any risks because there is full knowledge of the system in which is resides. Again, this would completely inhibit growth of the soul. Souls incarnate in order to fully experience situations, reactions, choices, and emotions. This is the perfect classroom in which to learn. At some point in a soul's evolution, they will have experienced, say, addiction. After many lifetimes of being the addict, they may pre-birth decide that in the next lifetime they will be the loved one of an addict. Then, perhaps in another, they would take the role of the child of the addict. In this way, with The Forgetting in place, the soul can live that life out with a completely "virgin" experience of each of those parts in the difficult challenge that is addiction. Souls within a family pod will often participate in multiple lives where they each take on all of the roles for each other. At the point where they have all experienced all of the facets of the addict's pain and relationships, with love and compassion they understand that lesson and release it. They will never need to visit that kind of life again if they so choose. That lesson has been incorporated into that soul forever. The forgetting is the mechanism that The Creator/God put into place to make this kind of education of the soul possible. The forgetting at birth is the hand tool of free will.

As a soul begins to embark into a lifetime as a small child, he or she will be within the family unit that he or she would have chosen to start the lifetime with. There are many challenging and joyful opportunities to use free will that can be set up like intersections or four-way intersections within a lifetime. I mean this to say that a soul will set up many large inter-sections or choice points in a lifetime for itself. Opportunities and decision points. that will need to be chosen upon. The decisions made with one's free will ultimately guide the direction of that life. Depending upon the soul's choices pre-birth, there will be relationship opportunities, emotional connections opportunities, work, schooling, physical issues, joys, chal-lenges, losses, accidents, lifestyles, and every possible combination of life situations which will bring that specific soul the opportunity to experience, react, and choose. Within all of the "possibility" crossroads that are set up prior to birth, there is also the free will of each soul. What this truly means is that there is no concrete destiny. There will be destiny points, where cer-tain roads may be taken, certain decisions can be made or chosen. The free will of the individual soul and its choices will in turn open the next myriad of choice points. There is no one set way for any life to be lived. There is only the one prerequisite that each life be lived to the best of the ability of the soul within it. Do, better, be better, learn, drop anger, fear, and hos-tility. Rejoice in the power of love, grateful joy, and every other powerful emotion. This is the intent of every soul. How does the soul move through life and all of its joyful and painful facets? How do you react to and choose around your most wonderful and painful situations? What is your choice? How do you implement your free will? These are all of the major life lessons that you will be on Earth to learn.

Death of the Body

The death point of the human body is the exact moment when the soul will return to The Lobby for rest and reinvestment of the whole of that soul's existence. The moment of death is often one that humans fear. The truth is, life and living of it in your body can and often is the most painful part of a lifetime. The days leading up to the death of the human body can be painful or completely free of pain. The death experience from a physical point of view will have been chosen by the soul prior to birth.

You as a soul had complete control over when, how, and what the circumstances of your return to The Lobby would be. I mean this literally. You personally will have chosen your time of death. Whether you die racing on a motorcycle at the human age of 50 or die peacefully at the age of 102 asleep in your bed with 30 of your children, grandchildren, and great grandchildren in attendance. If you die by disease or accident. If you die with many groups of other souls in a large disaster or alone from hypothermia in the Alaskan woods lost and cold or in a hospital battling a physical malady, you would have chosen that final day before your birth into the lifetime. The reason for this is that death, as important as humans make it in their emotional bodies, is on the other side, what can only be called a grand homecoming of a soul who has traversed a lifetime hopefully with amazing amounts of learning and expanding of itself. This information about death is not shared in order to glamorize or hurry that day. The opposite is quite in play. One of the soul's major objectives within a lifetime is to stay and participate to its highest ability for as long as it is possible. Souls are expected to fight to remain within their organic body and often times will have the lesson of surviving at very high odds in order to learn valuable lessons and continue on with the life.

There is no death of the soul and its inherent "character" traits. All of your most highly evolved and positive character traits, loves, talents, knowledge, spiritual gifts, interests, sense of humor, good deeds, and every other beloved of your traits are maintained within your soul from lifetime to lifetime. You do not sustain or keep the negative emotions or painful senses of being from lifetime to lifetime. You will return to The Lobby, look at the prior lifetime, and if you were not able to choose to grow past the negative lessons you will return again to release them in a new lifetime. The return to a new lifetime to revisit those lessons is always the free will choice of that soul. The whole process is about dropping and integrating all of the negative and more basic lessons over lifetimes in order to fill your soul with more and more beauty, giftedness, and gracious existence which is The Creator/God's wish for every soul. You are on a constant climbing learning curve which you ascend at your own chosen pace, with no judgment on your course beside self-evaluations combined with complete knowledge.

Suicide

Living in The Lobby as a teacher, helper, and guide, there is no other incarnate issue that pains The Creator/God and all of us more than the free will choice of suicide. When souls determine before a lifetime that they will all incarnate into the life plane together to learn, grow, and experience all of the emotions, situations, challenges, joys, accomplishments, and pains that will help them as a group to grow and transcend to new levels of understanding, it is a given, a hard and fast covenant between them that none of them will "un-naturally" leave the game before it is fully played out.

I use the metaphor of "the game" or "the play" in order to give you a very real and literal picture of what a lifetime *is*. You are reading this from the perspective of the soul/person living your life. You came into your life to spend it hopefully doing and becoming the very best version of yourself that you can. The most challenging days, relationships, losses are all situations that you would have agreed upon before your birth with those who are playing them out with you in this lifetime. If you can liken your relationships with others, good and challenging, as tennis matches that will never be won by either side but are meant to be played fully and with all of the best intentions and used to learn, grow, and enhance your skill level, you will easily be able to see how the whole and total meaning of that game becomes moot and untenable if *one player decides to throw down their racket and leave the playing field.*

That player would have made a covenant with all of the other players to remain in the game to the end no matter the outcome. The players would have all agreed to stay in the game in order to facilitate the growth of not only their own soul but also all of the other souls they agreed to inhabit the lifetime with.

Because of this covenant, The Creator/God has put into place a very specific and unchanged set of laws that go into play immediately upon a soul's free will decision to kill off its human body and leave the field of life play. These rules apply to every soul and have no caveats except **one**. The caveat to the rule surrounding human suicide is on the occasion of imminent death of the soul's body due to disease. Should the body be rendered unable to continue within the coming Earth year and the soul decides with the good wishes of its fellow soul family that more intervention will/ would not prolong the life of that body, and that soul chooses to stop any attempt to save the body, in this and only this situation is letting the body die acceptable and allowable. In most cases, this choice would have been made by the soul and the soul's covenant group to be a learning experience for all and fully planned as that soul's exit of the lifetime.

The Creator/God does not deem this action an act of suicide and or leaving the lifetime by free will. This is the one caveat. There are no other "reasons" within the Creation by which suiciding out of a lifetime is acceptable and without the immediate implementation of the rules that follow.

I could spend much time here and list the nine trillion reasons "why" a soul might be in emotional, physical, or psychological pain and determine why getting out might be the best idea, but none of those reasons are acceptable to The Creator/God and thus will not be listed here. What I will try my best to do is to outline the structure of the rules around human and all species' suicide and explain why it is to be considered *never an option.* Keep in mind also that within the Greater Milky Way Galaxy there are many, many species in which a suicide has not been implemented in many generations at all. Species do eventually evolve past this most violent act.

The first piece of suicide which should be addressed is that you will never have chosen and been born into your lifetime with the act of free will suicide being one of your chosen options or one of your possible choice points of leaving the lifetime. I say this with all gravity, as it is a hard rule here within the upper levels of Creation. You may say, "Well, how can this rule live within The Creator/God's free will rule?" The simple answer to that is that if human suicide only affected the soul who chooses to leave the playing field then it would be true free will. You would literally be leaving a game of solitaire where you were not learning through the experiences of joy and challenge that you have with other souls/players. It would be a completely non-game. Suicide and the choice to leave the field of play when there are others, even one other person *stranger or friend* who will be impacted by your action, means that your improper use of free will only leads to a complete stop in your soul's evolution until you have made amends to those you left. You have made a completely selfish decision to leave the field of play, which will reverberate through generations of your soul pod's lifetimes. By prematurely leaving the field of play, you have impacted your soul pod group against their will and in a very harmful way. Any of the agreements that you made with your group are now not possible to work through. You have broken your agreements with your soul's pod/ family.

Example of the Rule in Action:

Upon your decision to leave the field of play with your fellow humans, you begin a cascade of events for your own soul and the souls of those you leave behind. This example is meant to be a fully literal description. Please keep that in mind as you read. Please also understand that The Creator/God placed this rule into our Universe to keep the evolution of souls moving forward. If killing ones organic body were allowed by The Creator, there would be nothing to keep souls from quitting the game every time that challenges arrived in a lifetime. A soul who continues to leave the field of play may never transcend and integrate its own chosen lessons. It is simple and beautiful in its simplicity. You must play to the end of your lifetime in order to learn the lessons for yourself and be the lesson for those around you. Souls are in a complete symbiotic relationship throughout lifetimes. The following narrative is an example of how a human might come to the "decision" that making the choice to leave via suicide is the best choice available to them.

Ben's Story

On Tuesday, Ben decided that he no longer wanted to be in the world. He was divorced and his ex-wife, Katie, and their three children had moved back to their home town in Oklahoma. He had not wanted his wife to go, but she did, and took his kids with her. He loved her, but he worked in the oil fields in Wyoming and so they had grown apart. His sons, Jason, Trevor, and Paul were twelve, nine, and three. Ben had been battling 60-hour weeks on the rig, a smoking habit, a painkiller addiction from his old knee injury, and hadn't slept more than six hours in a night, in at least10 years' time.

When Katie left with the kids six months ago, he told her he would return to Oklahoma and work it out. He loved them all desperately, but he could not make enough money back in Oklahoma and they both knew it. Ben also had a 16-year-old son who lived in LA with his first wife, and although he had always paid child support for Dustin, he had not seen him since he was five years old.

Sitting in his one-room trailer on the edge of the oil fields, Ben was tired and just worn out from the work, the loneliness, and all of the missed opportunities. He could have gotten out of the oil fields years ago. He was smart and he could have gone to school. His father had offered to pay for his schooling, but Ben had ignored his offer and his dad had died back in 2016 without Ben making things right with him. Ben's dad had been a good man, and Ben had always rebelled against him. Sitting in his dark little trailer now at 48, Ben had no idea why. His family was gone, his depression was kicking in, he had four days off for the first time in months, and he was totally alone. Ben opened his first beer even though it was only 9:00 a.m. There was only one small window in the door of his trailer, allowing a sliver of hot white morning sunlight to cut through the dirty curtain filling up the room. It was July 4th weekend, and it was going to be hot and sunny. He was alone. He was alone with 12 beers, one bottle of oxycodone and two packs of cigarettes. Ben had not eaten in two days, he thought. As he finished the first beer and crushed the can, he opened another, downed it, and crushed the empty can on his leg. The top of his thigh began to bleed where he ground the crushed can edges into it. He could hear the drip, drip, drip of the blood on the dirty carpet below his leg. He did not move to stop the bleeding but just listened to the sound, pat, pat, pat, pat.

On the coffee table, his cell phone began to vibrate. It was Katie. He watched it vibrate with her name and photo showing. She was beautiful and he loved her. She had always loved him, but like everyone else in his life he had just used her up. He had used up everyone he ever loved with his anger and his isolation. He knew it. The phone went silent. Ben gulped his third beer down as if it were water and grabbed his fourth. In that moment, he decided that they would all be better without him. They could all go on and have great lives and he could rest. They would all be better without him. His four sons could go on and have great stepdads and Katie would find the right man for her. As he gulped down his fourth beer, he began to cry hard.

He was crying so hard that the tears coming from his eyes were running into his mouth and he could taste the salt of them mixing with beer and cigarettes. His guts burned with the painful emotion of loneliness. He had worked, drugged, and drunk his way out of his family and was alone. No one would even miss him if he walked out into the wilderness right now. Tears, regret, and fear were all running down his face freely as he opened his fifth beer and grabbed the full bottle of OxyContin. His nose was running, and a fly kept landing on his bleeding leg which was now beginning to clot. He didn't care and he didn't try to wave the fly off. He just sat there crying and watching it land and buzz, land and buzz. Even through the oncoming alcoholic haze, he could feel the fly's proboscis gently probing away at the wound on his leg. Absently he wondered if the fly would lay her eggs in that wound after he was dead. He sat forward and lit another cigarette. The smoke from his first exhale curled up to the ceiling line and then wrapped back down into a shaft of sunlight, creating a blue haze.

While mumbling to himself "no, no, no, no, no," over and over, Ben began to swallow all 40 of the OxyContin down one after the other with his beer. After he got them all down, he sat back, cigarette in hand, fighting the urge to throw them up. Crying silently and holding the pills down, he felt like he had made a decision. They would all be better off without him in this world. He had let everyone down that he ever loved, and everyone knew it. He had let himself down. It would be over for him and them. In the next 10 minutes, the urge to throw up left him and he felt his muscles grow very heavy. The sun through the small window of that trailer was the last thing that his earthly eyes saw. He could hear the vibrations of his phone off and on somewhere far away. The phone moved across the top of the coffee table with the vibrations and finally came to a stop, resting against his sixth beer can which was half full. The glints of dust and cigarette smoke rolling in the shaft of sunlight in rainbow hues would be the last visions that Ben would see. The last thought that he would remember later was, "Oh my god what have I done, I'm sorry, I'm sorry. Oh no, no, I'm sorry...."

The Rules of Post-Suicide Soul Engagement:

The first rule of post-suicide soul engagement is that *you, the suicide perpetrator, had no idea what was waiting for you in your future.* You had no idea what you had set up for yourself as possibilities, and those you loved in your future. You do not know until after you have gone what you were supposed to be doing within the future of the life you just left. Keep that fully in your mind as you read.

10 minutes following the heart stopping:

In the last moments of Ben's organic heart slowing and stopping, there would have been an alarm sounding in The Lobby. This alert would be going out to all of the souls in Ben's pod who had either stayed back during his lifetime to assist him or those who had moved over and were assisting after their arrival. Will's father who had died in 2016 would be one of those souls. There would be a quick meeting to see if there is any way to have his lifetime salvaged. By salvaged, I mean that his soul pod group in The Lobby would immediately search out any persons close to Ben's organic body who could intervene and save him from the decision and get him medical assistance for his body. In Ben's case, he was alone, and he was not answering his phone, so there was going to be no help on intervention for him and his decision.

At this point in The Lobby, the teams of guides and teachers who handle all suicide decisions on Earth and other inhabited planets arrive at the area and will take over the handling of Ben's soul when he arrives back at The Lobby. An immediate gathering will take place within Ben's soul pod at The Lobby as well because Ben's decision to *leave the field of play affects all of them as well.* Ben's decision acts as a stone thrown in a still pond and the ramifications will affect every other soul who was in his lifetime with him and those attached to him in The Lobby. All of the plans that were laid out for all of their lessons in the lifetime must be altered and those souls left behind will be under The Forgetting and have no knowledge of how it is affecting their life goals, plans, and lessons until they *naturally* return.

In the moments after Ben's heart stops beating, Ben's soul, fully aware and having full knowledge, will literally separate from Ben's body. Ben's fully conscious soul will stand in that tiny one-room trailer and look at his lax body sitting, empty of life. Ben's fully conscious soul will see the body he just left, he will hear the phone continue to ring and vibrate. Ben's fully conscious soul and mind will know what he has done to himself and every other person in his life. Ben has made the free will decision to leave the playing field early. He will immediately try to wake the empty form of his body, so that he can make a different choice. The choice unfortunately has been made. Within the next few moments, one or more of the teacher/ guides who work with suicide-choosing souls will arrive and embrace Ben's soul and consciousness into what is often called a resting energy field. Now you may think, "Well, if they take him to rest, that is what he wanted, so that's not a big deal. He gets to rest."

Ben is assisted to a resting area which is separate from the regular comings and goings of The Lobby. When souls choose suicide, it puts their soul and the souls of their group into a learning cycle which is long and may take multiple generations of lifetimes to overcome. This is why the choice of suicide is so, so detrimental to those in your family circle and even extended circle. Should Ben's act of suicide give any kind of strength or example for some other person to do the same, friend, family, or even the unknown person to him, Ben's soul will be held up from evolution and growth until his one act is worked out by every last other soul who he impacted with his decision. **I want you to really think about the reality of this.**

What I am telling you is that not only is Ben responsible for his own soul and the souls of those close to him, but if Ben's great, great, great grandchild also determines that because her great, great, great grandfather committed suicide and she follows that example, Ben is still held in account for that action. If a total stranger reads about Ben's action and then takes their own life because of his example, Ben is responsible for all of the repercussions of that suicide, even though he had no knowledge of that person. The spiritual and evolutionary ramifications are widespread and unknowable.

After Ben arrives in the resting area for those who commit suicide, he will be in rest for a period of what Earth might call two years, give or take some months. After that time of rest and rejuvenation, Ben is going to be gently awakened. It is at this point that all of his soul pod who are at The Lobby will be able to spend just a small amount of time with him in full truth. What I mean by full truth is that Ben is going to be shown and understand the lifetime he left and what that leaving is doing and will continue to do to those left behind.

Ben will understand fully that he made the choice to leave life early. His soul is fully aware of his decision and The Forgetting by which he was living the life will be lifted completely. Ben will meet with his soul pod and together they will mourn if you like the decision that he made. Each of his soul pods will also feel the loss of all that they had planned for the lifetime that he left. It is very important for you, the reader, to understand that this is not about judgment. There is no judgment set up by The Creator/God. The only judgment that is ever felt or experienced is that of each soul upon itself. After suicide, a soul will know, feel, see, experience, and look out into the future towards *all and every* other soul that is impacted by his/her decision to leave. Every feeling and decision that is changed by the souls left behind will be understood and felt by the soul who committed suicide. This experience is never forced upon the soul in any way, souls understand and choose the experience as one of the superseding laws of The Creator/God.

After the brief meeting with all of his soul pods in The Lobby, Ben will be guided to the re-entry area for the souls who committed suicide. A guide will accompany Ben back to the Earth plane where he will begin to witness, experience, and see firstly what his life looked like up till the point of the suicide. He will be given the experience of his life review in a very normal manner, right up to the point of his suicide. This process can take some time and is often some of the most painful for the soul because with full knowledge and emotional access to everyone else in their lifetime, a kind of balance occurs by which the soul can view and feel the whole of the experiences without their own filters of anger, loss, shame, pain, and self-inflicted separation illusions. This is true knowledge. When the lifetime is experienced up to the point of the suicide, the suicide itself is then seen and felt by Ben through the eyes and hearts of those left behind who are still within the lifetime and The Forgetting.

Ben will be with and experience the pain with his close family, children, surviving mother, siblings, friends, acquaintances. Ben will spend a lifetime with each of his soul groups left behind and physically SEE and FEEL how his decision impacts his loved ones. As you may be thinking, this can and will hold up Ben's soul progression for an unnamable amount of time upon the Earth plane and within his soul's growth pattern. Ben will be able to look upon his loved ones left behind and SEE and FEEL how they may make decisions in their own lives, which are completely against their hoped growth pattern because of his decision to leave. There is nothing that Ben can do at this point to change it, and he will need to wait for each of his generational soul pods to return to The Lobby in order to speak directly to them when they return.

I wish to impart upon you that I mean all of this to be taken literally and not in some mystical or unclear way. This is the actual way in which this process physically and energetically happens each time.

Ben will also be shown what points or opportunities in his life he missed and will miss, thereby changing the whole lifetime for him and his close family.

Back to the Scene of Ben's Departure:

Standing in the small room, Ben and his guide watch once again the inert form of his body, now lifeless on the couch. His phone begins ringing again for the eighth time. The guide standing next to Ben glances at the phone and the message being left can be heard:

"Ben, it's Katie, I have called you 100 times! Why aren't you answering? Okay, so anyway, your Uncle Chet called me last night. His project manager quit, and he wants you to come back and help him run the company!! Ben, please call me back, baby. The boys miss you; I miss you! We love you; this will be the change you needed. We can do this, baby. The money is twice what you make in the fields and Chet said he will even pay for you to do 30-day rehab to clean up if you need. He wants to help us! Ben, the boys are so excited that you can come home. We can do this. I love you so much baby, call me back! Please!" Beep. Silence.

The phone lays on the coffee table in the sun, and Ben and his guide stand and look at it in silence. The full impact of Ben's decision on that day impacts him. He now has full knowledge of what it means to prematurely leave your lifetime. He understands that decisions like the one to give up take moments or years to come to, but once the decision is made there is no turning back. Ben understands that putting down his beer, his anger, his fear, his own self-involved story for three minutes would have changed everything. Simply put, had he answered the phone the first, second, or third time that it rang, he would not most likely have committed suicide. He would have chosen to stay. His guide leans closer to him and he is shown how that one decision changed every other soul who inhabited his lifetime changed their trajectory as well.

There is a kind of parallel here which you may recognize in the movie It's a Wonderful Life. Suicide is not a lesson about what would happen to those you love if you were never born, it is truly about what happens to them if you chose to be born and then leave, and there is a much more painful and long-lasting ramification in this situation. Leaving by choice shows a much deeper and long-standing disregard for those you love than simply choosing not to engage initially.

Ben is shown how life for his family was possibly to go if he had answered his phone on that day and talked with Katie. No life is meant to be perfect, but Ben's would have been full and joyful. Ben was to go on and get sober. Ben was to begin working at his Uncle Chet's company, get out of debt, and eventually inherit that same company all the while taking care of his elderly aunt when his uncle died. Ben was to heal and reunite with Katie and his boys. Ben was to eventually stand at his eldest son's college graduation and wedding years later with Katie and the boys, his whole family reunited with him. Ben was also supposed to help other men with addictions get jobs in his company and get themselves and their lives put back together, and finally, Ben was to spend some time in the very last months of his life as an old man connecting with his youngest son's son talking about family and decisions and the fact that he too once thought about taking his own life, and how bad that would have been and why.

Every person that I described in the last paragraph was counting on Ben at least being in those places within his life in order to facilitate their own growth processes and they his. Ben's Uncle Chet needed to help Ben for his own soul's sake. Ben took that opportunity from him. Ben needed to be at his eldest son's college graduation for many reasons, and Ben was not there. So, Ben's eldest son had to live with not only the idea that Ben didn't love him but also that Ben didn't even love him enough to stay on the planet. Now Ben's eldest son will grapple with that painful belief when it most likely was not to be within his life plan at all. Ben chose for him, taking his free will away.

Now, Ben could have not picked up the phone on that day but not committed suicide. He could have used his free will to stay in an addicted and lonely life as one of his options. This would have always been one of Ben's free will options, but he would still be within the lifetime he had agreed upon with his soul pod, and by way of his mere presence on the

Earth plane, he could change his course to a more positive one at any second. By choosing to leave early, all of the positive growth possibility is removed immediately from the life field. There is a complete symbiosis within lifetimes for soul pods. Ben choosing to "opt out" of the lifetime completely de-rails and robs his soul pod of their possible growth lessons within the lifetime.

There is no way for Ben to make amends other than to spend eons of time (time as you perceive it) trying to wait and assist if he can with the damage caused to every soul his action touched.

The Forgetting Part 2:

When a soul has lived out its lifetime path, that soul will return to The Lobby and have full knowledge of the lifetime and all of his/her actions within it. The second part of the initial forgetting at birth onto the Earth plane is simply remembering everything that came before the life lived as well as all of the lessons achieved or sometimes not achieved within the lifetime just departed. Upon return to The Lobby, the soul will be met with the guides for its lifetime, family members who had returned or waited out the life just departed. There is a joyful reunion of all parties involved and after some rest period, the newly returned soul will have an actual meeting to look over the lifetime and investigate what was learned, what was failed to be learned, and there is a period of "experiencing and feeling" every possible angle of every experience shared with other souls. So, the simple truth here is that every emotion that you caused every other person to experience within your lifetime will be accessed by you and experienced as *they* experienced it. This applies to all emotions across the spectrum of human experience.

In this way, you will be accessing exactly what you put into the life-time. This is why, at this time on your planet, it has been deemed evolu-tionarily necessary for humans to become aware of how this part of the system of birth and re-birth is experienced. Humans need to begin to understand that while they are souls in a body, everything that they say and every reaction they have toward the souls around them matters a lot. With the knowledge that you will experience whatever you give to others to experience, the rule of "do unto others" takes on a very, very personal importance. If you spend a lifetime abusing other persons, emotionally, physically, or psychologically, you will not be allowed to progress upon your own growth journey until you have actually and literally felt your impact on those people you caused the pain to in the lifetime you have recently returned from.

This is a perfect system set up by The Creator/God in which there is no true judgment, there is no "hell" in the Christian sense but a much more active self-imposed system by which souls will experience the consequences of their actions with no outside judgment required. Burning one's own hand is by far a better teacher than the fear of another possibly burning your hand.

In closing this chapter, there is an uncountable degree of variations as to how these principles apply to our lifetimes. It is enough, I think, to impart upon you the importance of learning non-reactive negative interactions with your fellow souls in a lifetime simply because it is a Universal truth that you will reap what you sow. If not within the lifetime, then upon return, which is the very moment that you will realize that you could have chosen to course-correct at any given second within the lifetime. You will undoubtedly also return to lifetimes until you learn the lessons that you failed to learn in the last lifetime. Try to choose every day to respond and be as positive as you possibly can, no matter what is happening around you.

In this way, you will be able to gain the maximum amount of positive experiential growth from birth to death from lifetime to lifetime.

CHAPTER 5

The Universe

Your Universe
Aralamb

The Universe in which you reside is one of many hundreds in operation at any given time upon the field of Creation. I am not, at this time, at an evolutionary level that will allow me to give you the specifics of the "multiple universal creation" in a form which would explain the full form and extent of multiple universe actions. I can and will, however, give you a very simplified explanation of the Universe in which you, Earth, your solar system, your galaxy, all the other planets, and species reside within the Universal Field that we/you inhabit.

As I stated above, the Universe in which we reside is only one of many. This universe was deemed to be created by the combining/colliding/mixing of one Universe, which we will call MIL72/IV for this writing, with another Universe, LFP2/004. MIL72/IV was a very old Universe whose species had evolved well past the ones in which Earth resides now. MIL72/IV was specifically paired with Universe LFP2/004. Universe LFP2/004 was a very young Universe, which was very spare in planetary substance but had a very rich mineral, gravitational, dark/fabric/frequency, and organic content. LFP2/004 also contained immense amounts of inert and floating gasses as well as very high frequency-based dark matter. The two afore-mentioned universes were combined in order to "create" a new Universe, 6318XC/AN, which is the one in which you and your Earth resides. The numerical and phonetic symbols that I use in this text are meant to sim-ulate numeric coding that an Earth human can understand at the basic levels of mathematics. In reality, the numbers and letters listed are and would be of such astronomical size if given directly that the human under-standing of mathematics would not comprehend. So, for this book, I will continue to break down the mathematic symbolism to its largest common denominator for understanding. The larger point I am trying to make is that there is an "absolute" order to the creation of, naming of, frequency of, and characteristics of newly created universes.

I will explain, in general terms, what the Universe in which we live might look like from an "outside" view. All universes are roughly circular in shape. If you could look upon our Universe from the outside, it would *look similar* to a large soap bubble that has a layer of mercury or shiny mirror encasing it. This outermost layer is an electromagnetic, resonant, super-heated field of pulsing frequency vibration, which was put in place by The Creator. When I use the word "sound," I do not mean a sound a human or most any species could hear. I use the word "sound" only so that you might understand that the outermost casing of our Universe is a vibrational "place/time/frequency." Our Universe floats along with others in what I could only describe as an unending dark, velvety soup of ener-getic matter. It is an endless canvas of "possible creation." In this arena, universes float side by side, above and below each other endlessly. The exterior of each universe is generally circular and coated with the reflec-tive energies, so that they are able to float and gently bump against one another without ever infiltrating each other or "crashing" into each other in any way that would initiate a "mixing" of the two. The only time that universes are allowed to combine is if The Creator deems it so and combines them manually.

On the inside "wall" of the outermost barrier of our Universe, time actually folds back in upon itself, so that the outermost range of the Universal boundary cannot be traversed. It is impossible for any craft, vessel, organic species, matter, light, sound to break through the outermost barrier wall of the Universe in which we live. There is a self-cleaning mechanism at work that is much like a heart in a human body. A human heart constantly pumps blood around the whole body to clean, nourish, expel, move nutrients to the outermost skin of the body. In the same way, the outermost walls of the Universe will constantly pulse all matter coming upon its edges to be recycled back into the dark matter of *that* universe. In that same system lay the black holes/worm holes and supernovas that our universe contains. Although black holes/worm holes can and have been used for travel by species for many eons, if any vessel were to traverse them out to their final end, each one leads back to some frequency point which connects to the outside constraints or "skin" of the Universe in which we live. For example, if you were to traverse a black hole/worm hole to its very end without "getting off" at some destination, you would be recycled back into the dark matter possibility field in which we all live. That being said, there is no *physical* way to pierce this outer skin without being absorbed back into the dark matter of creation for our Universe. This is a law put into place by Creation in order to keep the evolutionary track of one universe from contaminating another. I use the word "contaminating" not as a judgment but as a purity issue literally. Universes are only combined, collided at the hand of The Creator/God, at The Creator's/God's time of choosing.

At the inception of the creation of a new universe by combing two older universes, the decision is made by The Creator/God, the determination of souls which will be transmuted to the new universe for evolutionary purposes. In this way, many souls from each of the predecessor universes may be joined together in the *new* creation.

When the decision is made to combine two universes, an energetic "skin" is created which encases the two preceding universes fully within it. At that time, the creator will allow the separate outer skins of the two universes to instantaneously dissolve. Upon the point of dissolution of the skins, the complete contents of each preceding Universe combust and assimilate within the new skin. This is what you refer to as "the big bang." Upon this instant mixing of universal "ingredients," a wholly new substance begins to take form. All of these actions happen over great spans of "time" in the understanding of humans. With the exception of the initial contact, and/or big bang, which takes place in less than a measurable flash of time.

With the big bang moment, two previous universes which existed in spaces that were practically unfathomably huge, touch and collapse inward through the "eye of a needle," after which one new universe expands and breaths outward. This new Universe will be, as you know, a primordial soup of energy, gasses, gravity, dark matter, and the most miniscule particles of what will congeal to become organic living and inert matter. Subatomic particles of every energy manifestation from each of the preceding universes are also floating in that soup. With time and the pulse of The Creator/God, these too will begin the evolutionary process. These will literally be the seeds of all "things", object, planets, species, energies, and levels of processing which will grow and fill the new Universe.

Your present Universe was created in just this way. I am told that this constant restructuring, rebirthing, and evolution of Universes goes on infinitely. What the Creation Field for this activity "IS" is beyond my scope of enlightenment at this time. What I am told is that the "hand" that creates is the hand of what humans call God. On other habited planets and planes, The Creator/God may be called by different names, but The Creator/God is still and always The Creator/God.

Every Universe, including this one, is multidimensional. There are scientists on your planet at this time who believe, mistakenly, that they may be able to traverse to "multiple universes." What they are actually beginning to discover are the multidimensional regions of our Universe. This Universe has approximately 2,200 dimensional regions. Earth sits at approximately at the 560th, although there is an evolutionary push for Earth at this time to move upward, which will change its vibration. Your whole galaxy is moving upward at this time, as well as many other close galaxies in your level/sector.

To explain this simply to you, although the Universe sits in a kind of circular shape, there are within it approximately 2,200 levels of energetic existence. You could imagine these energetic levels as stacking up one on top of the other. Many of the levels of existence in your Universe are lower than Earth, made up of rocky planets with no atmosphere, gases, inert frozen water, dark energy, gravity, radiation, etc. There are billions of planets which are close to Earth's level of existence, just above or below; they will be inhabited by some organic life, but the ones below rarely make it to the level of energetic travel within the Universe. There are many planetary systems which retain some form of "organic" bodies but are at much higher vibrational levels (600–780) who have fully mastered the travel capabilities that allow them to traverse the organic Universal levels at will.

Between the 780th and 890th level, there is a "buffer zone" of levels which acts as the travel line to The Lobby, where I reside at this time. All of the levels above the level of The Lobby are specifically for evolutionary processes of the Universe at any given time. These higher levels of existence are put in place by The Creator to assist all evolution of souls, planets, species, timelines of the Universe. This is why when any organism housing a soul moves from one lifetime to the next, they all traverse back to The Lobby in order to make decisions about that last lifetime.

In every universe, a kind of structure is in place for those species who begin to move out and travel from their planets. I could liken it to a kind of "energetic postal code."

As I stated above, our Universe is, if you can imagine, generally oval/ spherical in shape. There is a bit of sonic movement in the outside "skin" of our Universe as it pulses constantly in order to continue growth, recycling of energy, and movement. Our Universe is a closed system with its own tools and mechanisms of rejuvenation. All Universes that are in existence at this time, to the best of my knowledge, are working within this type of system. Our Universe at times may come close to others floating in the Creation Fabric, but is smoothly moving with no true contact, much the way two magnets will have polarity for one another. Keep in mind, when I say "moving," I am referring to movement that would traverse eons, and eons of Earth's perceived "time."

Outer Skin

The Outer Skin of the Universe is literally the zone or skin which holds all of the continually reproducing dark matter in place for the Universe within it. The Outer Skin of our Universe is based upon a combination of gravity, anti-matter, light photons, and frequency, all of which are mixing in a form that creates a completely new element. Suffice to say that this element, were you able to see it with a human eye would appear to you somewhat like a mirror or mercury. I am in no way indicating that the Outer Skin is made up of such, but that if you could imagine traveling to the Outer Skin, that is what it would look like too you. The Outer Skin is literally structured like a "bag" or, if you would, a "balloon." The whole of the Universe is held within it. Nothing from within a Universe ever touches this Outer Skin, as the Event Signature will always turn every particle of the contents of the Universe back upon itself, folding inward as an ocean wave into that Universe. The Outer Skin is not meant to be traversed. This has nothing to do with keeping species within their own Universes; it literally is just a mechanism of "holding." The Outer Skin is the vast holding mechanism for the Universe in which we live. Every Universe has an Outer Skin, I am told. At the Outer Skin of our Universe, there is no time, there is no movement, there is what a human might call "nothing." There is a complete lack of all movement and energy. The substance of the skin has no innate character. If you were sealed into a chrome box, you would just be there. There is a finality to this skin. It is only through The Creator/God that it can be taken down. I have been taught that the chemical, energetic frequency combination which goes into the making of Universal Skins, is only known to The Creator/God. I know that there are species in our Universe who have traversed closely to the Event Signature and were not able to see or sense with any kind of energetic or manual readings anything other than a "stopping point," where they assume the Universal Skin might start on the other side of the Event Signature.

The Outer Skin is a totally pristine area which we learn is able to ebb and flow to change its form somewhat as the Universe pulses and changes, but the general shape stays round, oval, or some variation of this. The Outer Skin has only the components which it is made of, and nothing from the inside or outside of the Universes is allowed to traverse it. It is pure. This pristine makeup is what keeps its integrity complete. There is a mirror-like perfection to the Outer Skin of the Universe. I do not have access to the number of Universal Evolutions that are in process at any given time. The Creation may have thousands of Universes floating, side by side, each in its evolutionary path. We are taught that only The Creator/God can decide when two should be merged to create a new one. We are also taught that due to the "Holy" nature of the materials that make up the Outer Skin, none of the components are wasted. There is never any waste upon the merging of two Universes.

Because the Outer Skin is always moving and undulating with the special needs of the Universe which resides within it, the area (in square miles) is constantly changing. I mean to say that should the Outer Skin be stretched in one area; it will balloon in another. The Outer Skin will move and adapt to the needs of the Universe within it. The one important quality that the Outer Skin has is that it does not get weaker in an area where it may be stretched or expanded. The tensile, frequency-based energetic strength of the components stay exactly the same no matter where you would measure it, *if* you could measure it. As an example, a 300-lb. anchor chain on Earth would have a completely different tensile strength to lift cargo, than would a 5-foot length of sewing thread. Obviously on Earth, the 300-lb. anchor chain would be millions of times stronger than the thread. At the Outer Skin, a section of the skin that was stretched to 300 feet in diameter would have the exact same tensile strength to hold the Universe in as a 300-million-mile section. The components of the Outer Skin remain at the exact same strength no matter what the size of the traverse. Looking at it another way, one drop of the Outer Skin components will hold in as much matter as the whole. It is statically strong in 100 percent form no matter the amount, thickness, depth, or percent of coverage. The Outer Skin is just that, it can be as thin in places as a human skin or as vast as a galaxy in another, and it retains a continuous tensile strength which is impenetrable and unbreachable, except to The Creator. It is the Universe's defense and safety.

Event Signature

The Event Signature is the region which is also "skin-like" in its construction. The Event Signature resides between the Outer Skin and the Dark Matter Fabric (DMF) of the Universe. The Event Signature is 100 percent fusion in nature. It is in continual rotation in the manner of what you might imagine is the shape of an ocean wave folding in upon itself. The Event Signature is in an unending folding upon itself, and its sole function is to allow every kind of Universal matter, energy, and substance to be slowly pulled into its wave, and gently redirected back out in the form of Dark Matter Fabric, and back into the enclosed Universe. The Event Signature is not a region of space time which can be penetrated or "gotten through." The Event Signature is the place where all of the contents of a Universe are eventually recycled into the original formless potential matter that is the Dark Matter Fabric. All worm holes and black hole activity finds itself eventually leading back to the Event Signature. In this way, when a black hole consumes galaxies, stars, and matter around it, that matter is recycled out to the edges of the Universe and the Event Signature to be recaptured and reused at a future time in the Dark Matter Fabric. Please note, however, that no beings or species who have a soul at any given time or Universe will find its "soul" recycled. Only organic matter and measurable energies are recycled to the Event Horizon. Should an Earth human be shot into space and eventually die in a capsule, the soul of that human would move on to The Lobby for reconciliation. The organic body of that human as well as his or her capsule could float in space for eons of Earth time, finally to be gravitationally absorbed into a black hole and that energy would eventually make its way to the Event Horizon and be reconstituted as Dark Matter Fabric. This process may take time expanses that would be so large as to be nameless on your planet, but that is the cycle. If a vessel were to be at the edge of the Universe and near the Event Signature, they would only see the Universe mirrored back at them. The image that would appear would seem to indicate that the Universe went on forever. It is, however, the mechanism of the Event Signature to mirror back the space from which it is creating Dark Matter Fabric. I am in no way insinuating that our Universe is not unfathomably large, it is, and has many regions, energetic levels, and dimensions. The Event Signature is a very simple fusion band which keeps everything recycling and new for constant evolution in our Universe.

DMF: Dark Matter Fabric

The DMF is what your scientists are now calling the "God Particle." This energy is the basis for every possible thing created in our Universe. The DMF is everywhere, in that it is the literal space between anything that can be seen and measured and is constantly "waiting" for new instruction for creation. It is literally The Creator/God's clay if you will. The DMF is gravity-based, and what your science is missing at this time is the spiritual dynamic of the DMF and its function. All matter whether it be organic or energetic is literally the DMF slowed down to a fraction of its normal vibration/frequency in order to "become" something tangible. When I say "become," I mean this literally. In order for the DMF to "become" or "take form or "BE," it needs the intent of either The Creator/God or some (in a group) or one of the many sentient species in our Universe to agree upon it "becoming." I intend this in its most simple and literal meaning. The Creator/God literally "intended" our Universe into being. The DMF has no ability to decide upon its own, where to come into being, how to come into being or what it should be. The DMF is pure possibility which resonates or dismantles its "beingness" upon the intention of a sentient being. You might ask, "Who intended the planets, gasses, and other objects in our Universe?" The initial intentions would have been The Creator's/God's movement of intending into being in order to be a "stage" if you will for the evolution of sentient beings of all kinds as well as organic, microbic, amicrobic, and all other manner of life. The DMF has no ability to "intend" itself into any form; it is literally formless until such time that an intention is directed upon or toward it. Then, and only then, through the gravitational reso-nance/frequency manipulation of the "intendor," or "observer" if you will, that the DMF will coalesce in the intended form. The strength of the inten-tion, the focus of that intention/observation also has a very large impact on the intricacy of what is created. Emotion is also a very large aspect of the intention/observation. The more emotion a sentient being places with the intention/observation, the more core energetic information will be cast into the gravity of the DMF. When the oldest species in this Universe who are now long gone began to become sentient and aware of themselves, the DMF began to resonate to their intentions/observations. This is a basic fundamental truth that humans are just now beginning to look at. There are organizations on your planet at this time that are well-studied in the intention/observation energy uses of the DMF. However, those few orga-nizations are not public at this time. It is time for the whole of the human species on Earth to understand that the DMF is there, responding to your intentions/observations whether you know it, understand it, or believe it. This being true, as a species you would do well to begin to look at what you are intending/observing either consciously or unconsciously. You are more powerful than you know and are creating every moment, whether you are concentrating or not. Many species have fallen to dust because they did not grasp the power of themselves as a species intending negativity into the DMF. Perfection is not the aim, but certainly benevolence and soul growth should be foremost when understanding the use of the DMF. The DMF through its sympathetic gravitational frequencies is also a fully functioning and ever generating power source. Many species in the Universe have learned to harvest this power to travel through galaxies and power whole planets. There have been two species that have visited the Earth in your very ancient history who had this technology. The DMF was placed as the fabric of Universes to basically be the pen, paper, clay, food, and substance that can "BE" all things with the correct intention/observation. It is truly The Creation substance. The DMF is in infinity literally sitting in wait, until it is observed, intended, or acted upon.

Zone:

The Milky Way Galaxy is located in Zone NI. The Universe in which we reside is broken up into approximately 8,872 million Zones. A Zone is a structured area of space within the Universe. A Zone may have over 1 billion galaxies in it. All zones of space within the Universe are not exactly the same size, but they follow the general shape of a multidimensional square. The Zone specifications are literally used in the galactic sense as an address for species that can travel. It is quite rare for species to move from Zone to Zone without also moving through dimensions as time/space/frequency becomes a constraint to such movement. If you are a species that can travel from Zone to Zone, you are traveling such distances that it is necessary to remove yourself from the dimension in your Zone in which aging is a natural occurrence or you would not "live" long enough to travel the distance.

If you are a species that can travel from Zone to Zone in a corporal body, you have learned to adjust your energetic/frequency blueprint to jump dimensions as well. For example, if you wanted to hang glide from one high rise in New York to another next to it, you would need to go up to the roof in order to hang glide to the next building. You would need to bypass the floors below you in order to do this. You could not hang glide from the 30th floor to the 30th floor on the next building over as you would run into the side of that building. You would be constrained by the "form" of that building. However, if you were able to move to the uppermost roof dimension of the building, you could easily hang glide from the roof to the next roof and then go back down to the lower floors of that building. The Zones of the Universe are just so. You can only move from one to the next by moving up dimensions in order to bypass the organic time issue. There are, to my knowledge, five species habituating the Zone in which Earth resides who are capable of this at present. Needless to say, it is enough to know that the Zone that Earth resides in is as big as what scientists would call "the known Universe." What they are seeing as the whole Universe at this time is really just the NI Zone.

Strata:

Within the Strata of each Zone, there exists what you would call a three-dimensional structure/grid that is held together with a fourth-dimensional time/energy/frequency signature. The fourth-dimensional time/energy/frequency signature is a pure energy source which allows for instant lateral, vertical, and free form movement throughout the Universe. The fourth dimension of energy is what your scientists call "Zero-Point Energy." This source will and can "become" whatever is asked of it at any given moment on the time continuum. This energy is literally "potential." This energy IS everywhere, ALL of the time. The Zero-Point Energy is one factor *within* the DMF. It is wholly purposed to be in waiting for molding into the intention of sentient beings. The Creator's/God's clay if you will. What this means is that if, for instance, you were to visit a planet in the 62 Strata where Earth resides, but the planet was at a different frequency Level of the 62 Strata than Earth, you would come to rest at the exact frequency of that planets (S) Sun and Node space time. In order to travel to Earth, you would need to have Earth's exact time/spatial /frequency, Zone, Strata, Level, Sun, Node "address" so to speak. The fourth dimension of energy is connected directly to the dark matter fabric and is the "key board," if you will which allows for physical movement and time direction throughout our Universe. This Zero-Point Energy is what allows my group to coalesce at a specific point in order to work together. It is the same energy that Einstein referred to as "spooky attraction." The fourth-dimensional energy/Zero-Point Energy actually responds to intention by sentient beings. Your scientists are attempting, at this point, to "mechanically" find, maneuver, and control Zero-Point Energy, and what they should be doing is understanding that "intention" must come into the picture to fully utilize it. There are species in this galaxy who have learned to equip AI to have this correct "intention" in order to control and maneuver space craft/vessels throughout the Zones. These species have actually evolved the understanding of how to impart upon artificial intelligence the ability to "intend" itself, and thereby a vessel filled with beings along the lines of the fourth time/space/frequency to specific "addresses" in the Universe. Earth is quite far away from this knowledge, evolutionarily speaking, but it is in the future for humans from Earth should the planet survive the shifting times to come.

Level:

There are an almost uncountable, at least in human terms, "Levels" in each Strata. This is because each Level has its own frequency. Frequencies are divided by such miniscule changes in the numerological system that the counting of them becomes beside the point. There are different numbers of Levels in each Strata of each Zone. Not unlike very populated cities on your planet when compared to rural regions of your planet, the more populated planets there are in a galaxy the more closely aggregated the energetic/frequency Strata and Levels of a Zone will be. Overlaying the whole of a Level will be all of the energetic species' levels which I spoke of earlier. This is held together by the union of the dark matter and the fourth-dimensional time/space, Zero-Point Energy.

Galaxy:

The Milky Way Galaxy in which Earth's Solar Node resides is within Level 4.2963 of Strata (62) of Zone (NI). You will notice that the Galaxy itself does not need a particular frequency for "travel." The frequency of the Solar Node of the Earth's planetary Sun and Node are all that is needed to travel. The galaxies within a particular Level all carry the frequency of that Level. What is needed is the particular Sun/Node frequency that is specific. As an interesting aside, humans on your planet who are beginning to learn the art of "astral travel" are actually accessing the fourth-dimensional time/space/Zero-Point Energy/frequency system. Unknowingly the "travelers" are accessing this plane in order to "be" at that exact frequency. I digress. I will speak more on that later.

With the simple explanations given, you might liken the frequency, time space, and "position in reality" of your planet to be similar to a very, very, distinct mailing address. Keep in mind, this example is not to be taken as a metaphor in whole, as the distinct Z(NI)S(62)L4.2963(S)129734.9(F)N(P)(18) is the actual place in time/space/frequency that Earth resides in within this Universes structure. With this information, species that have mastered traveling in the multidimensional space/time/frequency will, and have, been able to travel to Earth's very point of being. I use the term "point of being" because the Universe is set up in so many Levels and Strata that it is a system of "time/place/frequency," and as Earth might understand it does not apply. The "point of being" is the most functional process for all that exists in this Universe. I also want to delineate that "multi*dimensional* space time/frequency" within this Universe is what I am speaking of. There is no allowable "multi-*universal*" travel allowed at this time. Earth scientists at this time are only just realizing "multidimensional" space time, and mislabeling it as "multi-Universe theory."

The realization of this is only approximately 25 Earth years from full evolution. That is to say that within 25 years, science on this planet will understand fully and embrace the "multidimensional" space time movement in its actual reality.

If you were, for example, a species living in Zone (F), your species will have fully embraced and evolved the ability to travel to most areas of this Universe. Should a scientific party of researchers on your planet be interested to seek out a very primitive species which was a distant cousin to your own, Earth, for example, they would first apply the "points of being" that they already knew may harbor planets which support those kinds of life-forms, that is, humans.

The procedure that this highly evolved species would employ in order to determine where it might visit would be by seeking out not only the "address" of such planets but also the energetic "signature" of the *species* that lived upon that planet. You as humans have an energetic, organic "signature" which can be read. All species have such energetic signatures, and they are linked to the same address signature which the planet or planets upon which they reside, a sort of "home" energy signature.

For example, if a human was taken up in the vessel of some much more evolved being from a higher Zone, even if that human was transported to Zones well above and beyond Earth's evolution, he/she would retain the energetic signature of Earth and humans. This would be the same for any humanoid from any planet. If, for example, a humanoid much like yourself was taken from a planet well across your Milky Way Galaxy to Zones above his/her own, that humanoid would share the "humanoid" energy signature but not the "Earth" frequency signature. He/she would have his/her own planets energy signature mixed with the humanoid signature. I also want to be sure that you understand that only species that have been gifted souls will have the full energy signature "address." There are, throughout this Universe, "species" that are no longer or have been constructed not to possess any organic soul or material. All species that have fully traversed the bridge of robotic or non-soul-based intelligence have no connection to The Creator/God. On Earth you would call these beings AI or artificial intelligence. At the point that a species replicates its intellect without retaining the "soul's connection" with The Creator/God, the soul is released for a final time. This is not the intent of The Creator/

God, as mechanical evolution has no pure growth potential in the sense of dignity, love, artistic endeavor, mathematical elegance, innovation, color, or intellectual diversity. Machinery can only realize itself and ultimately becomes a statue in the end. Again, this is not The Creator's/God's wish. Free will requires a soul. Free will is the objective of growth and manifestation after all.

The being that is fully robotic and has fully computerized memory will have the energetic signature of its original planet of origin but no kind of energetic species marker from The Creator/God will be present. The species of origin will only be discernable by manually searching its functional history for the original species or "maker." The offspring of these species, if there are any, will be created or born without any connection to a soul or The Creator/God.

Earth is only in the past few thousand years becoming capable of understanding the space/time/frequency in which it resides. With the shifting evolution of the whole Milky Way galaxy at this time, humanoids on this planet will begin to understand that there is a multidimensional Universe existing just outside of Earth's view, and it is literally teaming with life.

CHAPTER 6

Good Morning

Good Morning
I truly loved my mom...and she was scary as hell!

I can remember distinctly being about 13 years old when I started my period. I remember this time because of the smell. When a woman of any age has her period, bathing or showering becomes a really huge deal because menstruation, although completely natural and wonderful, does have an odor.

In Sally's house, there was a real issue with bathing for some reason. I was beginning seventh grade in the latter half of 1976. It was the 200-year anniversary of the U.S.A. and at our school it was a big deal. I had started my period that summer and I became really sensitive about being "clean." Unfortunately, my need to have a shower or bath every day before school was completely at odds with Sally's weird obsession with linking the need to bathe every day with "evil," "vanity," "trying to seduce her 19-year-old boyfriend," or some kind of "religious wrongdoing." For a long time, there was no shower in our house, just a big ole claw-foot bathtub, which we were not allowed to use freely. Don't parents usually have to fight their kids to get in the bathtub? In our house, it was mostly off-limits. The baths I do remember taking were far and few between until I got to be around 15 or 16 and insisted on a bath at least once a week. Prior to that time, bathing and self-care in general were activities to be done on the sly.

I was about 11 or so when my militant ability to wake up quietly 10 minutes before the alarm went off each morning came into play. I would grab the radio shack alarm clock with both hands, gently turn off the switch that would blare the alarm, and gingerly place the alarm clock back on the piece of cloth upon which it sat, all while keeping so silent that even my sheets did not rustle. This skill was honed to a precise number of movements which had the grace and silence of a ballet. On the rare occasion when I would accidentally set the thing off, I would wrap it quickly in a blanket until I could get it shut down. Waking Sally up in the morning before school was a very, very risky, and frankly, terrifying proposition. Sally was not a great morning person, which is funny considering that both my sister and I grew up to be sunny, happy morning people.

I had started the hypervigilant wake-up routine in the fifth grade when I figured out that it was best, and much safer if you simply woke up, got ready for school, and left the building without waking Mom up. As I said, Sally was not good in the morning. I have since realized that those first morning hours between waking and leaving the house were the hardest for her because I believe that any self-medication that had been administered the evening before, that is, alcohol, weed, "crank," would have worn off in the early morning, leaving her raw, emotional and on edge. As a kid, however, I did not know that. I simply knew that I would need to get myself and my sister out of that gauntlet of a house without waking mom up.

To wake her up meant a complete crap shoot of crazy, scary, burn the house down mental illness which could become an all-destroying fire on any given day. I had learned this very early; I would say by six or seven years old probably. Whatever mental illness that plagued our mother came with a healthy dose of paranoia, and the need to look for issues like lying and other wrongdoing, even when they were not truly present. She was convinced from a very early age, in my case, that I was always plotting against her in some way. My one and only directive when I was a child was to survive her. Literally, that was it. These outbursts would and often did devolve into being emotionally and verbally abused until you were ready to "admit," or even make up an incident of wrongdoing, so that you could escape her wrath. Once you confessed to the imagined deed, you were expected to "hug it out and feel better for admitting your sins." The problem with all of that is that it was such a full-frontal mind screw for a kid of any age. Having to go through the admitting, begging for forgiveness, hugging it out for an event that was totally made up in her mind was crazy and terrifying.

It *was* terrifying, it was exhausting, and it was too much for any child to carry really. All of this screaming, crying, interrogation about imagined wrongdoings accompanied by insane rants, laughing, Bible-hugging breakdowns and threatening could happen for as much as an hour in the early morning hours before school, ***if you woke her up***. Once this happened, you would have to go through it, hopefully get out of the house, and then try to seem as if everything was: just fine," by the time you got to the bus stop.

Our house was 200 years old and was one big creaking hulk. If you have never lived in a very old home, I mean to say that every door, floor, wall, window, and surface creaked like an old boat hull when you moved around in any and all directions. I mean, it was noisy. Added to that, was my mother's need to add bells to the door handles of every door in the house. The front door had brass bells hanging from it. The door between the living room and the tiny, steep stairwell to the bedrooms upstairs had bells on it, and the door to the upstairs literally creaked like a barn door when you opened and closed it to pass through. That door also always had to be closed and tied shut, so that the bedroom cat would not escape from our mother's room. Because of that cat, there was also a kind of rope which needed to be tied when going in or out of that door.

Writing about this now, reading it out loud, makes it all seem even crazier and just confusing. The most important detail in getting downstairs and out of the house without waking Sally up was the art of picking out all of your clothes the night before. I would insist that my sister had her clothes picked out as well. Stephanie is four years younger than me, and it was much harder to get her out of the bedroom, down the stairs, and ready to go than if it had just been me. It was imperative that both of us had picked out socks, undies, shirt, pants, sweater, whatever we would be wearing. They had to be neatly folded into piles on the dresser. The idea was that no drawer, closet, or basket needed to be moved, touched, or rummaged through to find what we were going to wear. All of these activities would create noise, movement, and might wake Sally, or worse her bedroom cat, which would dig at the door if it heard us, thereby waking her up. Our room was always a filthy wreck, with clothes on the floor and everywhere. This fact actually worked in our favor because at least walking in ankle-deep clothing was quieter.

Our room had a door which opened onto a 2x2-foot landing at the top of the very steep and narrow stairs. Sally's bedroom door was on the other side of the 2x2 landing. Once the alarm was turned off, I would quietly sit up in my bed, wake my sister with a finger to my lips in the "shhh" sign. She would wake up, like a well-trained little soldier. I would hand grab our clothes bundles, again with a finger to my lips, and send her toward our bedroom door. Our door, for whatever reason, would not creek very loudly if you just swung it hard and smooth toward your body. I would swing it open just enough so that we could both pass onto that 2x2 landing. Stephanie knew that she needed to be soft and quick on the stairs in order to avoid making them heave and creek with noise. I was just a bit too heavy and would often step directly from our bedroom door threshold down onto the first-stair step in order to avoid the landing. That landing would creek loudly with my body weight, so I avoided it. Once we got to the bottom of the stairs, the door between the living room and hall needed to be opened. It had, however, as I said, bells on it, so I would hold the bells in my right hand, Steph would untie the rope, and swing the door open enough for us to get through. I would then retie the rope or ribbon or whatever was holding it shut. Getting out of our house always felt like getting out of some crazy, scary carnival box to me. I think that is why now, in my own home, I can't stand closed doors or blinds drawn or locked spaces.

Once we were safely downstairs, we would still remain very quiet. I would often wet or wash my hair in the tub, because it was too risky to try to bathe fully. If Mom woke up and found that I was washing my hair or taking a bath, she would devolve into a raging meltdown of "Oh the sin, the vanity" usually followed by "who do you think you are, you dirty little bitch" craziness. Stephanie was also not allowed to bathe enough. For the life of me, I still have not been able to ferret out just what the bathing issue was.

Cereal would be quietly poured into bowls. I figured out how to pour cereal onto my hand while it lay against the bowl, so that no cereal sounds were created. It would just roll it into my palm and not make any noise on the transfer to the bowl.

Being that our house was a pre-Civil War building, it had many nooks and crannies. One of these nooks was a strange cut-out hole in the wall between a pantry room, and the stairwell just below our mother's bedroom door on the other side. What this meant was that anything we did in the kitchen or bathroom to get ready for school in the way of sound waves would travel up through that nook in the wall. If we were too loud in any way, bowl clinking in the sink, bathroom door shut a bit too hard, refrigerator door let swing to close on its own without a guiding softening hand, IT COULD WAKE HER UP.

The only great thing about that nook in the wall was that if Sally decided that she had heard something, something that would let her know that we had not left yet, she would get up, untie the ribbons that held her door shut from the inside, fight with the bedroom cat a bit so it wouldn't get out, swing that creaking bedroom door wide, and hit that loud stairwell.

We would hear all of this clearly and have approximately four minutes and 17 seconds to get out of that house before she could get down the steep stairwell, through the hall door, and out into the kitchen. That weird little pantry wall nook was our savior and our ruin on many occasions.

Our successful morning program was pretty much the same on school days. Get dressed either on our beds or downstairs. Bathroom, silent cereal, coats, hats, snowsuits, depending on the season. On a day when we had not woken Mom up, we would approach the front door to the porch to exit. This door again was old and super creaky, and on top of that, it had a literal "bundle" of old brass bells hanging off of it. I still have this bundle of antique brass bells in my home. Until recently, I actually had the very same bells on my front door. I finally figured out that having those bells on my door is somewhat Stockholm Syndrom-ey! I have taken them all down. The front door was better actually because even though there were more bells, they were much heavier, so that if I really slowly and smoothly opened the door, I could do it without any bells even moving. I would open the door enough for us to get out. Close it quietly and we would quickly, very purposefully and silently hurry off the porch and out onto School Street. I can still remember that every day that we successfully moved out onto School Street without waking Mom up was so liberating. The feeling of having gotten through the morning without her interaction was like a snake of terror unfurling from your stomach and moving away across the road to terrorize someone else. The problem with Sally was that due to her undiagnosed psychiatric issues and alcoholism, she was totally free to ter-rorize and love us any way she deemed correct. It was only much later that I would understand how completely "war-like" this morning scenario was.

Now if we were fed and close to departure and heard movement of any kind from upstairs, we would, in a kind of silent "the house is on fire" panic, coat up and get out the front door without being quiet. Winter was the worst. We could not leave and walk to school and/or the bus stop with-out mittens, hats, snow suits, snow pants, boots, etc. Snow gear added its own noise hazard. Between the years of 1960 and 1990, snow gear was made of what I can only deem the noisiest blend of polyester ever known to man. The zippers, the snaps, the hoods, the whole friggin' deal was noisy! Then once it was on, every arm and leg rubbed together like a hellacious buzz saw when you tried to move at all. Not the best gear for moving out of your building like a ninja trying to get off the field of battle. If we could get off the porch and up past Canal Street to Forlie Balou's Clothing shop without looking back, we could feign the idea that even if Sally was yelling at us from the front porch to come back, we did not hear her. I cannot even count the number of times that the flight up the street happened with the opening creek of that bedroom door.

I think at some point when I was about 15, and Steph was maybe 11-and-a-half, Sally started to really get wind of our silent morning ritual because if she woke up, she would start yelling our names from the stair landing instead of coming all the way down stairs first.

The real issue with Sally and the school morning was that you absolutely never knew what kind of an experience it was going to be. I believe that about 75 percent of her mornings were bad experiences at least prior to Nelson's arrival in our home when I was about 14. After Nelson moved in, and they got married, Sally for sure was a bit more reined in. Thank you, Nelson, for that. I truly believe that Nelson's arrival in our lives saved my sister's high school years. So, prior to Nelson's arrival, I am going to give Sally a 75 percent horror show of a morning ritual. The real mind crusher about her morning mental issues were that every once in a while, she would catch us completely unaware and wake up happy, making pancakes, smiling, and hugs goodbye at the door. This was particularly mind-screwy, however, because it was so far and few between that you knew, in your goddamn bones that you were going to pay for it at some later time. At a later time, when your guard was down, she was going to come at you with the force of a full-blown psycho, and this soft, kind person making you pancakes would be the most terrifying human you had ever stood before. This was Mom....

Looking back on the scenario now, it occurs to me that this kind of experience as a child really makes you grow up in a very "black and white" way. I can remember being very young and knowing that the way our life was set up was not right. There was no safety in it. There was no soft, safe secure place for us. I was very young, maybe six or seven, when I became fully aware that this woman was not right mentally. I obviously didn't put any kind of real name on it, but I knew that even as a kid I was more capable of getting ready for school and getting Steph ready for school in some way that was not traumatic to either of us. I knew that the "crazy" was not normal. Aralamb tells me now that all of the childhood trauma was a facilitator for a kind of evolution that might otherwise take much longer. I don't buy into the "must suffer for growth" mantra and neither does Aralamb, but certainly I was at 11 years old thinking like a like an adult trying to survive. Survival was the rule of thumb. I just wanted to survive it. I wanted Steph to survive it. Thus, the ninja morning routine.

To this day, both my sister and I are militant happy morning people. My son refers to me as being the only human, other than his aunt, who has the "morning dirt bike syndrome." If you are not familiar with this term, it means that I wake up very cheerful and ready to head off into the woods at a high rate of speed, bantering the whole time about how great the day is going to be. Thus, the dirt bike sound, "Baaaa, baaaa, baaaaaa, baaaaa." Like a dirt bike rider shifting quickly through gears and happily speeding away into the morning sun! I would fight this description, except that I have often seen it in my sister Stephanie and, truth be told, do have it myself.

Aralamb is telling me that this is a great time to bring up the subject of "choice." Aralamb always tells me that there is a place for making choices in every second of your day. No matter where you are or what you are going through, no matter how "fucked" things may seem, you can choose. (Aralamb wanted me to tell you that I used the word fucked, not him.) No matter what your Earthly circumstances are, you can make a choice about how you will adapt in situations or be run over within them. It is that simple. You adapt and choose your reaction to any situation, or you refuse to adapt, and you choose victimhood. I have often complained to Aralamb that this rule seems a bit hard, and he assures me that it is a truth. No matter what is going on in any second of your day, you always have the option of adapting and choosing how you will react to that situation. In that way, you actually retain ultimate power over your own soul's experience. Our "morning routine," although I did not realize it at the time, was a perfect example of this rule.

Although just kids, we chose to adapt to an untenable situation by coming up with a way to completely avoid that situation. We adapted and determined to have a reaction that was safer and more conducive to NOT being targeted by terrifying craziness in the morning. Stephanie and I took it one step further, which was to look at that adaptation as adults and decide to be super annoyingly happy and positive with our loved ones in the morning! Thus the "morning dirt bike." We learned from our mother how NOT to be.

The takeaway here is that you are in total control of how you feel and react to difficult situations in your life. As a soul, you always have the choice to adapt and react in any way you see fit. Not to be clichéd, but you actually can take crappy situations and decide how to adapt and react in a positive way that ultimately facilitates you! Use that muscle, feel it as your reality, and The Creator/God will send you options. Also, if you can, avoid polyester!

CHAPTER 7
Energy-Sound-Frequency

Energy-Sound Frequency-Music
Aralamb

Every Level, Strata, and cubic space/time area of this Universe is energetic/
frequency. There is nothing in existence that is not composed of energy/
frequency, and in turn composed of vibrational field. The speed/frequency
at which energy is vibrating is the only indicator of what that energy will
be manifested into or out of for the experience of the souls or soul who is
coming into direct contact with and within it. Every experience that you
will or ever have had in your incarnation upon this Earth is at its most base
element an energetic/frequency experience.

Because of this scientific and spiritual truth, energy/frequency in all
of its forms is completely and utterly at "the will" of any and every sentient
being that it comes into contact with. You might ask, "If that is true, who
willed an asteroid belt or a black hole into being?" Those manifestations
would have been intended by the will of The Creator/God initially upon
inception of this Universe. Plainly stated, energy/frequency and its control
and flow and congelation into form is completely at your will and under

your control in your life at all times, whether you choose to embrace that fact or not.

Should you determine that this is not a truth that you can accept, you will simply be buffeted by the energy/frequency of those around you who may or may not have this knowledge or "belief" as well. You can, should you so determine, literally be a feather in a veritable sea of rolling energy, or you can "decide" that you will not be a loose and aimless "floater" within the system of scientific and spiritual reality that is the ever-present energetic and gravitational frequency field in which we all reside.

If you are at all sensitive to the energy/frequency fields around you, you will be able to think in your mind's eye to a time when you would have entered a room and immediately "sensed" the people, space, feeling and/or energy/frequency of that space. Most humans at this point only "sense" the energy/frequency that is around them within approximately a two-foot circle of where they stand, sit, or locate their bodies. Because of this lack of outward experience with the energetic/frequency field, they assume that "what they can see, smell, feel, or hear" is all that there is. This is a very young and limited view of the reality of our Universe. There are at this very time many species living in our Universe who literally can sense, see, hear, and experience realms and worlds that may physically be separate from them by light years or levels of time/space/frequency. This is because these species understand that due to the scientific and spiritual nature of energy, frequency, magnetism, and the DMF, no location in time and space is ever truly closed to you. You may know this in its practice as remote viewing or astral travel.

From a human standpoint, it is time to understand that the ability to sense energy and frequency in a very real and visceral way is an evolutionary process that your brain is undergoing. This unfolding ability through your frontal cortex "faith" tether is completely natural and normal. It is time on your planet for this knowledge to be understood and evolved both physically and spiritually. This is a tool that humans were created to embrace and use when the time was right for that growth. Now is the time.

Trust and the Connection

Only very few humans up to this point have had true knowledge of this ability or the knowledge of the nature of "energy/frequency" in the Universe. The religious and political machinations that have been put into place on Earth were set there specifically to subvert and hide this knowledge from humanity. A population of humans who truly understood how their soul and mind are connected to the actual movement and creative forces of energy/frequency would be very difficult to control in a way that would be to the advantage of the controlling group. We will speak to the geo-political nuances of that story in another chapter, but suffice it to say here that as a race on Earth, your true connection to energy/frequency and your talents to move, mold, and create with it have been hidden from the knowledge of the whole up till now for the furtherance of the goals and desires of a very few human/hybrid groups at the very top of your Earthly pillars of control. You as a human were created to embrace and advance your mental and spiritual skills. The time of being controlled is well past and evolution is on your doorstep.

Trust in The Creator/God is a very integral part within the system of sensing and understanding the energy/frequency field in which I, you, and every particle of the Universe resides. It is not necessary to "believe" in The Creator/God to access your natural and organic connection to energy/frequency sensing and manifestation, but if a knowledge of The Creator/God is accepted and embraced as the omni point of all energy/frequency that exists, it is much easier for the newly awakened human to access his or her connection to the "faith" tether by which all energy organically must pass to and from the energetic manifestation field that I refer to as the DMF.

Having a level of belief and faith in the system put in place by The Creator/God enhances the overall feeling of support that we as souls enjoy and, therefore, enables a relaxation and trust that energy/frequency manifestation, healing organic transmutation matter is possible. I would liken it to learning how to ride a bicycle. One of the often unspoken but integral parts of this operation is that either a child has training wheels or a parent's hands on the handlebars or a combination of both happens while learning the skill. Either or both of these "safeguards" is pivotal in that child feeling secure in and having faith in the process of learning the new skill. A conscious connection with The Creator/God is the same kind of tool which is very helpful in learning and expanding this human ability and talent. The Creator/God gave every human body and soul the ability to grow and evolve the gift of energy/frequency sensing and manifestation, so acknowledging and being grateful for The Creator/God who gave you these gifts and opportunities simply enhances the growth potential exponentially.

Energy Sensing and Manifestation Types
General Situational Energetic Sensing and Netting

General situational energy sensing and what I will call "netting" is on its face very simple and should be employed by all humans all of the time. By this, I mean that the general resting state of all humans should be in "sensing" the changing and subtle energies around them. Many humans already access this without even realizing that they are doing it. This skill, however, can and needs to be honed, acknowledged, and accepted at this time as an evolving trait for humanity on your planet.

As an example of what this might look like in your life right now, have you ever been walking down the street and crossed over because of a feeling you get about the person walking toward you? Have you ever decided at the last minute to make changes in travel plans or taken a job that paid less money because you "felt" like it was the better thing to do? Have you experienced meeting a complete stranger and felt an immediate "connection" with them and they end up being an integral part of your life? Have you ever made a change in the direction of your life because of a "gut feeling" rather than logic? Have you ever avoided another person because you don't "feel" good around them? Have you ever had the sense that every time you are around certain people or places, you come away exhausted or conversely uplifted? Have you ever travelled to a location on Earth and "felt" completely at ease, comfortable, and at home even though you may have never been there before? Have you ever met a stranger and wished you could spend more time with them simply because they make you feel good? Do you ever have dreams in which you are somewhere, living a life, even on some other planet or in a strange city which feels familiar to you but you have no recollection of how that can be?

These are all examples, and I could go on, of your body and soul using your energetic/frequency sensing mechanism. Take into consideration as well that I am not implying that you are constantly sensing the "negative" in other people, situations, or locations. I am simply telling you that your soul will constantly give you energetic/frequency feedback on everything you do, every person you come into contact with, and every possibility outcome that is presenting itself within your lifetime.

Should you have a friend who you love but who is also energetically constantly sucking your energy away, you may find yourself exhausted by their presence. This does not mean that you avoid them, it simply means that your energy/frequency sensing ability is there to help you determine whether your own energy/frequency field or your own energy/frequency stores on a certain day are willing and able to allow that person to syphon from you what they need, or what you are willing and able to give. Energy/frequency is constantly in an ebb and flow from person to person, location to location, and situation to situation.

Keeping this in mind will help you to understand why you might visit a certain place on the planet, or city, and even though you should feel like a stranger in that location you may not because it is most likely that your energy /frequency field is very compatible with that location and is, therefore, refreshed by that place. Some human souls are drawn to oceans, some to mountains, some to deserts or jungles. The resonance of those places will be in keeping with the soul's own resonance and this is why being able to read and sense your own energy/frequency needs as well as of those around you is so critical at this time. In the next 15–28 years, humanity on Earth will have full knowledge of the immensity of this Universe and understand fully that there are billions of habitable planets upon which organic humans or cousins thereof reside. This enlightening knowledge will suddenly open up the opportunity "literally" for humans to decide to travel and relocate to these other planets. If you can extrapolate what this means for Earth humans, it means that you may feel drawn to relocate to some other solar system, some other planet which actually enhances, and is symbiotic with, your own soul's energy/frequency field. This is becoming a possibility and thus the need for your species' evolution at this time.

Again, I wish to stress the point that should you sense energy coming from a person, situation, location, or activity that brings the fear sensation to your physical body, it does not mean that there is nothing but negativity there. It simply means that it is not the right situation, person, environment, or location for you. The stronger the "positive" or "negative" feeling you have in your body through the sensing, the more important it is to listen to it. When you begin to run your choices daily through this sensing filter, you will see that your decisions begin to move you forward in what can only be described as your highest good. This is the lesson of this tool. The more adept you become at giving attention to and trusting your energetic/frequency senses, the less difficulty you will encounter in creating your life and making good choices for your possibility arc with The Creator/God.

When I use the word "difficulty," I do not mean in the basest sense of the word, as in doing something wrong. I mean that the sole purpose for your time on Earth in this incarnation is to begin to learn how to steer your own life path in such a way that you do not have to keep experiencing over and over those situations that are painful to yourself and others. Should you be, in this lifetime, more able to use your energy/frequency sensing tools, you may decide not to date that woman who will ultimately make you once again go through pain in a relationship regarding addiction. You may avoid a life of missed opportunities by moving to a place that "feels" right to you instead of staying in your city of birth to please others. Avoiding those painful mistakes in experience and judgment is much, much easier if you are fully engaged with you energetic/frequency sensing mechanism. Faith in yourself and a faith in The Creator/God and the system of energy in which we all reside is the best strengthener that you have for enhancing your sensing tools.

Your energy/frequency sensing system is at once linked to your physical endocrine system as well as your third-eye chakra and your soul's connection with The Creator/God. There is no "time/space/frequency" signature between the sensing and the knowing. This process is instantaneous and in past millennia has been fully the domain of the "reptile" brain. At this point in the physical history of humans, the reptile brain is giving way to the higher portions of the frontal cortex in this implementation. As the reptile brain gives this piece of its responsibility to the frontal cortex, the frontal cortex is lighting up and energizing locations of itself that have until now lain dormant and the reptile brain is expanding its ability to "keep the bodies' systems safe and running cleanly." There is no difficulty with this transition, and this ability to evolve was genetically dormant and waiting for this particular time in organic human history, should the human species on Earth find itself surviving to this specific history point in our Universe. Bravo! You have arrived at this point in Universal history. This evolution will continue and is unfolding on the Earth plane at this time should humanity accept it or not. Should a human fully reject these inner changes in him or herself, there will simply be a feeling of being overwhelmed and exhausted. There is no judgment or retaliation should a human ignore or refuse to accept these changes within themselves. I will stretch to say that as the whole of humanity on Earth shifts in this awareness, those who literally refuse to see the change will suffer within themselves, as inner evolution is a process which happens to every species in the

Universe and is a gift not to be struggled against. Should that be your will, however, you will be allowed to struggle.

The organics and genetics that surround energy/frequency sensing for species is completely linked with that species' ability in the areas of *telepathy, telekinesis, frequency movement, astral travel and frequency toning,* that is, *musical toning.* I would also insert here the idea that human's obsession with electronic devices at this time is literally and figuratively overriding the ability for many to sense this change within themselves. I would advise that every human take 24-hour respites from any kind electric device in order to release those energies and better hear, feel, and assimilate the natural evolution that is in process. To be quiet within oneself and listen for The Creator/God is a more powerful tool than any that humankind has ever invented. The abilities listed above are actually completely natural in our Universe and many, if not most, long-lived species will have embraced these inherent genetic qualities and accept them as freely as a human on Earth accepts that seeing, smelling, and feeling are all just "givens" in your worldview. There is a time upon Earth coming in the next 100 to 187 years when these "new" abilities will weave themselves into the human experience and be taken out beyond the shores of this planet with you. I am honored to be able to bring some of this knowledge to your species now.

You were seeded by The Creator/God originally, and then given a "leg-up" in the evolutionary process prior to the last Ice Age. In that prior time, the genetics for "full" evolution were given to you as part of a treaty which was conducted by the Tochal species who engineered your speedy evolution along with the higher counsels of The Creator/God. The agreement was loosely that your species was to be given the full array of possible genetics to incorporate yourselves into the Universal Community of Species adequately and peacefully. The floods and Ice Age would be allowed to "wipe clean" the planet of the off-world others who had come and "meddled" with The Creator's/God's plans, leaving some behind to pay for the unsanctioned "creation" of the new human species, and should any groups of you survive and flourish on your own to this point, you would then and only then be allowed to begin an evolution into your full and functioning selves as Universal beings. That time is now. You have stepped across the threshold of the timeline and The Creator's/God's agreement must be allowed to stand. You as a species now have the right and complete free will to do, be, and create whatever you have the will to. Your genetic inheritance from The Creator/God is now waking up and in full accordance with the birth of Earth's human species. I will speak of the treaty and its ultimate brokenness in the "Off World Others" chapter of this book. Suffice to say that the original treaty that was agreed upon by those off-world species on the seeding piece of Earth Human genetics was broken by those off-world species and thus the cleansing of the Earth. You as a species are now free from that timeline treaty and fully able to move forward as The Creator/God intended.

Energy as Sound Frequency

The secondary and most important piece of the energy/frequency reality is that "energy," all energy, has sound frequency. Humans believe that there is a finite sound frequency arc by which all sound is bound within physics. This belief will be undone publicly in the next 25 years of Earth's history. Energy in all of its forms has an infinite number of sound frequencies and qualities. At energies' highest sound frequencies, the waves are so highly charged that they coalesce into the very background vibration of the full Universe. At energies' very lowest sound waves, particles coalesce in deep and infinitely continuing waves which may arc over uncountable distances of space time years out to the edges of the Universal plane, and ultimately enmesh themselves back into the DMF. Humans only hear a very miniscule swath of the never-ending sound of the energetic universe. Humanities scientific equipment at this point only sense a very small arc or window if you will into the energetic/frequency realm. It should be stated, however, that sound/energy/ frequency is the powerful left hand of the DMF and manifestation. Energy/frequency/sound vibrational waves can be used to literally create matter, transmute matter, and relocate matter. Many species in your galaxy alone are able to use energy/sound/frequency as a tool to create, move, travel, and dissolve matter. Understanding that energy/sound/frequency can be used for this kind of manifestation is integral at this time of human evolution on Earth.

Sound Frequency as a Tool

Energy/sound/frequency vibration is the tool of the DMF and intention. The DMF responds to the intention of a soul and begins to merge "frequency" in such a manner as to create that which the attention/intention of the soul focuses upon. Depending upon what that creation is intended to be, *attention* and *intention* may need to be held upon the DMF for larger increments of time (as time is experienced by the intender).

This is why in ancient times on your planet, there was a belief that objects could be "sung" into and out of existence. Enough skilled singers/chanters could, with concerted attention, actually sing through vibration situations, objects, and creations into and out of being. The full understanding of energy/sound/frequency is simply that skill. Through frequency and the welding of it, matter can be coalesced and broken down by way of the DMF. This ability was given to the human species on Earth through its DNA. The knowledge of this ability was fully suppressed by the systems put in place to control the future populations, that is, YOU, by the original renegade DNA manipulators, or off-world species.

Tones, frequency, and sound can be used to heal organic matter. The same tones can be used to move objects through time and space. There are many species in your Milky Way Galaxy who use tone frequency to move themselves and their space-faring craft from timeline to timeline and solar system to solar system. Tone frequency was used millions of years ago for clean power on Earth by creating resonators (pyramids and stone circles), which tapped into the Schumann resonance of the Earth, magnified it, and created energy. This knowledge is only just now coming back into the fringes of the scientific minds of your time. Energy/sound/frequency is the chosen energy of the Universe.

Music on your planet is another arena where Melissa would say that "the machine" has taken over what the frequencies and styles of music/ tones you hear. These frequencies are tightly controlled. By controlling the tones which resonate on the face of the planet, humanity can be kept in a particular state of being. When you listen to any piece of music, you are resonating with the signal which that music is sending to you. Whether you enjoy the sensation of listening or you don't, it is strictly in the vibration that you are receiving from the music. This being so, imagine the power that vibration/music wields on your planet. Music in all of its forms can be transcendent. Musical vibration can and often does put you in full physical contact with the vibrational codes that are much closer to that of The Creator's/God's vibration. Music can also block you from and separate you from your natural connection to The Creator/God.

Vibrational frequency is a paintbrush, the DMF is the paint, and your life is the canvas. Within certain and determined frequency combinations, the DMF responds and "creates" the energetic signature of what the vibrational combination is signifying. To simplify, should a human determine that they wanted to lift a car and move it down the street, it is completely possible for one humanoid to engage in this activity successfully if they have full use of their ability to understand, wield, and activate the correct frequency/sound/vibration with their voice. In the same way that a human voice can shatter a glass goblet, at certain known frequencies, objects can be moved within time, space, and Universal Strata in any way the wielder of that frequency desires. This is a true Universal Law, and humanity on Earth is capable. This knowledge needs to come into the present known paradigm for the evolution of your species. With this knowledge will come great responsibility.

In order for your intention and use of frequency/sound/vibration to impact the DMF for a result, the DMF uses gravity. With the use of mechanically or organically created frequency/sound/vibration fields, gravity is "tuned" if you will to a certain mode or stance. Once enough gravitational matter is "tuned" to that frequency, the DMF will begin to coalesce into the substance that the gravity's "field/body" has been tuned to. If a human can, by vocalizing, drumming, or tuning by way of electromagnetic device, maintain a certain frequency into the DMF, thereby merging and mobilizing the gravity within, a skyscraper could be raised and moved to any location. Objects, planets, people, anything really can become visible, invisible, moved, travelled, or created from nothing across the time space Strata. In this way, Jesus could feed thousands from a few fish. When gravity is activated with concentrated intention and vibrational force within the DMF, manifestation is guaranteed. Rain can be manifested in the desert by indigenous people chanting. You can find the perfect parking spot just where you need it. You have the full ability to change your frequency/sound/vibration in ways that either help or harm you, and those around you in your life as you are right now. Every day you choose either consciously or unconsciously "what" and "how" your general frequency will be, and thus you CHOOSE. Humans can spontaneously heal, transform, and grow within this system.

Your thoughts, your actions, your lack thereof, ALL have vibrational qualities or "sounds" if you like. This is true whether you become conscious of the fact or not. Should you actually study and begin to use frequency/sound/vibration to your growth and advantage, the changes in your daily life will be substantial, almost immediate and put you more fully on the path that you have incarnated to fulfill in your lifetime. You need not be a musician in order to learn and integrate this knowledge. However, music is a powerful tool for growth, expansion, or oppression and is used by your control sectors to keep humanity as a whole separate from this knowledge and heritage. It is no mistake or accident that in 1939 Joseph Goebbels determined that the Nazis' push for the arbitrary A=440 standard (which is "disharmonic" vis-à-vis the physio-acoustic laws of creation governing reality). This tuning, which is now used worldwide on your planet, literally creates a dissonance which completely inhibits the creative force of frequency/sound/harmonics which humans need in order to connect with and use the DMF and gravity. Your species have been fully cut off from the use of your gifts and evolution by the systematic cutting off of your ability to connect with The Creator/God and the gift of creation/manifestation you were given. This is why on your planet now, music and frequency is being controlled, sold, created, and doled out in such a ruthless and processed way. You are meant to forget who you are, and the easiest and most wholesale way to disconnect you from your memory and knowledge of who and what you are is through frequency/sound/vibration, and the control of those.

Sound frequency is so powerful a manifestation, travel, and creation tool that there are whole planets that are made up mostly of water. These planets are inhabited by humanoids living on and caring for hundreds of islands similar to the Hawaiian, Fijian, and Caribbean islands on Earth. These humanoid species are fully engaged upon planets like these by where the whole of the civilization spends the bulk of its time creating healing, growth, inception, and high-end vibrational tones which ring and are sent like a bell toll from their oceans out into our Universe. The planets' inhabitants are singularly involved in sending frequency out into our Universe from their water planets in order to uplift whole sections of the Strata of Universe in which they reside. This tool which most of humankind on Earth is completely unaware of is at work in your life as I speak.

CHAPTER 8

The Garbage Room

Melissa & Aralamb

The smell was the thing in the summer. Humidity, blue resin-y pot smoke and the light smell of decay that over hung the season. Our house was very old, I mean old, 1798 old. Stories in town had our house as part of the Underground Railroad which led escaped slaves to freedom to the North in Montreal, Canada. The cellar was lined along the walls on two sides with fieldstones, but the other two walls and floor were dark, damp dirt. The house had that New England kind of layout that you found pre-Civil War, many small rooms leading into bigger rooms kind of like a maze in places. Many times, as an adult I would have dreams that the rooms were all closing in like an *Alice in Wonderland* scenario where I was too big for the rooms, and as they shrunk my head would be poking out a window while my arms and legs were trapped in tiny rooms.

The "garbage room" was an annex between the kitchen and the laundry room that had been added at some time in the past before we lived there. It was a kind of unheated shed-like hallway which looked out onto an empty 18x18 square of yard that was unused between the kitchen and the barn.

The garbage room was maybe 5 feet wide and 14 feet long. The floor was cement and the interior walls were actually just the exterior walls of the house and barn which it was built along. This is where all of the plastic trash bags full of our household garbage were placed until we would "supposedly" every week deposit it to the dumpster across the road, which was attached to the Survey. The Survey was my grandfather's business, and it was where we got all of our garbage bags, toilet paper, and other supplies clandestinely on the weekends when no one was there. Looking back now, I guess it was a bit like stealing toilet paper from the gas station on the corner except you were never going to go to jail for it. I don't think that I ever wiped my butt on anything but stolen toilet paper from the time I was maybe five to 18 years old!

The garbage room would have been a fine idea, if it had been used in the way that it was supposed to be. Bags of random food, paper, and refuse building up over the week to a manageable six bags maybe, then dutifully taken across the street to the dumpster. The issue was that it never seemed to happen that way when I was a kid or even into my early teens. As our house was a veritable hippie commune in that 1970s sense of the word, the garbage was copious. I tell you this story because Aralamb feels like it is a great illustration for how we humans tend to have hoarding situations take over our emotions, spirit, and experiences in our lives and how it is like an emotional, psychological, and spiritual cancer when not addressed.

The garbage room was never managed with any kind of schedule and in fact it was not unusual to have 20, 30, or even 50 bags piled up in that space rotting, festering, smelling, drawing flies, and generally being a massive pile of, well, garbage at any one time. Our mother would let it get to such huge proportions that eventually most of the bags on the bottom of the pile would be broken open, maggot-infested, and reeking. As an adult now, I understand how unhealthy that was, and I also remember about once a month, my grandfather would send some maintenance man from his business with a shovel and wheel barrel and clean it all out of there. I can remember as a kid looking at a newly cleaned out garbage room, the black stains on the floor, the stray white maggot rolling around in a panic as the only world it knew was destroyed and think that it smells worse now than it did before the pile was gone. One particularly hot summer that whole room had to be cleaned with bleach because it was so infested and horrible. The stains in the cement floor were so deeply soaked in with rot from the leaking broken bags that bleach was poured to kill the smell. The bleach bubbled when it spread over the floor and it looked like blood stains. It was the early 1970s and our home was a drugging and drinking haven, so the garbage room was just like some world away from the party that was behind a door and until the sweet smell of old food and dead maggots crept underneath and started to get into the main house, everyone thought "Screw it, let's just leave it." Honestly, I think that everyone who lived in our house, regulars and transients alike, were just too drunk and stoned to care. At some point, in my high school years, we stopped using the garbage room because my grandfather told us to leave the trash on the porch and the maintenance guy would come over and grab it. Even so, some things in life cannot be unseen, and it was horrific.

Aralamb believes that the garbage room is a great example of how we as humans often let whole areas of our emotional lives become completely overgrown, rotten, and out of control rather than address those areas. He likens this kind of emotional hoarding to any kind of hoarding that humans tend to do. Now, when Aralamb talks about emotional hoarding, he is not talking about someone who "collects." There is a real difference between a person having a beloved collection of "art" or "skateboards" and the emotional dysfunction of having 300 million, old Zip Lock baggies or newspapers, OR collecting garbage until it is rotting and stinking to point where the town might force you to clean up when the dumpster is literally 60 yards away from your front door and it's FREE.

Holding on to any kind of "garbage" until it is actually eating you alive or festering in a room in your house is due to an emotional issue and nothing more. Aralamb tells me that the outward manifestation of this kind of "hoard" is simply your own soul trying to get your attention and get you to address the problem. If you have a garbage room full to the brim with rotting bags of trash just 20 feet from your kitchen table and you just continue to ignore it till the neighbors complain about the smell, then the garbage is not your true problem.

Looking back at it now, I understand that the garbage room, like many other issues in our mother's life, was a symptom of the undiagnosed mental issues that were occurring, for which she was constantly self-medicating. The garbage room was an actual outward symbol of so much of the pain she was feeling on the inside and as a child it was monstrous to me.

I can never un-see one particular occasion after a pretty raucous four-day weekend of 20 people eating, sleeping on the floors, couches, beds, fighting, screwing, and partying. I carried a bag of trash out to the garbage room and when I went to open the door, it would not open all the way because in the night some of the bags high in the pile had rolled back down in front of the door. I pushed hard and the edge of the door broke a bag open, and masses of maggots came rolling out in numbers that would rival any Stephen King movie. I remember gagging and throwing the bag I had on top of the broken one. The smell was so bad that I can't even really describe it with any kind of specificity. I slammed the door shut and for days I could not get to sleep at night without seeing those maggots rolling in a huge mass out of that bag. People don't always get to see or know that if maggots are left to their own devices, they eventually get a kind of black shiny head on them. I don't know if that black shiny head can see. I wondered for many years after that if those giant black-headed maggots saw me spilling them out of their safe haven onto the floor that day. That picture is still so real in my mind even now as I write these words. Filth, maggots, terrible, nightmarish.

Aralamb on The Garbage Room

Humans have a very strong propensity to internalize and compartmentalize emotional traumas, real and imagined. The issue with this tool of survival at the most basic levels is that it fully and forcefully cuts that soul off from the openings and intended growth through obstacles in the most productive way possible. To internalize emotions which are painful and counterproductive builds a fortress of caged and inaccessible "feelings" that will inevitably surface for the soul later in life, coloring and informing all future decisions and directions. It is a soul's main purpose to "see" these tendencies and understand their nature and origin, and ultimately overcome, learn from them, and release them.

As a soul spends more and more time upon the Earth plane, that soul will gravitate more and more to other souls, life situations, experiences that will allow them to either "double down" on the protective behavior, that is, "filling a room with actual garbage" or other negative experiences within relationships, addictions to emotional upheaval, substances, food, and a myriad of other situations that will continue to support and play out the negative emotional situations and beliefs that the soul is literally running from.

Example: (Not from Melissa's Past)
Aralamb

It is a very real situation in which a female child who is beaten by her father time and time again while growing up will then enter into relationships with men in adulthood who continue to abuse her. This behavior is the reinforcement and "doubling down" of the emotional belief that was rooted in her childhood. No matter how many times she may "think" that she will "never do this again," her emotional state, having been set so early in the opposite experience, will continue to bring her back to itself, "being abused," until she makes the decision to change course. The painful growth aspect of this for every soul is that the initial pain and reality of the lesson must be re-visited in order for the soul to truly learn, release, and grow forward from it. It is impossible for the soul to bury and compartmentalize the painful growth experience while simultaneously try to grow through it. In fact, the moment that a human soul decides to even look at past painful growth in a whole and truthful way, the door is no longer able to be closed on the learning curve. This is the very reason why souls in their learning path on the Earth plane will often get much worse in the healing path before they get "better." As Melissa often says, "You cannot un-see certain things."

Example: 2
Aralamb

If a child is constantly caring for a psychologically crippled parent, as in Melissa's case, that child may spend the rest of that incarnation "caring" for a world full of crippled psychological souls rather than "see" the truth of the experience and grow through it without judgment or challenge to the other souls. The reality of this is that whatever perceived horrible experience you may have had involving another person, you would have agreed pre-birth to experience those painful situations together. It is often that the relationships within an incarnation that are the most challenging are those that are decided upon by the souls before birth in order for both of them to have the opportunity to grow through that challenge, no matter how difficult. The decision to grow through these challenges is totally in the hands of the souls involved. The souls may choose to spend a whole lifetime ignoring the possibility of loving growth and stay locked in sorrow, hatred, and a revisiting of the relationship through self-abusive addictions, relationships, and losses. These decisions are totally the venue of the soul or souls involved. The truth is that you as a soul have the ultimate decision as to whether you are abused by another and go on to revel in victimhood, wallow in the same behaviors, and use that as an excuse **not** to grow. Often souls incarnated to this lifetime do not want to hear that it is "all up to them" or "their own decision" to remain in victimhood, disease, and pain.

This is a hard truth to hear because if you understand the truth of this rule, then you are completely in control of your own experiences, and, therefore, you can no longer blame another for your suffering.

Example 3:
Aralamb

Should you be born into a family in which both of your parent souls abandon you at birth, or decide to die and return to The Lobby soon after your birth, your life path is still fully "up to you." Within this lifetime scenario, there is the real option for you as a soul to grow up bouncing from foster home to foster home with anger, abandonment issues, loss, pain, maladjustment emotionally, and a complete mistrust of family relationships and the feeling of being "useless and unwanted" as well as a hatred of any kind of Creator/God. The truth in this matter, however, is universal in that you could just as well determine at a young age that your origins and experiences were just those—situational—and not an indicator of your true soul's path or worth. You may ask, "How the hell is a kid supposed to know to do that?" I used Melissa's exact thoughts to me just now as we write. This is where your "tools" come into play.

The Tools:

There are many tools that every soul created have at their disposal at any time. These particular connections to The Lobby and The Creator/God are always present and unable to be detached or taken from a soul. A belief in this connection is not necessary. The connection is within the very energetic fabric of every soul in this Universe. Your particular connection is uniquely your own. However, all of these connections lead back to The Creator/God. When every human child is small and newly arrived, there is a feeling of non-judgment. Within that initial feeling of "trust," there is an innate knowledge of the "idea sense" that they came from something, somewhere "bigger." Somewhere bright and unendingly loving. You may not remember this feeling with your mind, and in fact it cannot be accessed with the mind, but the physical body and the heart remember it. This feeling is actually an energetic place which is the connection with The Creator/God and any of your family and pod souls who have traveled with you.

This is your first and strongest tool to remember why you incarnated to the planet in the first place. This "connection tool" is the energetic thread that holds every human in a place of possibility. With one human decision, the possibility to choose a different trajectory exists in every moment of human time. I want you to understand that I mean this literally. Every single second of your day is broken into all of the uncountable moments of decision. If you as a soul were to begin to see this in your own life, you would begin to *feel* your connection to The Creator/God. You would access your tool for beginning to understand in a different light, all of those situations, relationships and reactions which you deem horrific, painful and insurmountable. This would allow you to make different decisions or thought choices about them resulting in positive growth and change in even the most challenging circumstances.

At the very moment that you access your connection to The Creator/God and "see and feel" these situations through the light of that truth within yourself, you will begin to make different decisions around how you want them to affect your life within this incarnation. If you become less reactive and victim-based, you will begin to see your abusive father as an abused soul himself with whom you agreed to try to stop that painful cycle within this lifetime. Should you determine to see and feel the situation from this stance, it becomes impossible for you to continue and repeat his behavior in your own life. By doing this, you are changing the energetic stance of the lesson, and it begins to be "felt" at both of your soul levels as a lesson that is being transmuted into soul growth. Should you begin to see yourself as not a victim of his abuse but as a fellow traveler who decides to forgive the abuse and use that experience to grow, assist other souls with releasing the lesson, and move forward in a lighter and released way, then the possible soul lesson is learned and will not need to be repeated in another incarnation.

The soul of the human who was your abusive father may or may not determine to follow your growth pattern and healing. This is totally up to him. He may continue his negative behavior, but you will translate the experience into a growth pattern and grow from it. In this way, you will have disconnected yourself from the lesson and done your part. Releasing these kinds of emotional lesson traumas in a giving and blameless way is the only way to internalize the lesson within your soul and move forward. Should the soul who was your father live out the whole lifetime without reconciling the painful lesson, that soul will most likely incarnate again to "see" the situation from many different perspectives, but you can choose to never revisit that lesson again.

Often a soul who has released a lesson that is painful will come back many lifetimes later to "be the aggressor" for a family soul who needs to "see" the lesson from the side of the victim. In this way, the soul who wants to grow through a painful lesson will be assisted by the one who has already fully released that energy. This is again why I will often tell Melissa that your lives are populated with souls who are the difficult lesson purveyors and souls who are the loving "soft places" to heal and grow with. Every soul will play both parts until certain levels of growth are acquired through incarnations. For example, from my level here as a guide/teacher, it is very unlikely that I would ever feel the need to incarnate into a lifetime anywhere where I would re-live some very negative aspect of incarnate life as a "perpetrator." This is because of the fact that most of my soul family has grown and assimilated past those incarnate experiences at this point. There is no soul in my family of souls who has been "left behind" in the lower levels of incarnation. Please let me be clear. In using the term "lower levels of incarnation," I do not mean to imply a sense of "better" or "worse." I would liken it more along the lines of your Earth schools. A Kindergarten-level human child is still learning possibly that fire burns the skin, whereas a third-year medical intern at Harvard would have internalized that knowledge prior to many years of education and it would not even be a conscious thought for him. This is what I imply when I say, "lower levels of incarnation." None of my soul family at this point is still within the "grade school" levels of incarnation. Because of this, I would not be called for any reason to become the "perpetrator" incarnate soul for an abused child, let's say.

Bringing this conversation back to Melissa's garbage room…
Aralamb

The point of the garbage room illustration is so complete because in order for you to feel, truly feel and experience your connection to The Creator/God, you cannot have mental, emotional, or fearful "baggage" piled high and rotting around your connection which is most likely hidden in the deepest part of the trash pile. Human souls often continue to place their most painful and festering emotional and psychological issues into these "trash bags" in order to suppress and hide them from the truth of their own soul, so that they do not have to be addressed. Melissa's mother actually outwardly used this trash hoarding as well as other behaviors as a symbolic way to "hide her painful insides."

Melissa was in a way given this great gift from the soul who was her mother because it was a horrific yet actual, physical way for Melissa to SEE that something was not right with her mother and to separate her own energy out from that pile of trash. She was given this very real symbol of her mother's struggles with painful psychological and addiction issues which allowed her to SEE and FEEL the energy, its darkness, and the fact that it was NOT coming from her, and that SHE was not the reason for it. In this way, Melissa was at a very young age terrified of her mother and also saddened by her suffering. It allowed the tiniest sliver of pity and love for her mother to creep in, which in turn allowed Melissa to have some access to her soul's tools.

The garbage room gave Melissa a literal way to observe her mother's mental and emotional suffering and gave Melissa a way to see it as outside of her own soul. The garbage room allowed Melissa to see her mother as a suffering soul and not just a perpetrator. The garbage room with its smell, maggots and black ooze was a literal picture of how her mother felt on the inside and it allowed for Melissa to begin to see the possibility of forgiveness without blame. When you can begin to see your abuser in this light, the soul's lesson begins to unwind and pass. It would be many years until Melissa truly crossed and released this soul lesson, but I give you this explanation and example because you have the ability to begin this process here, today, where you sit. You need only stay in pain and victimhood if you choose to. You can literally change that in the next second, or the next or the next.

Should you choose to stay within your own garbage room for a lifetime, you will not be judged back at The Lobby upon your soul's return. You will not be judged by The Creator/God, but you will most likely decide to incarnate again and try to learn and release another time. I am simply here to tell you that this time can be your last time should you choose to release the victimhood energetic signature and the pain that accompanies it. You could decide to address the lessons, and just grow, now, here, in this time.

CHAPTER 9

Off-Earth Others

Aralamb

There are some scientists at this point on Earth who are studying the Grand Procession. The Grand Procession is the mechanism by which every 26,000.00 years or so in Earth time, the whole of the Universe does an energetic shift upward in frequency. This number can be broken down into its derivatives of numerical value to smaller shifts in the cycles of planets and solar system throughout the Universe. This procession exists in all the Strata of this Universe as a kind of "clean-up" system which forces change, growth, or in the alternative, destruction and rebirth of planets, civilizations, and species of organic and energetic nature. Within this Universe, uncountable numbers of civilizations, species, planets and plains of existence have grown up through and been dismembered by the Grand Procession. There is no corner of existence in this Universe which is not within this mathematical and energetic procession. This procession and the shifting up of energies are not just unseen energy in process; it affects every corner of energy lowered in frequency to "solids" as you would perceive them. This shift upward in frequency affects every last molecule in the Universe, lifting the whole of the experiential planes at the same time.

Thus, even The Lobby in which I reside will lift upward in frequency. This is a celebrated event in all timelines and corners of existence.

The reason that I want you to understand this is that The Creator/God is the originator. The Creator/God is the only complete creator in the Universe. Although The Creator allows many off-Earth species to learn and utilize the history, uses, and implementation of the movement and mixing of DNA for a species inherent growth and evolution, those species are always, with no exceptions, required to be given the right to that knowledge only *and* only when The Creator/God gives permission to do so. The Creator/God must give the permission to control, grow, or create any new species, new evolutionary lines of species, any implementation of the change of a species DNA, or any cross-implementation which creates a new species by way of "mixing" one with another. This information is solely and fully the domain of The Creator/God. This is a full and true law of the Universe. Should a species determine to use its free will to step outside of this law of The Creator/God, that species will be dealt with very aggressively and by particular means. Should the leaders of one species determine to take creation out of the hands of The Creator/God for its own power, it has the free will to do so but will be dealt with harshly by The Creator/God.

This is where the history of the "modern Earth human" begins. The human species was set to evolve on the Earth for as many 26,000 years to the 33333.9 multiplied number. Your species was meant to evolve with no intervention for another 45 million years from the 2024th year of your knowledge. You were meant to be still a mix of Neanderthal and Savanna human to remain for many more cycles of the Grand Procession. This changed approximately 86,000 years ago. Your planet was visited by those who would ultimately show up in your mythology as the "makers," the "Nephilim," "giants," all of those supposed creators. The one point that was not lost in your supposed mythology was the thread of innate knowledge that there is one Creator/God. That is the one truth that your young souls were fully tied to and no amount of genetic intervention by the off-world species that arrived could disconnect you from it. I would have you know that removing you souls was tried by them as well. The very first genetic seeding was meant to disconnect your very young and not evolved souls from The Creator/God and The Lobby in order to create a fully organic but compliant slave/worker species. Those failed. Creation in this Universe was specifically set up so that no matter the youth of the organism upon its inception, there is a soul given. Upon the evolution of that species either being evolved naturally or seeded by a higher sentient being, that organism will have the one growing, evolving soul. To be clear, I am speaking of only those beings that presently or will have the ability to become sentient. I am not implying that a "rock" has a soul, but I am meaning that early Earth humans who were pre-seeding did indeed have the ability to contain a soul from The Creator/God. These pre-seeding humans would have lived for many millennia more, as I have said, without full self-awareness, but eventually would have come into complete sentience on their own. This did not happen on Earth, due to the full intervention of two main off-world species, and one interceding species whose DNA can still be traced and seen upon the faces and within the DNA of all Earth Humans to this day. Please understand that there is not one human being on Earth today who did not come from the mixing of these three off-world species and the pre-sentient humans of ancient Earth.

I am going to outline the three major off-Earth species for you, so that you can begin to understand the manipulation of your DNA, the manipulation of your species, some of the Universal laws which were broken, the treaties that were agreed upon in rebuke of the broken laws, and the ultimate release of the modern human species upon your Earth which began in 1961 and the changes that are underway now upon your planet.

The Creator/God put into place the restrictions on DNA splicing and the "making" of new species because inherent in the incarnation process is "free will." With free will, every sentient being must make decisions every second about what they will do. What energy will they work with, how will they "be" in their corner of the Universe. Will they be prey, will they be predator, will they rise above this kind of lesson and understand the true beauty and power that lies with The Creator/God's system for growth here in our Universe? These are all questions which every soul must ask itself every second of its incarnation. This is the truth of The Creator/God no matter if you are a soul incarnate on Earth or a soul incarnate on the other side of the Universe on a completely different planet as a sentient being who is not of any human origin. The law of free will is final. Because of this, The Creator/God has in place some other hard and fast rules of "being." The second rule is the "creation of species rule." This is the rule that was broken so long ago on Earth. The three species of which I will speak came to Earth and determined for reasons which I will outline to take the DNA and species altering into their own hands without the decree and good blessing of The Creator/God for their own means. Not all of their reasons were nefarious. However, in the end, the new human species were, and consequently have been, subjugated and controlled. That epoch has ended, and at this time, The Creator/God is releasing Earth Humans to their own history. What humanity on Earth does from here will be of its own accord and within the Universal Laws of The Creator/God. You as a species are finally becoming free from the control grid placed upon you so many eons ago by those renegade off-world species who changed your DNA without the permission of and fully in opposition to The Creator/God who lovingly made us all.

A Short History of the Off-World Others
Anunnaki

This is the most well-known species that is coming into your world's consciousness at this time of change. This race of beings is biped like humans, and they share much of the general building DNA of the early humanoids which resided upon Earth when they arrived in ancient history. The Anunnaki are a much longer-lived species than the Earth humans were but had much less physical strength and were not able to procreate in the same manner as early and present-day humans. This was one of the reasons why they came initially with their science teams. Their initial visits to Earth were to simply take DNA samples to "study" and possibly understand where their own breeding practices had failed them in their home worlds. The Anunnaki home worlds at that time were spread widely across the Milky Way Galaxy but were dwindling due to their free will decisions to make their lives much longer at the cost of their breeding and reproductive organs. Simply said, they had maneuvered themselves into a situation where they were genetically able to live many hundreds of Earth years but were unable to reproduce as easily as they had in the past of their species. The Anunnaki had been given permission by the upper levels of The Creator's/God's energy workers to seek Earth out, and "study" by way of taking, without harm or manipulation, samples of the early human DNA for its reproductive qualities. At that point in Earth's history, Earth inhabitants had pristine DNA, and were to remain so.

The Anunnaki came to early Earth and found three specific populations of pre- and full humanoid Earthlings. They were evolving from apes, and doing so at a very, very slow pace, which was as The Creator/God wished it. Upon arriving to Earth, they determined that of the three species which were in small pockets on the Earth, the Neanderthals and the Savanna types were the closest to their own base DNA and determined to get samples from each. They were supposed to take a sample of hair and skin from each and leave. The visit was to last for what would have been four Earth days. Upon arriving to the Earth, they were accompanied by what would have been considered in your day a "military unit" for their own protection. This was also deemed acceptable by The Creator/God's energetic counsel. This same unit, not unlike those in your history, had come, unknown to the scientists, to also look at the planets resource base. This was not deemed appropriate by The Creator/God. In that time, many of their home planets were dealing with issues of atmospheric losses, which were creating the need to come up with new chemical and mineral combinations of "spray mist," which would create a protective layer of shield from their planet's suns. This same technology is now being implemented on Earth and will end in the same manner as their own technology did so long ago on their own planets. You would know this as geo-engineering. Because of this need for minerals, the military end of the expedition began mapping and searching Earth for gold, platinum, lead, copper, and silica deposits. Many were found and at that point, the Anunnaki sent word to the second off-world species for their assistance in mining the minerals from the Earth.

Senchali
(Zen'Chale')

The Senchali races are more closely related to humans in their DNA makeup. They were completely free of the reptilian and animal DNA model. In your present day on Earth, all of the Asian peoples would be the most closely related to the Senchali races of antiquity. This species was highly traveled and strictly lived in a trade-based society. The Senchali races were not a warlike species but to this day still travel the Milky Way Galaxy and currently inhabit more than 16 planets on the far side of the Milky Way Galaxy from Earth.

The Senchali race is at this time restricted to those planets and has not been allowed the technical ability to travel through time portals due to the incidents in which they became entangled with the Anunnaki on Earth in that earlier time. After arriving upon ancient Earth, the Senchali met with the Anunnaki military and crafted an agreement to quietly transport gold, lead, copper, silica, and any deep crystal deposits that were found off the planet. The Senchali were also very involved with the Anunnaki and their ongoing DNA splicing within the early human populations. This DNA manipulation was in no way sanctioned by The Creator/God and was carried out in the most secretive way. The Anunnaki and the Senchali created a base at the Earth coordinates of what now would be called the cradle of life on Earth, in Northern Africa.

The initial DNA splicing was attempted in a fully artificial embryonic state where by the Anunnaki would harvest the eggs from the early Savanna humanoid females. The egg would be fertilized with partially DNA scrubbed versions of the Anunnaki DNA. When I say, "partially scrubbed," I mean to describe the means by which they would literally need to "clean" or "simplify" their own DNA to remove many of the higher knowledge genes by which they had evolved, as they were not compatible with the unevolved human psyches. Many failures were endured by which an embryo might be started in an artificial womb only to become too monstrous to live outside the artificial womb. At that time, there was a push by the Anunnaki military to "create" a worker who was acclimated to the mixture of oxygen in Earth's atmosphere, as many of the Anunnaki were at a disadvantage. Earth was not at the oxygen level that was optimal for them, thus leaving them unable to maintain long-term physical exertion.

The Senchali were brought in to add their DNA to the possible mix as they were more "humanoid" within the DNA structure and the experimentation continued with a bit more success. Still the Anunnaki and Senchali scientists were trying, mostly in vain, to build and birth the human hybrids in an artificial womb. Part of the reason they were doing this was that they did not want to build a humanoid slave species that would automatically be given a soul by The Creator/God. If they were to build said slave species in an artificial womb, it would have no contact with The Creator/God and thus be "invisible" to the Creation. In the end, their greed for power and the need to press forward compelled them to make compromises, and thus opened them to the attention of The Creator/God.

Tall Whites
(Toshal)

The species that is often referred to as the "Tall Whites" on Earth are not exclusively white in coloration and at this point in the history of this Universe are only about 68 percent corporal in nature. The Toshal species are one of the oldest and most diverse humanoid type species in this Universe. The Toshal races have in great numbers evolved away from organic bodies and are mostly now at the levels of light beings who inhabit many planets and strata. The Toshal are also among the first species who were evolved to be a sort of "Universal Counsel" in service to The Creator/God. The Toshal are and can be any color they choose in many shades.

At the time in history that the Anunnaki and Senchali were busy on Earth manipulating the DNA of the natural Earth humanoid species, the Toshal were called in by The Creator/God to put a stop to the unsanctioned DNA manipulation that was going on as well as to mitigate or manage the new species, "you," that had been created. Upon their arrival to the planet, they began to put into place sanctions which would cease and desist the activities of the Anunnaki and Senchali species. There was also work done by the Toshal which would incorporate their own DNA into the DNA structure of the new human which had been seeded to Earth. The Creator/God did not condone the action of the new species seeding on Earth, but nor does The Creator cut off those species which receive a soul. Humanity was born from these three species blending in the end with The Creator's/God's intervention through the Toshal.

The Toshal have the DNA structure to allow them to have the skin color, facial features, and physical attributes of all of the "humanoid" species which dot the Universe. The Toshal evolved to be the Universal example of the "O" blood type on Earth. They can as a species literally mix their DNA with any human-like species who do not have a high animal mixture in their DNA. Humans on Earth today have a heavily weighted Toshal DNA mixture. The mixture of the DNA in humans of your time on Earth is roughly 83 percent Toshal, 16 percent Senchali, and 1 percent Anunnaki. There is obviously some deviation in these ratios over generations of humanity, but they are engineered to stay mostly in line with this ratio. The Anunnaki have a relatively high ration mix of humanoid/reptilian DNA and due to this fact, they were having a very hard time importing their DNA strands to the new humanoid they were attempting to create.

The Senchali have a fully non-animal DNA mixture and, therefore, were very helpful to the Anunnaki in moving their engineered humans along.

The Toshal are a species that will be seen in every color seen by the human eye. Black, white, tan, brown, red, luminescent, clear, and opaque are all colorings that you will see in the Toshal species. In some far reaches of our Universe, they will be in bodies of shades of blue, red, and green. Highly evolved Toshal soul/sects have actually moved away from organic bodies and are fully light beings who appear opal in their energy sphere. Often The Toshal will appear in physical form to a human in that humans mirrored skin color in order to create calm in the human. The one attribute that the Toshal do embody which humans on Earth have noted is that their eyes are a bit larger than that of the Earth humans, and they are tall compared to Earth humans. The average Toshal woman might be between 6'9" and 8'5" tall. Toshal men will averagely be between 12' and 15' tall. The Toshal species is also capable of unisexual physical orientation. As a group of Universal travelers, the Toshal are often described by species on planets like Earth as "The Tall" you add the color, red, black, blue, white, yellow, greens. They are the Universal Counsel/Order Keepers in the most hands-on sense of the word.

Upon their arrival to Earth, the Toshal immediately halted the experiments that the Anunnaki and Senchali were conducting. Some numbers of highly Anunnaki-like new "humans" had already been genetically created and were being used as slaves. These humanoids consisted of more reptilian DNA strands than was accepted as the standard for The Creator/God to have had souls imparted within. The Toshal set about creating a mixture of new Earth humanoids who were at the corrected 83,16,1 ratio of DNA. In so doing, they also determined that the very best way to "clean" the new humans of the Anunnaki DNA structure was to implant the mixture of DNA from Toshal, Senchali, and Anunnaki males into the living womb of a clean original Savanna female Earthling. This procedure was successful in the very first attempt, and the program to raise the new humanoid species was underway with the approval of The Creator/God.

During this time, however, there was much infighting between the Anunnaki and the Toshal. The Anunnaki did not want to give up its specimens of the fully integrated Anunnaki/human DNA species, and the Toshal began a concerted effort to find those Anunnaki hybrids in order to send them off Earth for safekeeping. The Toshal and the Anunnaki spent what would be ultimately 3,000 Earth years stewarding the new Earth seedlings through the earliest stages of your development. The Toshal stayed in this endeavor as emissaries of The Creator/God, but the Anunnaki stayed as penance from The Creator/God. The Senchali were allowed to leave with other sanctions from The Creator/God. Remnants of the Anunnaki and Toshal bloodlines still reside on Earth today.

A covenant was signed by the Toshal and the Anunnaki handed down by The Creator/God stating, in its simplest form, the following:

The Anunnaki would stay in some capacity on the planet for however many eons it took to teach and guide the new "species" of humans forward in their evolution.

1. The Anunnaki were not to enslave the new species in any way but guide them in their growth as souls living in The Creator's/God's Universe.

2. The Anunnaki were to put into place a system by which the new species might govern itself as they grew and flourished.

3. The Anunnaki were to cease all DNA splicing, testing, creation of new species or further integrating their own DNA into the human population as it moved forward.

4. The Anunnaki were prohibited from any kind of physical procreation with the new human species in any combinations.

5. The Anunnaki were to live in quiet and unassuming ways while reporting back to the Toshal after long intervals the evolution update of the new human species.

6. The Anunnaki who had lifetime expectancies of approximately 1,500 Earth years were stripped of that lifespan by The Creator/God and given 200–400-year lifespans on Earth, in order to slowly have the final remnants of themselves, "the Anunnaki," die off, leaving the new humans alone to evolve naturally.

7. The Anunnaki who arrived with the first exploring team of scientists and military were sanctioned and not able to leave the Earth for any reason until such time as was indicated by The Creator/God. There were 18 of them.

8. The Anunnaki were not allowed to call in assistance from others of their species in order to destroy, exterminate, or expunge the new Earth species' population.

9. The Anunnaki were not allowed to portray themselves as "gods" to the new species.

10. The Anunnaki were prohibited from aligning themselves with new kingdoms or as the communicator or spiritual bridge between The Creator/God and the new species.

11. The Anunnaki were given thousands of years to accomplish the enlightenment and care of the new species on the small planet that they had encroached upon.

12. The Anunnaki would teach the new species about their true connections to The Creator/God and the workings of the Universe.

13. The Anunnaki would only be allowed to leave the planet when these covenants were completed.

This covenant was to be ended on the turn of the last Baktun. As you may realize in the reading of the simplified covenant above, the Anunnaki held and kept none of their covenants with The Creator/God.

They instead made themselves kings of the continents, enslaved the populations of new humans, set up language, financial, and religious institutions in order to further control and enslave the new human species. They fought against each other and set up all manner of control systems in order to keep the new human species working for them in such ways that the true nature of the DNA that humans possessed as well as their potential would not come to light. The very DNA that had been imparted by the Toshal to Earthlings was the same DNA that was **not** within the Anunnaki species and kept them from being as powerful as the new Earth species they had inadvertently brought into being. The Anunnaki were left to shepherd a flock of newly souled beings who were many, many levels above them in energetic evolution. They determined that enslaving the species for eons was their only option for continuing their personal lines of genetics on the planet. This option and the covenant have come to an end. The Creator/God is stepping in now.

Off-World DNA

Within the DNA of the Toshal is the ability to move, create, and form simple matter with sound and energy vibrations. Toshal are fully able to understand complex connections in the mathematics of this Universe that we live in. They have an innate ability to communicate fully with mental visionary and non-local speech. The Toshal have evolved to have complete knowledge of the arts of what humans would call, telekinesis, energy healing, physical and spiritual bi-location, precognitive ability to read the future possibility lines of any situation, the ability to astral travel energetically, healing abilities, physical interstellar travel, and many other abilities that humans are just now beginning to accept.

The truth is that humanity on Earth is 83 percent Toshal in its DNA makeup. The massive amount of unused DNA in the brain of humans is finally being allowed to wake up. Earth humans were given all of this potential at the time of the corrective seeding by the Toshal. This genetic makeup is and was freely given. In order for Earth humans to begin to open and access these genetic markers, they need only to place their attention on the abilities.

I mean this in the most literal way possible. All of the above-mentioned abilities in a species must first begin with the attention of the species on those abilities. If you believe you have the ability to change matter with sound and energy vibration, then you can. Simple.

After the initial movement by the Toshal of the newly corrective seeding, there were a number of radical changes upon the planet. It was determined by the Anunnaki who were left that they would carve up the planet and become ruling gods to the "savages" that The Creator/God had left them with. Free will, as you know, is always held at the highest level of consideration and so the Anunnaki used their free will to decide to disregard the Covenant they had agreed to. The continents were fought over and decided upon. It was also decided that the Anunnaki would need to breed with the new human species to continue its own bloodlines. The Anunnaki's life span had been dropped by over 1,000 years and they wanted to set up a line of descendants, some of whom are still in the ruling classes today on Earth. As of 1961 A.D. Earth time, The Creator/God's Covenant ended with the Anunnaki and their descendants on Earth. Being free of the covenant, it has been decided that the descendants of the Anunnaki are to leave the planet and release the enslaved populations of Earth. It is imperative that Earth humans understand that they are just one small inhabited planet in the Universe and that they are now on the precipice of decision. It will very soon be an option for humans to migrate to other planets in the Milky Way Galaxy that are inhabited by humanoids. There will be no need for any Earth human to stay within the present system if they should choose not to. The power brokers are falling and quietly leaving the planet.

The whole of the Universe is shifting upward, and Earth is shifting up with it. In order to shift up through energetic evolution, the reality of your place in the Universe must be fully grasped and understood. You are no longer in a position to "pretend" or "go along with" the systems that you have been sold for hundreds of years to keep you blind to your own power and growth potential.

As you sit and read this, you have within you an 83 percent Toshal DNA line which will and has marched you forward in evolution to this point. Now is the time to take the next step and trust in the innate knowledge that was imparted within you by The Creator/God. Embrace the inner knowledge of who you really are. You are not a slave species.

CHAPTER 10

Manifestation

Faith and Manifesting, Energy and Attention

"Manifesting is as easy as being, and as difficult as you would like to make it." (Aralamb smiles at me.)

Aralamb:

Manifesting any reality into being is as easy as connecting your soul through your crown chakra to your faith tether at your frontal cortex out through your third-eye chakra and your sixth sense, then in reverse while attaching the DMF/energy/frequency/gravity and completing the circle. Once that has happened, you simply need to continue that connection of "beingness." The DMF has no other choice but to, through gravity, begin to coalesce energy to the "beingness" that you hold in your connection. As long as you hold that energetic circle in place, the manifestation has no other choice or ability to manifest other than that which it has been instructed to manifest." That is a Universal and Energetic Law.

Melissa:

"Okay, well, I might need a bit of a breakdown here, as I am not certain I can get all of that rolling at once! Hahaha!"

Manifesting
The breakdown in scientific and spiritual terms

Faith is the unwavering interior knowledge that there is a support system for you, your soul, and your life's purpose even in the face of supposedly concrete *evidence against* such a notion. Faith is the most important tool in the manifestation process. Faith is a complete function of free will and the connection of every sentient being to its creator, God. Faith is the all-powerful glue which holds the intention of being upon a path which may or may not have any "proof" of itself prior to it being brought into being-ness. Faith is every being's gift from The Creator/God. Faith is an actual energetic frequency which acts as a muscle connecting your frontal cortex with your soul.

The Mechanism of Faith

There is an actual ener-spiritual mechanism by which faith works. I use a word which I understand is a hybrid of the word's "energy" and "spiritual" because the actual mechanism of faith is a combination of both of the literal and concrete substances of each.

The soul of a sentient being, "human" in this case, is its connection to The Creator/God which can never be severed. A human soul can be quieted by its owner. A human soul can be ignored or bypassed by the choice or free will. The soul can be quieted by the presence of the mentally ill mind, sickness, or injury of the physical brain, but even in those extreme situations, the soul is never fully disconnected from The Creation and will return to that same Creation upon the physical organic death of the body. Every human soul has this innate connection to Creation, and it is through this connection that "faith" operates. The "DMF," the dark matter fabric, is waiting for the smallest inclinations of the soul to exercise its faith mechanism. Faith then becomes the tool by which the energy of the soul interacts with the DMF in order to bring into being the circumstances, objects, and realities that the soul needs and longs for in order to fulfill its lesson plan within whatever lifetime it inhabits at a given time.

The DMF responds directly to the soul through the tool of faith and intention. Intention is the actual tool by which humans might and do interact with the DMF through faith. It should be noted here that simply having faith that you will acquire say, in a lottery win the amount of money that you think would heal your life experience, while possible, might not be within the scope of what you came into the present life to learn. You will have chosen certain lessons to learn. Whether you follow your life plan in any given lifetime is up to you, but often what you might pray and have "faith" for may not arrive in the way that you would have it. Now, please do not misunderstand what I say. With faith and intention harnessed through your soul's energy, all things and experiences are a possibility. There is no limit to what faith and intention when harnessed through the soul can accomplish.

Faith is an unwavering picture attached to an emotion that you hold in your mind and body as truth. In the presence of the human soul when it is fully in line with intention, vision, and emotion, the DMF will begin to coalesce the energetic nature of itself to bring that three-pronged reality into being for the soul which is holding the vision.

Faith is the "gut feeling" in your body that what you are "intending" in any situation already exists and you are just "being" in that experience. Your scientists and scholars are just now beginning to understand the reality of the relationship between the soul, intention, emotion, and the DMF. The dark matter field in this equation acts upon the clear intention as paint on a painter's brush. The DMF immediately begins rearranging itself into the very intention that the clear and joyful soul is holding. Faith is the constant and unwavering "belief" or "knowing" that what is manifesting is present and real already. The soul only needs to sit with it while it manifests and becomes concrete.

During this process, The Creator/God will often bring into your energetic sphere by way of the DMF many opportunities to progress the "vision" forward with your own hands. It is always the soul's decision as to whether it accepts those opportunities to smoothly incorporate those ladder rungs into the manifestation process. For the soul who sees and implements this assistance in manifesting, the process will speed up and "appear" much faster. If the soul does not stay in faith and continues to take assistance from the DMF, then the faith pattern is broken, and the forward-building manifestation will stall and/or discontinue. The idea that faith is a one-time experience should not be the norm for an Earthly soul. Faith should be used daily as a tool.

As an example, let us say that you, as a soul, would like to pay off $15,000 in debt that you have accrued. Being in faith and utilizing the DMF to the very best of your ability would look something like this: You would need to take a few moments every day to thank The Creator/God for breathing life into your soul, and for giving you the tools of faith and the DMF. Truly feel the gratitude in your body. At that point, you would imagine yourself paying off the final amount of the debt. You would picture that in your mind's eye, and you would feel it in your body the same way you might "feel" a wonderful memory from your life. You need to truly "know" that the image in your mind is real. You will need to be thankful and feel how good it feels emotionally at that time of that debt being gone. The longer and more often you can stay in this "space," the more quickly the DMF can begin to attract and arrange its energetic gravitational pull toward your soul's energy signature, and that "reality" in which you have imbued emotion, joy, gratitude, and physical well-being. In this way and by this mechanism, you truly can manifest into your world and the world of those you love all good things, material and otherwise.

Faith is in essence the actual "switch" that engages the electrical connection that your soul has to the DMF. The DMF was created specifically to allow for the progression, growth, and organic evolution and dissolution of the whole of this known Universe.

The ability to have and access faith is located in the connection of the human frontal cortex to the soul fiber that runs up through the crown chakra in the human body. There is an actual chemical and organic synaptic response in the frontal cortex of humans, which "turns on" at the inception of the soul's need to access the DMF via faith. Faith is also a "spiritual construct" in that it is the one true tool of the human soul in its organic host and the one tool which gives us direct access to The Creator/ God. Faith is also one of the few attributes in humans that during a lifetime are connected to the organic matter of the body, and passes back over with the soul when that human organic body dies. Faith and the ability to use it is the only piece of energetic matter that moves with a soul from lifetime to lifetime and connects with the frontal cortex of that new body upon re-entry at birth.

Faith is not just an intellectual construct; faith is a functional energy which holds its shape by way of its connection to the DMF and reconnects to the human frontal cortex again and again. It could be likened to a small muscle-like energetic tether which affixes itself to the human frontal cortex for a lifetime and then disconnects at the time the soul leaves the body to return to The Lobby. With each lifetime, the faith mechanism/tether can be strengthened by use and can and should grow stronger with each lifetime. If the human frontal cortex is damaged by disease, accidental trauma, or genetic mutation at birth, the faith tether will usually connect at some point or space in the brain, but be less active in that lifetime. It should be said that in situations like these it is usually because the soul has chosen these particular set of events to employ certain lessons for that lifetime. The faith tether will not have been damaged in any way, and will travel back out in tact when that lifetime is ended.

Faith is not a static employ in the brain. Should a human completely ignore its own connection to faith, that human will be buffeted by the faith of others. This action will be explained in a subsequent chapter which deals with prayer. Faith and prayer are closely related, and very different in nature. Prayer is a human construct that actually blocks faith from expressing its most powerful strengths when used in the "lack" forms of itself.

The most efficient use of faith for one who is not versed in faith, or has chosen to ignore or dismiss it as a non-actuality would be this: Simply begin to accept and address faith as a "real" physical place in your frontal cortex where you are connected to your soul and thus, by activation, the DMF. In just the open acceptance of the faith muscle/energy path, the human begins to use and open that very place. You do not need to "see" anything, or feel anything at this point, although you may. Faith is a tool that will begin to work in your journey as you place your attention on its existence. That is all that is needed. At the very moment that you put your attention on faith's existence as your bridge to your own soul and the DMF, it blooms into activity.

At this time, you will be able to begin the process of "knowing" what I spoke of in the first paragraph of this chapter. Once you have engaged your frontal cortex's connection to faith, you can begin to manifest those experiences that you would have in your life and the lives of your loved ones.

Faith and your Third-Eye Chakra

Faith is connected to your reality in this lifetime by the area of your physical forehead known as your Third-Eye Chakra. The Third-Eye Chakra is the physical and energetic place on all humanoid bodies in this Universe which connect the physical and organic third to fifth dimensions to the body. On Earth at this time, you are transitioning up to the fourth dimension organically, which is the reason for the work we are implementing here. The energetic faith tether attaches itself directly behind the Third-Eye Chakra because this chakra is where the sixth sense for the human mind/

body lays. The sixth sense for humans on Earth, although only now truly waking up, is the "hand" of Faith. The Third-Eye Chakra and its sixth sense is where information is gleaned, which will facilitate faith in connecting to the DMF to move forward manifestations of the soul. Information gleaned by the Third-Eye Chakra will move back and forth in constant communication to and from the soul.

Example: 1

A soul's lesson journey in a lifetime might be as an artist, Monet's for instance. Monet begins to feel the impression (Melissa would say, pun intended) from his soul to paint in a certain place with a certain feeling and emotion. That impression moves into his faith region in his spirit and brain. From the faith tether, this information moves to the Third-Eye Chakra in the body and sends this information out to the organic world. Through his sixth sense, a picture of a place on Earth that will inspire his work comes in. This information is "known" by the sixth sense and into the Third-Eye Chakra without any time or organic sense being used. From that point, the information will move through the faith tether into the soul and imprints on the DMF as a command, not unlike the computer on which Melissa types these words. From that point, as long as Monet holds in his person and spirit the impression that there is a special place in which he will paint and do great work, the DMF will begin to arrange itself magnetically to that soul signature that is wholly his and bring that experience to him in the real-time organic field. He then is drawn to Giverny and paints his lilies. When I discuss this issue, please know that I am intending this to be a literal organic/spiritual/energetic experience and not philosophical in nature.

Example 2:

Candice wants to be a mother. She and her husband have tried to have a child for years to no avail. If Candice were to disengage her fear and loss around the issue, and just decide to have faith that she will be a mother and see herself being a mother to happy children, the following will happen: Candice will engage her faith. At the moment she engages her faith tether through her Third-Eye Chakra, she will begin to feel as if she will be a mother. At that point, the Universal DMF will begin to send that energy signature through her soul, to her faith tether and out into the organic world through her third eye. In this way, the signal is sent, and the faith tether can begin to use the DMF to literally put Candice's need to be a mother with the soul's wish to come in and have a mother. It may even be that through this action, Candice will be activating a group of souls who made connections with her upon her return from her last life. The DMF gravitates to moving as many souls forward in groups for positive aims as it can. Should Candice continue to open and use her faith tether, holding the idea in her soul that she will be an amazing mother to children who need her, the following will often happen. Candice and her husband will be approached by someone who has a baby to adopt, and then become pregnant on their own after that. The Creator/God loves and lives for the elegant building up of lifetimes that assist many souls who journey together. Again, I feel the need to stress that this system of sixth sense, Third-Eye Chakra, faith tether, soul, DMF is not to be taken in a philosophical manner but in the most physical literal sense. Humans use this system daily, and almost never truly understand **the power that using this gift or ignoring this gift has in their lives.**

Example 3:

Melissa connects to me through her sixth sense, Third Eye, faith tether, and soul, and then on up through her soul's connection to The Lobby which is where she will return as all beings do at the time of the body's organic death upon the Earth plane. This four-part system of connection to and from The Lobby is in constant flux and constantly exchanging information between the energetic Earth plane and the organic body of the soul. The DMF is sitting in the middle section of this exchange. It can be activated at any time or it can be bypassed during regular daily energy exchange. The important fact to take note of here is that this system is in constant movement and flux with or without the conscious attention of the soul. It is your lifeline to the Universal energies and The Creator/God. It is more "real" than the organic body and mind that you inhabit as you read this book. You truly are an energetic being inhabiting an organic body. When that organic body is dropped at the time of death, the whole of your soul and its energetic makeup will move back to The Lobby for its review with other travelers, guides, loved ones, and Universal teachers.

These are just few examples of the power of your faith tether. Faith for you should be viewed as your inherent right as a being in the Universe. You will never lose this part of your soul's system and it cannot be given, taken, or transmuted to any other soul. There is some work on your planet to experiment with the actual physical part of the human brain that houses the "tether." This work is being blocked by The Creator/God, and will not be allowed to move forward for a few reasons. Free will is the First Law of Creation and it will stand. To attempt to examine the actual physical domain of the faith tether impinges on the free will of the soul. Secondly, although the faith tether does connect to the human "mind," and has a physical component, it is not purely physical in nature and thus cannot be dissected.

The faith tether cannot be distinguished from its soul and thus it cannot be removed from you as a toenail might be. As with all of the gifts of The Creator/God, your belief in faith is not a prerequisite of its existence. You as a soul upon Earth have your faith tether and connection to the Universe, whether you believe in it or not. You can make the choice to ignore it if you wish with no negative connotations. I would assume, however, that if you are reading this book, you are interested in using it.

The Power of Attention in Manifestation

Attention is the "engine" of manifestation within your reality. Your rapt attention upon any situation, object, activity, emotion, or space within time constructs is the strong fuel that attends the strength and connection to the DMF of your manifesting activity. There is no manifestation available to a human incarnate without attention to the hoped outcome in any instance. Attention is the ability to hold on to a certain focus for a time which is not changed by circumstance or any other persuasive stimulus. Attention is the ability to hold a very concrete and certain feeling, vision, sensation, and physical sense of a completed outcome in your mind's eye, in your imagination, and in your emotional and physical body no matter what stimuli might be coming at you from the outside world.

Attention in the manifestation process is the ability to NOT lose the emotional sensation of your vision and keep that feeling for as long as you can within your "personal" reality and scope. You must always keep the emotions around your attention joyous, grateful, excited, loving, and positive. Attention upon your manifestation should never be laced with doubt, self-doubt, fear of lack, fear of loss, control, fear of failure. Your attention should only hold the highest emotions and visions of the FEEL of success. How ARE you FEELING within your manifestation as truth in your organic real life? You also must direct your attention upon your manifestation goal as if it **already IS**. Your attention must not be focused in a "will be" or "can't wait till" or "someday" emotional package. You must feel and BE within the attention to your goal as if IT IS here now, and FEEL that reality with your attention. You should keep that vision and attention as much as you can each day. I understand that in the reality of human daily life other activities will come into play here, but the more times a day that you can BE in that emotional and intellectual attention state, your attention muscles will strengthen, and your manifestations will grow along with it.

I would be remiss if I did not also draw your understanding to one of the more powerful aspects of the attention tool in the human experience. Attention is a powerful tool by which positive manifestations can be activated in your life. Just as powerful is the negative attention that is so rampant in the human condition upon Earth at this time in your history. When a human directs attention to negative emotions, negative thoughts and actions toward others, negative beliefs about their own bodies, negative beliefs about relationships, negative fear-based attention to all things barbaric and apocalyptic, that energy is also set loose into those souls' lives as well as the lives of those around them. This is why it is so important for humans at this time in evolutionary history to fully and finally understand how powerful a tool the human brain is when it is linked with emotion and soul.

Example:

Everyone knows of one person in their family's history who lived a wild, exploratory, joyful, not always "lock step with society" life. These humans often will do, say, and follow their own soul's desire and, much to the fear and loathing of their family members, live long, happy, generally healthy lives with much adventure and growth thrown in. I am not talking about perfect lives, I am talking about lives well lived, well-loved and well-learned. I can tell you that the emotional and spiritual attitude and attention of these kinds of souls will not have been to live in fear, loathing, loss, fear of society's disdain, or lack of joy. Our attention, fueled with emotion, states our life's general timbre. This is a Universal Law.

If a human being decides consciously or subconsciously to imbue his or her life with the emotion and attention of "suffering" in a life, that will be his or her truth within that lifetime. The Universal Law of attention and manifestation will be happy to coalesce into a life of suffering for the human who chooses such a life. If a human being decides to live in poverty because "the meek and poor shall inherit the Earth," the Universal Law of Attention and Manifestation will oblige once again.

I am not insinuating that every cancer patient, rape victim, or accident victim used their own attention to those situations to bring them into being, but I am saying that there is a very, very strong attention/manifestation rule at work in every human's life. How you think/feel about yourself in your own quiet moments *is and will dictate* much of your physical experience of your lifetime. If you fall and sprain your ankle, you can look at it two ways. 1) My ankle will never be the same, I am doomed, I hate having to sit for six weeks while this heals, I will never hike again, this is the end of so many things that I wanted to do in the future; or 2) My ankle will heal and be stronger than it was before, I can spend a few weeks catching up on some books that will further what I am manifesting in my life, I will use this time to rest and regroup my spirit; I will use this time to call friends that I haven't talked to in a while; I will exercise the rest of my body while I start exercising this ankle; I will take this time to reevaluate my life a bit; I have faith that this happened for all of those positive reasons and only positive outcomes will come from it; I will feel, see, and experience my ankle fully healed and better than it was before.

Now, with those two scenarios in your mind, I want you to understand that the DMF and the Universal Law of Attention and Manifestation are completely unbiased in *either* of your approaches to the sprained ankle. The DMF is fully willing to accommodate whichever of these scenarios YOU wish to experience. I do not want you to miss the gravity of what I am telling you here. The DMF will respond in multiplied kind to whichever scenario YOU CHOOSE. You can choose the growth scenario, or you can choose the victim, never, can't scenario. This law is concrete. The DMF responds directly to YOU, in all situations, **every time**. Whichever scenario you choose to hold in your attention and emotional body, the DMF will begin to coalesce and bring the building blocks of them to you.

Emotion and Manifestation

The final piece in the energetic form signature for manifesting within the DMF is emotion. Humans were given, even before the seeding, the genetic and spiritual ability to feel and incorporate emotion into its experience while incarnate. The soul is also able to experience emotion when not incarnate as well. Emotional attachment to a vision or manifested upon outcome is the actual key and fuel to the successful manifestation of that which the soul is seeking.

In order for the emotional input to be fully successful in the manifestation process, the emotions attached to the vision of that which the soul is seeking must be positive in nature. Negative emotions carry with them a highly charged persuasive quality upon the human body. Negative emotions, while originally intended to aid in the survival of the human organic body, are now becoming an antiquated piece of DNA, which need to be slowly and systematically removed from the toolbox of being human. I am not suggesting that fear is wholly unnecessary. Fear of freezing to death should be used when the decision to seek shelter or lay down outside during a blizzard is made, But, in all of the higher levels of surviving and growing within the arc of humanity at this evolutionary period, fear, anger, hatred, fear of loss, fear of shame, fear of lack, fear of failure, fear of death in the psychological sense, fear of winning, fear of love needs to be actively and daily tamped down as a response.

Within the manifestation realm, all of the negative emotions will and do immediately stop, hinder, and derail whatever the human soul is trying to bring into being which is positive for the experience within the lifetime. I mean this in the most concrete sense possible. Should you blindly worry/ manifest negative, fear-based emotions into your lifetime, you will have that outcome as well.

For example, you are manifesting for a lasting, loving relationship, but your emotions tell you that you are unworthy. You fear being alone. You fear loss. You fear the unknown. You fear that there are no "good" people out there. You fear that true intimacy will bring pain. You fear, you fear, you fear. You fear the good outcome, and you fear the negative outcome that you "secretly" know will occur because it always has in the past, not only for you but your parents and all of your friends, and on and on with the negative emotional input to the DMF. With all of this fear and negativity, you are bringing to the table the "actual" energy with which the DMF is directed to manifest your lasting, loving relationship. Within the emotional input loop that you have set up, what kind of relationship do you think you are drawing to you? The emotions that you attach to your manifesting vision are so very powerful and will bring you what you are feeling or fearing. The choice is always your own.

If you begin to embrace the actual nature and power of your soul in the Universe, you will begin to see that if you use your emotional power to infuse your visions and manifestations with love, joy, grateful thanks, wonder, happiness, the joy of accomplishment, the thrilling feeling of winning, the actual quiet graceful joy in attaining that which you manifest for will come to you. You must learn to BE in the emotion of the arrival of your vision. You must be able to be quiet and truly FEEL the awesomeness of **what you have manifested**, well before it is a reality within your daily life. Hear me when I say that this is an unchanging law. Even if, while you do the work that you can physically do toward assisting the Universe with your manifestation, you spend moments each day physically and emotionally FEELING the truth of that vision as true in life NOW. You must not use words, feelings, and emotions such as "When this comes true," "if this happens," "I wish for this," "I hope for this situation," "I will be," "I will have," "I will do." All of these statements carry with them the specifics and emotions of the idea that the vision of what you are manifesting is *in the future*. That it is *coming to you*. That you hope it someday *comes to you*. That you want it to *come to you in the future*. I realize that I am repeating this piece of the manifestation scenario, but it is imperative that you understand the full importance of the power of this seemingly small change in emotion and vernacular.

You must learn to feel and see in your mind's eye and imagination what you want **as real now**. You must feel and see in your mind's eye the final outcome in all its joyous glory as being right now within time. Spend time imagining in your mind's eye the feeling and senses that you feel when you have reached your manifestation as present and real. Feel the joy of accomplishment. Feel, see, smell, and imagine how the arrival of your manifestation **IS**. It does not matter if you are living in a "van down by the river, with an old cassette player of Journey blaring in the blown-out speakers eating beans from a can, alone." This was added as a humorous aside by Melissa just now. She tells me that you, the reader, will "get it." No matter what your situation, if YOU begin to feel, act, and see into a completely different manifestation of your life, and you listen to your intuition, you cannot help but be in full use of The Creation, your soul, and the DMF, which will immediately start to align itself and all of the creative energy in this Universe to bring your vision into place. The one key to begin this process is that while you are sitting in your van eating those beans from a can and Steve Perry is wailing away, you MUST start to envision and feel yourself in the new situation while being completely grateful and trusting in the place from which you start.

Incorporating all of this will, like any other talent or skill, require some amount of attention and practice. The beautiful point of this skill is that The Creator set it up so that the more you place your emotions, attention, and vision on being grateful, the more exponentially your skill will grow and hone itself. You will no longer find solace in your self-imposed negative emotional thought loop. You will begin to see the DMF moving in directions that support your manifestations. This process will speed up as you strengthen your ability to focus and release all of the thousands of years of political, religious, and societal programming around this subject put in place to keep humans from grasping the true beauty of the Universe.

In closing, I will leave you with this. You must have faith that The Creator/God has gifted you with the ability to manifest your very best lifetime now. You will need to have high-level positive feelings and emotions attached to any vision that you hold of the life experience you want to achieve. You will need to believe that the DMF is there working for you at every moment. You do not need to see it to have faith that The Creator/God gifted us all with it. You will need to only see and envision your manifestation when you can hold with it only the feelings of it being real and joyfully yours NOW. Go forward and manifest your most excellent destiny. It is true that what you see for yourself deep in your soul will be tied to what you decided to work toward before you were born this time upon the Earth.

CHAPTER 11

Religion

Religion and Religious Doctrine

The first idea that needs to denoted is that "religious doctrine," "religious law," and the "implementation of species" erected rules/law which rely upon control through religious institutions are not usually meant to uplift the spirit of humanity. That is not to say that ALL religious institutions, laws, hierarchal structures, and belief systems cannot lead you to The Creator/God. However, the bulk of religious institutions are meant to control the masses of humanity and separate them from their true connection to The Creator/God and the gifts that were bestowed upon you at the initiation of the human species as it exists today.

Within the world's leading religious organizations, threads of some of the true tenants of The Creator's/God's few rules were implanted in order to give weight and credence to the religious structures with some Universal truths in order to cement the "goodness," the "purity," the "correctness" of these religious organizations. It is also worthy to note that most if not all religious paths hold certain "laws" to be truth. I am in no way telling you that you should not be a part of a religious movement or structure if it truly enhances your connection with The Creator/God. The issue would be if the structure to which you belong begins to cover, block, control, condemn, and or cut you off from what you know in your soul/heart to be true.

I often tell Melissa that if a Christian, Muslim, Jew, Catholic, Shinto, Native American, Pagan, Norse, Protestant, Baptist, Orthodox Jew, Tibetan Monk, Amazonian witch doctor, atheist, and on and on were all on a bus together and were hit by a train, killing all aboard, there would be surprise by all to find themselves all, to the number, showing up in The Lobby in front of the very same Creator/God to look at the life they had just lived. There is but one Creator/God. There is but one path to The Creator/God, and that one way is ALL paths as long as the few true laws are obeyed.

For the control of humanity to be fully imposed upon the planet, the powers that be needed and still need to create the illusion that there was only ONE correct way to connect with and have a relationship with The Creator/God. In most cases, the religion in question will proclaim itself the "one true path" to The Creator/God. There is a thread of this indoctrination in most large, organized religions on your planet today. This was put into place by the original seeding species to keep large masses of humanity on Earth too busy being correct, being special, being part of a large group of the "chosen" in order to keep them occupied, either trying to convert or destroy those who were "outside" of their chosen religious body. Within these structures of religion are the perfect tools for control. If you are not among the "chosen" humans who belong to a certain "right" group, then you are outside of the protection of that group, and possibly outside of the protection of "God." This control through religion is all based upon fear and the possibility that you could lose your soul's connection to The Creator/God. This is impossible. If you were indeed gifted a soul in the beginning epochs of time, which you were if you are reading this book, then you can only be disconnected *by* The Creator/God, and that is not in the nature of this Universe. It cannot happen.

Should the human species on Earth truly understand their connection to The Creator/God, there would be no more control or suffering. The Creator/God does not create or condone suffering in any way. When a "clergy person" stands at the pulpit and preaches to any congregation about the "grace of God" and suffering, they are simply incorrect. The grace of God is real, it is constant in nature, and it does not come with suffering. Suffering is a needless state of being that humans have literally "bought into," as it has been fed them for hundreds of thousands of years by controlling religious states as they are run through off-world species.

This may seem incredulous information as you sit in your church or place of worship and listen to your pastor or leader. The true nature of the issue with control is not in the people that you see weekly or daily in these religious organizations. The issue is with the structure of them at the uppermost levels. There is a pyramid-like structure to them that is simply meant to keep the masses of humanity on its knees in supplication and suffering. If you take in only a bit of this information understand this one point: The Creator/God is happiest when souls are living lives filled with joy, gratitude, good choices, a lack of suffering, and the ability to get off its knees and feel its power, then choose to go and do, be, create more joy and good. It is that simple. Humanity on Earth is not and never was born of sin, or into any kind of sin.

That is certainly not meant to imply that humans or any other species cannot make decisions that lead to the suffering of others. That fact is fully obvious at this time in Earth's history. The point I make is that the "original sin," which the Christian and Jewish writers were encapsulating in the various versions of the Bible, was not humanity's "sin" or "error" at all, but in truth was the chosen broken law of the off-world species who originally seeded and created humans' non-sanctioned evolution on the planet. They were the original "sinners." It was necessary for them, if they were to hold power on the planet during their enforced stay, that they use this to their advantage by placing the blame on humanity for the sake of holding control.

The other and more basic issue with many of the religious ancient structures on Earth is that they are inherently political and monetary in nature. This particular piece of the puzzle is even more scary for the souls of humans because it implies within it very deep-seated, fear-based ways that political leanings, monetary needs, and full social control is somehow "sanctioned" by The Creator/God. To be outside of these beliefs and systems is somehow to be separated from The Creator/God. This could not be further from the truth. The Creator/God has no interest in politics, control of nations, control of fortunes, control of species, control of anything. This notion that The Creator/God is concerned with or involved in any way is fully false. The Creator/God looks upon this type of religious doctrine as "enslavement" of God's own creations. As I state in this book over and over, free will and the choices we make are fully the most important and most SEEN by The Creator/God. You, because of your soul, which is fully yours and never to be taken or sullied, is firmly connected to The Creator/ God and is in reality a part of The Creator/God by way of connection. Your soul is a brilliant thread of The Creator/God. The life you are living as you read these words or listen to them was given to you freely. You are meant to learn, to grow, to be better and better. There has never been a religious doctrine that is truly sanctioned by The Creator/God as the *one way*. This applies to all structured religions on Earth and all other inhabited planets within our Universe.

The Creator/God does not care how you get back to The Lobby and The Creation. The Creator/God cares only that you did your best to leave the path of life behind you littered with other souls who you did well by, including your own. That your path upon leaving the Earth was full to the brim with positive connections, love, and joyous opportunities that you took advantage of and that you extended to others all of the learning and love you could contribute. How many other souls did you lift up? How many fellow souls did you bring with you in love and joy? What was your "body count?" How many people did you hurt, how many people did you leave feeling better because you were present with your God-given light in a room? You want to ask yourself these questions because many, if not most, traditional religious structures do not give you that power. YOU are the power, the light, the growth in the world. Get up off your knees. Pray to The Creator/God standing in your full power with gratitude for the ability to look up toward the heavens and give thanks. Then, move out into the world in your power by doing good for other souls. It is a very simple concept.

The list that follows has many of the abilities in the human species which the Tochal shared with you genetically to assist you in this time of evolution. Jesus knew of these abilities and spoke of them in parable, as did other religious leaders on Earth over your history. Every human on the Earth is *capable* of ESP, spontaneous healing of themselves and others, astral travel, energy transfer, bi-location, energetic manifestation through the DMF, ascension, communicating with off-world others through channeling, communicating with those passed to The Lobby, communication with guides and teachers through channeling (Melissa and I). There is the ability to sense upcoming geomagnetic changes on your planet, prophesizing evolutionary shifts (Melissa), knowledge of past events, and possible future timeline threads, as well as sensing the true nature of time, time shifts, energy manifestation, time travel, and age reduction while in an organic body. All of these abilities are inherent in humanity. All of these abilities have been suppressed and written out of most of the major religious bodies at this time. The reason for this is obvious. A fully understanding humanity would be in direct relationship with The Creator/God, growing positively and learning of these skills, so the need for controlling bodies would evaporate like sea mist. It was imperative to the species that seeded and were contained here to control the masses and keep them from their true nature. This was most easily done through religious doctrine which encompassed monetary and political systems as they do today on your planet. For the atheist population, money, politics, and the race to succeed becomes the religious system, and the same outcome is seared onto the planet. Control and separation from the true nature of humanity.

There are a few religious paths which encompass some or all of the abilities of humanity. They are growing at this time, but are not considered by 68 percent population of the planet as "true," and thus the tipping point of realization has not been met for full change or awakening as of yet. Yoga, meditation, Buddhist, Pagan, Indigenous systems, the Essenes, all religious systems which condone free will, music, prayer, chanting, and one-to-one connection with The Creator/God as well as group meditation, singing, chanting, and the "esoteric" abilities of humans are in the scope of a more well-rounded and less controlled concept of religious rites.

Again, I am in no way vilifying your weekly pilgrimage to your church, synagogue, shrine, temple, or any other place that you spend time with other positive souls in gratitude or worship of The Creator/God. But if those institutions are taking from you in guilt, gold, or the impingement of who you are, and the infringement of your positive free will on the planet, then you may want to look at the history and larger agenda of that organization. The Creator/God does not care who you love, what you look like, whether you tithe to one church or another. The Creator/God cares about who you care for, how much positive light you put out into the world, how much joy you leave in your wake every day. There are no rules about food, words, marriage, sexuality, body type, clothing, or any other skin-deep issue. The Creator/God is concerned with you doing as **little harm** to any other soul as you can, by *your own choice*. You have the right to *choose* every thing, experience, person, action in your lifetime. This is meant for you to be a bigger, brighter, more powerful soul every time you incarnate. You are free to be involved with any religion you choose, if you choose to do so. What I would implore you to do is read and research the history of some of these major religious organizations and see them for what they are. Then, choose what is right for you.

In ending this chapter, I will give you the example I once gave Melissa to explain how the soul's path to The Creator/God is to be traversed within each incarnation on the road back to The Lobby. This journey does not require any certain, correct path.

Imagine a beautiful lake in the center of large, forested island. The lake is perfectly round with smooth wide granite rocks all along the edges. This lake is approximately 5 square Earth miles around its shore, and has small, beautiful beaches ringing it. Were you to be in a small boat, you would be able, from the center, see all the way around the lake shore. The water of this lake is crystal blue, and the sun or moon is always shining upon it. There are never any clouds. The water is soft, beautiful, warm, and placid. Were you to lay on your belly in the boat and peer over the side into the water you would see forever. Looking long enough, you might realize that you cannot determine if you are seeing beautiful multicolored fish in its depths or twinkling stars. If you were to pick any place on the shore of that lake and begin finding your way out to the ocean in which the island sits, you would find that no matter which way you walked away from the lake, toward the ocean, a path would be made for you. Every step you took would simply lay out a path before you, always allowing you to make changes in direction.

Upon your birth into the Earth plane, you find yourself on the edge of that island's forest, looking toward that beautiful lake in the middle. Every soul born to this Universe is similarly placed. The Creator/God is that beautiful lake in the middle of the island. You are a soul who is now in a life on a journey toward that lake, home, and back to The Creator/God. The Creator/God does not care which path you take through that forest back to the "lake" (The Creator/God) and home. It is simply important that you keep moving forward with gratitude through the forest and back home to the lake in the center. There are no right or wrong ways to get through the forest and back home. You will all traverse the forest to get back to the lake and home. You create your own path back to The Creator/God. There is no one way to get there.

Free Will
Melissa

Free will in my opinion is the very best thing ever while existing in tandem as the full-blown most terrifying thing in our universe. It puts everything down to the atoms in your own hands and it completely takes away all excuses. Excuses are so easy and so available in every given moment that, I guess, The Creator/God had to have a rule that overrode all the others in order to make us as souls fully responsible for our lives. Free will puts all the decisions *in our own hands*—the crappy ones, the great ones, the right ones, and the obviously stupid and wrong ones…. Man, it makes me want to go for margaritas on a Tuesday morning at 10:00 a.m. while chain-smoking Newport Menthols sometimes just thinking about it. Ha!

Aralamb

As Melissa so aptly put it above, free will is the one overriding rule that The Creator/God put into place upon the inception of this Universe that you abide within. Free will has such a tapestry of meaning and uses as well as impacts on the soul that there is no real way to quantify its effects on every particle of energy in the Universe, but here I will try to extrapolate for you at least how this law affects humanity and some of the closer species in your galaxy.

Free Will: self-imposed, uncoerced, unforced, volitional, voluntary, volunteer, willing, accord, autonomy, choice, self-determination, volition, willing. (Websters, 2022)

As you read, free will is defined as above for humanity correctly by the Webster Dictionary. The Creator/God defines free will as the law which holds in place all other Universal laws whereby souls can have the opportunity to move forward in evolution in the direction of better and more positive experiences back to the place of origin/creation. Free will can also leave a soul mired in lessons for eons of time with the choice of either direction being fully within the Free Will Law for each soul in all and any given lifetimes and existences they inhabit. The Creator/God overlaid all actions, decisions, and natural and synchronistic gravitational pulls and manifestations fully within the Free Will Law. The law of free will literally and figuratively ties together every possibility that lies within the sphere of your Universe. There are actually no accidents in any way. Energy and the DMF are infinite and everywhere. Your Universe swims within those elements and by that immersion, there are no accidents of chaos or nature. Free will is always in play within every action, both finite and infinite.

Free will is the one law and tool by which a soul can control the general traverse of the lifetime in which it finds itself. Free will is the mechanism by which The Creator/God gave all sentient beings the freedom to determine the direction in which they travel. The Creator/God did not determine to create souls who were enslaved to The Creator's/God's essence in such a way that there was no choice in the matter. Without choice, there is no field upon which to grow, learn, and progress. Without the law of choice in place, there would be no understanding of consequence in either positive or negative experience.

As a soul inhabiting a human body on Earth, you decide within every second of every day how you will feel. You determine what you will do, what you will think, how you will go about your day, and how you will feel about all of those actions or lack of actions. Humanity is only now coming to terms in small pockets with the actual idea that everything within your sphere is a choice. Free will gives you the choice to "decide" at every moment how you will feel and what you will think or do in any situation. It is the law.

You might be asking, "How is this true?" "Things happen all of the time that are out of people's control." In this observation you would be correct. However, it is always within the soul's ability to choose what to feel or do in any situation. Below I will give you some examples of the law of free will in action and how the myriad uses of this law, for better or worse, color and insinuate the direction of the soul.

Leslie

You spend your days staring at the television watching game shows and taking care of your two children. Your husband left and so you are living in an apartment which is luckily only three blocks from your son Jerry's school, as you had only one car and your ex took it when he left. You are depressed and your house is a mess. You are just able to live with the help of State assistance and the small child support you receive from your ex-husband. It's just enough money but not really enough sometimes. The only exercise you get is walking your oldest son, Jason, to the main street. You stand and watch him as he walks the two more blocks to his school. You spend hours a day staring at the TV and social media on your phone intermittently and at the same time. You are tired. You are depressed. This is life. You are 36 years old and do not work. You take a long nap in the afternoon when the baby sleeps in her playpen in the living room near the TV. Your daughter Rebecca is three. All and all, it is just your life.

There is nothing in this explanation of a life that cannot be radically changed by the law of free will. Nothing. Here are some of the free will choices that the woman in the short story is using to keep herself in this loop of inactivity, non-growth, non-movement, and depression.

1. Chooses **not** to turn off the TV.

2. Chooses **not** to walk her son the whole four blocks to his school.

3. Chooses **not** to put on some music and slowly tidy up her house.

4. Chooses **not** to pack up the baby and go down to the ground floor and do her laundry.

5. Chooses **not** to wonder what she might do for extra money, even if from her home, while her son is in school.

6. Chooses **to blame** her ex-husband for "not being there."

7. Chooses **to continue** feeling like a **victim.**

8. Chooses **to ignore** the fact that maybe him leaving was the best thing for her to move forward, as they were not happy together.

9. Chooses **not to walk** to the food bank to volunteer where she was invited to do so in exchange for childcare services and a monthly food stipend.

10. Chooses **not** to give herself a cap on all TV watching and social media time in order to spend those hours in a day thinking about what she wants to do for herself and her children so that they might progress to a better place.

11. Chooses **not to reach out to her family** because she is too proud to let them see that her marriage failed, and her ego will not let her accept and release the shame of the failure.

12. Chooses **to remain in the role of victim** in her own life because it is easier to deal with "the devil she knows."

I think that you can, from my examples, get my meaning. All of the things Leslie is doing every day are connected to all of the hundreds of small choices she makes. Every small free will choice that is made will compound and compile more of the same all day every day until a whole lifetime has passed by and many of the initiatives that the soul might have come in with will have passed by unacknowledged. Okay, same woman, same situation, same Tuesday morning in May, but *different choices*.

1. Chooses **to turn off TV** and walk her son all the way to school with the baby in her carriage. Meets son's teacher and is told that the school will start a free class on women's small business. Gets a flyer for this class and finds out that there is financial help for those interested.

2. Chooses **to keep TV off when she gets home**. Puts music on her phone in the kitchen and drags the playpen in from the living room. Cleans kitchen for the first time in weeks while listening to music and watching the baby.

3. Chooses **to walk to the Rec Center** after lunch with the baby and check out the free mommy/baby fitness classes they offer there three afternoons a week.

4. Chooses **to sign up for those classes**, and on the way home stops by the coffee shop to get one to go. Nancy, the nice owner, asks her if she knows anyone in her apartment building who might want to go to her mom's apartment to cook her breakfast on Monday, Wednesday, and Friday, as she can't be there herself. The job would pay $100 a week?

5. Chooses **to accept the breakfast job for Nancy's mom** and asks if it's okay to bring Rebecca with her? Nancy says "Absolutely!" Mom has a highchair in the kitchen for the great grandkids, and she would love to see Rebecca for breakfast.

6. Chooses **to continue on home and calls** the number on the flyer she got that morning from her son's teacher about the women and small business classes. She speaks with a really nice woman who also lets her know that if she does not have a laptop for the class, one will be provided for her.

7. Chooses **again that day to walk** the whole way to her son's school to pick him up. She also signs up for the business classes while she is there and gets her class instruction list. She leaves with a laptop and her schedule.

8. Chooses **finally that day to sit down with her kids,** on the couch and watch a bit of TV. Puts the kids to bed and starts to read the class schedule.

9. Chooses **to be happy** for all of the seemingly synchronistic things that had happened that day. Every one of those opportunities were there waiting for her, but she had to use the law of free will, and just make one small decision—to turn off the TV. She needed to engage her universal right to choose to be a victim or not.

10. Chooses before going to bed herself **to call her cousin** who lives a few towns away and chat about what all has been going on in her life. The cousin invites her and the kids to come and spend a weekend by her pool and offers to come and get her, so she won't need to come up with bus fare. Two years later with her business classes under her belt, she moves to that town with her kids and starts her own hair styling shop where she meets her next husband, and they go on to have a very productive and loving life together.

While making specific choices in one's life is never a certain guarantee of success, The Creator/God has given you the right of free will because with forward decision-making, your experiences cannot help but change. The other aspect of the active decision-making process is that without the decision/choice being made, The Creator/God cannot put in front of you any "new or novel" opportunities for growth. You cannot, by the rules of gravity and inertia, make positive changes if you refuse to make any decision to move differently, feel differently, and frame your current circumstance differently in your logical and feeling mind. You must make the decision to do, feel, act differently even when there is no logical reason to do so. When you decide to make a choice, a decision, The Creator/God can and will put into your path every tool you need to begin to grow and change. If you sit and refuse to use your free will, however, you have stopped the creative force of the DMF from manifesting for you and with you.

Jamie

He had been in the intensive care unit for three months, although it was hard to remember most of it. The doctors and nurses had kept him very medicated for pain control while his body was slowly coming back from the trauma of the accident, and it was slow going. Funny thing was that he knew he couldn't move much of his body, and he was unable to speak, but everyone who came in to see him now seemed to yell and talk loud like he was deaf too! He wasn't deaf. His hearing in fact seemed to be getting more and more acute. His vision too was really still good.

He could not remember the accident per se; he knew that he was in a hurry to get to court. He can remember feeling really rushed and angry at traffic. He knew in some hazy way that he was an attorney for a good firm. He had been late for a court date and was on the phone. He could remember yelling at someone about meeting him at the courthouse with some paperwork. He had hung up and thrown his phone hard into the passenger seat. He was about a mile from the exit to downtown Denver. He could remember that he was speeding toward that exit and was happy that for whatever reason, like some act of God, there was not much traffic in front of him. His phone started ringing, but it was down between the seat and the passenger side door where he had thrown it. It was vibrating and as he began to enter the exit ramp on the right to Speer Blvd., he just reached over to grab the phone where he had thrown it. He reached it easily as he was driving his 1969 Porsche 911 and the seats were close together. His hand curved around the phone and the last thing he could remember was seeing the speedometer in the sun which read 78 miles an hour. He could not remember any pain or any of what he was told later came next. He could only remember the slowed-down feeling of knowing that 78 miles an hour was too fast for the exit ramp to Speer, and that he had pulled the wheel to the right when he reached for that fucking phone. It seemed as if he had 20 minutes of slowed-down time right then with that bright Denver sun shining in on the left side of his face, warm and comforting, to understand and know that he had just screwed up majorly. He knew it. He had really fucked up. Blackness followed that last thought.

Jamie's parents drove in from Wyoming that night, and his fiancée Devon was there too, he had been told. He had been taken to Denver Health Medical Center, with barely a pulse. He had then been transferred to University of Colorado's Intensive Care Unit. Jamie had arrived at University of Colorado Health with two broken ankles, a broken right femur, a right hip fracture, and the capper, a fully broken cervical spine at the C1, C2, C4, and C5. For whatever reason, his C3 had sort of survived which, his mother told, him probably saved his life. He had survived six surgeries in the first two weeks in order to fuse, correct, and surgically implant many plates into his fractures, and a fusion of his cervical spine in order to keep it stable for healing. He was left incapable of speech at this point, on tons of meds, and everyone just kept telling him to "rest, Jaimie, take it easy, you will heal in time."

He had been kept in a medicated sort of coma for weeks as his body healed in the initial stages and he had just been allowed to start to come out of it and back into some sort of clear consciousness, he thought, for maybe five or six days. His mother and fiancée were moving around his room this morning and saying that Dr. Gimacheyls was coming in this morning to talk about the next steps for treatment, and get things scheduled. Devon was holding his hand and looked tired and strained. This morning he was so much more awake. He could smell the breakfast carts moving by in the hall outside his room. The smell of bacon, coffee and tangy orange Betadine mixing in a weird acrid and comforting haze. He was covered with the Betadine every day at his surgical sites by a parade of nurses and interns. The sun was streaming in, he wondered if his room was facing the Rocky Mountains, or the far-flung Eastern Plain. He tried to move his head to see, and it hit him again that nothing in his body was responding to any thought or command he had. It dawned on him right then that though that he was breathing pretty much on his own, and he could blink his eyes, he did not have any conscious feeling of being able to take a deep breath because he wanted to. He could not fill his lungs on purpose and exhale deeply in a sigh. The foggy memory of the days before came back to him of Devon and his folks all holding their breath when his intubation tube was pulled out to see if he would breathe on his own. He could faintly remember voices talking about what was to be done if he did not respond and breathe on his own. Devon's voice was a memory too, crying and imploring his parents to re-intubate and give him more time if he didn't breathe right away. He supposes they would have agreed.

He could not speak, and it was pissing him off hearing Devon, his folks, and the nurses talking about what was next, without him having a say, like he was a big piece of furniture that had been left in the entry hall and needed to be moved. He wanted food, but knew that he was being fed through a tube somewhere below his chin. He couldn't feel it, but he knew that six times a day, the "feeling" or "emotion" of hunger left him, which must have been right after his stomach was filled with some kind of mush. He had also, the previous day, begun to hazily remember the moments of sunshine on his face, the phone in the Porsche vibrating, him reaching without looking or thinking for that stupid phone, the feeling of finding that phone between the seats, the vibration in his hand, seeing the speedometer, that last vibration of the phone in his hand, knowing that he had just screwed up so bad, the warm sun on the left side of his face. His rage now knowing that the last actual physical sensation he would have been that stupid friggin' phone vibrating in his hand.... Jesus, he did this to himself. He did this to himself and now the rage of that knowledge was a huge balloon in his head. He could not move or feel his body, but he was left with this massive fucking balloon of rage in his head. This was not his plan. His life was supposed to be different right now. He was an attorney. He had chosen that; he loved the battle. He needed to feel life in that visceral kind of way, and right now, he could not feel anything. The anger was so strong, but it was all in his head, just living in that space with no connection to his body.

The doctor came in and looked into his eyes. She said, "I am going to ask you if you understand me fully and I want you to blink one time for yes, and blink two times for no if you can." Obviously, she said, "If you don't understand me at all, then don't worry about it," and she smiled. He blinked one time, slowly and deliberately. He realized then that Devon and his folks were pushed in hard, watching and listening to this. They all gave a huge sigh of relief at his obvious one blink, and he could hear them crying and holding each other somewhere out of his peripheral vision. The doctor explained to him that everyone was going to use the one-blink, two-blink system with him from this point forward while his treatment plan progressed. She said that he would need to try to answer as many possible questions with yes and no as he could to begin to regain control of his life and the choices that he was going to have to make in order to heal.

The doctor went over his laundry list of initial injuries and told him that when his car drifted over in the exit lane, he had hit a cement abutment at 78 miles per hour without ever hitting the brakes. She said that he may never remember the actual accident because of the severe nature of his injuries, but that with hard work and concentration on recovery, it was possible that he would be able to bring part of his body back to 50 percent functioning. It was her opinion that he would regain all of his mental clarity with hard work and that although he might be in a wheelchair, he would most probably be able to have full use of his upper body down the road a bit with hard work. Before the doctor left the room, she told him that she would be sending in the speech therapy team with the computer system that would allow him to look at the pad and create sentences through that computer in order to be able to communicate until he could begin to retrain his vocal center.

He could feel tears sliding from his eyes and down his face. His instinct was to wipe them away quickly, but his hand did not move, and his mother reached in and wiped them away. The doctor smiled at him, at his family, and moved out of his small field of vision and out of the room. So, there it was. He was starting from just about zero. His life, as it had been, was gone. He was a 34-year-old cripple, ex-lawyer, with a wedding supposedly happening in sometime, he had no idea when, and he was a vegetable laying in a bed with only his thoughts rolling around in his head with a blinding rage that had nowhere to go. Devon leaned in and hugged her body to his face. He could smell her perfume and hear her muffled "I love you," against the top of his head where her face rested. Tears bloomed out of his eyes, unchecked. He had never remembered so many tears ever falling from his eyes. What in the goddamned fucking hell was he supposed to do now? Devon looked into his face closely and asked in a too loud voice, "Are you okay?" He blinked one hard time.

Aralamb

In this example, Jamie has lost most of his physical motor skills. Jamie is very angry, and rightly so. Anger in this situation is a reasonable and expected human reaction to such a life-changing and painful event. Jamie is sitting at a very serious juncture in his lifetime possibility spectrum. He will have set up for himself different options for moving forwarding fully depending upon his grasp of, and use of, free will. Below are the two examples of what his possibilities are moving forward. There, obviously, would be many variations upon these two themes, but I will give only the two for the process of the extrapolation of my teaching here.

Example 1

1. Jamie stops answering questions with the blinking system because he is so angry and depressed that he wants to be left alone. He rails internally against a The Creator/God for "doing this to him," even though he has never believed in God at all.

2. Jamie only slightly begins to respond with the blinking system and does this only to tell his family to leave and stop being so present all the time in his room. He wants to be alone for fuck's sake!

3. Jamie only works a bit with the speech pad when the therapist comes in. Jaime stays in his own head and keeps reliving his angry phone calls in the moments before his accident. Eventually, he refuses to work on speech therapy.

4. Jamie will not agree to have a therapist come in so that he can talk through some of his emotional issues. Jamie is prescribed pain medications and stays on them for the rest of his life even though he is not in any physical pain.

5. Jamie will not respond to Devon when she comes, which is every day. When Devon comes into his room, he closes his eyes and will not engage with her. Jaime believes that she should just "go and have a life" and move on without him.

6. He does not agree to physical therapy and decides that he would rather just stay the way he is than to try to build a new life.

7. Jamie is moved to a long-term facility because he will not agree to sell his own condo and move in with Devon. He does not want to feel like a burden to her.

8. Jamie goes to a long-term care unit, and breaks off his relationship and engagement with Devon after three months there.

9. Jamie languishes in the long-term care facility with only small improvements to his mobility. After two years in the long-term care facility, he is released to his parents' care.

10. Jamie is confined to a full body wheelchair. Jamie has no speech ability. Jamie has done a minimal amount of physical therapy and is unable to move his arms or any of his upper body.

11. Although Jamie can fully understand all speech and has lost none of his cognitive ability, he mostly refuses to communicate with anyone and prefers to be parked in front of a television during his days and evenings. Jamie dozes many times a day.

12. Jamie accepts very little visitation from his old friends and colleagues, and refuses to engage in any kind of physical or speech therapy even when it is offered within his parents' home.

13. Jamie dies in his sleep at the age of 40 from a kind of paraplegic sleep apnea.

In this first example of free will, Jamie chooses, which is his right, to completely disengage from his life process. I am in no way insinuating that Jamie is being weak or wrong. That is the true beauty in the law of free will. There is no right or wrong, there is only outcome and the fully unknown path that you might choose through faith and movement. In Jamie's case, he might have used his free will to be very, very angry and emotionally hurt for any given amount of time. That is his right under the law of free will. He could, however, after some amount of time, have chosen to engage his free will and make a decision. In this first example, he decided to remain in the hurt stages of his situation and block out completely the infinite colors and possibilities that free will offer him. If your soul is still housed within your body, there is always a choice to be made. Free will is always available to you no matter how dire your circumstances may appear, and it is in those most dire circumstances that the law of free will is the most powerful. In the second example of free will, I will extrapolate many new and different outcomes that Jamie could have affected for himself and his family, not to mention the idea that the law of free will is very intertwined with the Three-Minute Rule, which I cover in a later chapter.

Example 2

1. Jamie immediately meets with the speech pad therapist that afternoon. Jamie is able to communicate through the speech pad well enough to let the therapist know that he wants to meet with her every day. His family is pleased with this, and they begin talking to him and conversing through the eye blink method. They all laugh when he gets tired, and he can feel his eyes laughing even as the tears flow down his cheeks. He is going to fight to get back to himself. He is so angry and so scared, but he decides to take his life back.

2. Jamie requests to have a psychologist come and speak with him every other day in order to work through his fear and anger. He refuses any medications for mood because he wants to "get clear." Jamie engages in the therapy for two years and later tells people that "talking about it and getting out all of it out of my head really saved my life, I think."

3. Jamie spends every afternoon for three months with the speech pad therapist and is becoming very good at forming sentences. He asks if he can begin actual physical speech therapy, and that session is added to his regimen as well.

4. After the first four months of physical therapy, Jamie has regained full feeling of his face and neck to his collarbone. Doctors tell him this is because he has been working so hard to reclaim his vocal cords and the muscles are finding new pathways to begin to connect his brain with his vocal cords.

5. Jamie begins a program of neuromuscular electro stimulation of his upper body, arms, and chest in order to have better control of his breathing, which facilitates his speech.

6. Six months into his treatment, Devon and Jamie buy a duplex in Denver with his parents so that they can all be in one area, and Jamie leaves the hospital for home.

7. Jamie and Devon have put the wedding plans on hold while Jamie regains his ability to speak.

8. Eight months into his healing process, Jamie is able to sit up in a wheelchair, he is speaking freely, and doing four hours of physical therapy a day. The rest of his days are employed in the single-minded effort of researching cutting-edge healing technology for spinal injuries and healing.

9. Jamie still holds his attorney's license and begins to talk with the attorney general's office about a possible position which would be in the office and at home in equal parts.

10. Jamie is contacted, after sending an email to them, by a stem cell company who would like to start trials on a treatment with implications for his injury and would pay him as well as facilitate all of his physical therapy.

11. Jamie and Devon are married three years after his accident. He and Devon are planning to start a family, Jamie has 100 percent use of his upper body, ability to speak, is fully employed as an attorney, and has invested in that same cutting-edge biomedical company for stem cell research. He is able to stand with the use of exoskeletal leg braces and the stem cell work done on his spine thus far. With those braces, Jamie is now walking briskly three

miles a day with Devon and their dog Burt. Jamie feeds, clothes, cleans, and takes care of himself fully independently.

12. Jamie is a working attorney, surrounded by family and friends, using his free will to accomplish his own full healing and in that way working toward healing others. Jamie decided to write his journey of healing in a book called *Blueprint for Healing* and has given thousands of copies to families, hospitals, schools, and other public communities which assist spinal cord injury victims in looking at how to begin healing for themselves. Through his use of free will, he "decided" to make his life.

The most important issue to be aware of within these examples is that this is the exact same person. The same man who found himself in the same untenable situation. The same broken body, the same broken mind, the same broken heart. The only thing that changed within these two examples is that his free will was used in two completely different ways. That's it. The only difference in these two outcomes was the "choice" of the man using his free will. It's that simple. The Creator/God can only give you more of what you are asking for with your own free will. If you continue to follow a path and never "choose" to diverge from it, then it will continue in a loop. You choose by your free will what is to come next. I am in no way insinuating that free will guarantees an easy, smooth change of path or experience instantly. I am in no way saying that every day will be seamless and perfect, but I am saying that with the use of your free will to choose how you see, feel, experience, and use every single day that comes into your life, you can and will change the outcome going forward no matter what. It is the law of free will. It cannot and will not be changed in this Universe. It is a sacred and concrete truth.

Free will and the use of it is the literal "hand tool" of life on your planet. If you give over your free will to circumstances, other people's need, situations, relationships, corporations, addictions, fears, anger, hopelessness, and any number of negative impulses, you will be at the free will of those situations, institutions, and negative forces.

Picture yourself standing in front of your home. You can see a hole in your roof. You can see the wood you need to fix in front of you, the nails are there, the shingles are there, the ladder, everything you need is there. On your tool belt, you have a hammer. Free will *is* the HAMMER. You always have this tool in your proverbial "life belt." The issue is that most or many of you at this time on the planet are choosing, through fear, complacency or 100 other excuses to NOT grab your hammer and fix the hole in your roof. You choose to live with, live under, survive with, suffer with, be in pain, be in fear, live in anger, as a victim, rather than just using your hammer. Free will is the tool every soul has. I use this example because no matter what you are facing at this time, no matter how bad you perceive your situation to be, no matter how painful or untenable, you have that hammer. You own that hammer. You have your own free will with which to decide what you will do or not do at every moment of your life. Period. Free will is the most powerful tool that you have in conjunction with the Law of Faith. The only thing that you have to understand and realize is that you can use it. You have to use your free will every day.

The secondary aspect of free will that needs to be addressed is the inherent nature of the negative or positive uses of it. Free will by its nature is the tool that will allow the murderer to kill other souls. Free will is by its same nature a tool by which immeasurable good can be imprinted into a given lifetime. What you choose to do with your own free will is, by way of the nature of energy, your own "free will." YOU are fully and finally responsible for everything that you do, think, embark upon, choose, condone, implement, start into motion, agree with, physically or mentally engage in, or with, accept, and imply with your actions and thoughts throughout the lifetime you are presently within. You are the only one who is choosing for *you*.

You may at this time wish to argue the point that, "I am not always in control of other people and situations. I am not able to change this or that." Actually, in the most basic ways, you are always in control of how you feel, react, respond to any, all, and every situation through your lifetime. Even as your plane is falling from the sky or your neighbor is about to shoot you, you receive a positive or fully negative diagnosis. Or if you are about to do, say, conduct negative business, you are given an opportunity for good or evil, take advantage or lift up another soul. YOU always have the control of your free will to determine what you do in *those* moments and the moments that follow. You are always in control of your reaction, your emotion, your response, and fully knowing that that will change your relationship to your world, your Creator/God, your future. You hold all of your own free will. Go forward and use it wisely. Pull that hammer out of your tool belt and stop being a victim. Build your life and soul as you will.

CHAPTER 12
The Kidnapping

The Kidnapping

In February of 1976, I was 11 years old. It was the bicentennial birthday of the U.S.A and my elementary school was in full swing celebrating the event. This event is cemented in my mind as somehow being connected with the kidnapping. The whole of the country was waving flags and celebrating, pumped up with pride. My elementary school had put into place a flag cake rule, which I loved. Every Wednesday a giant flag cake was served at lunch after we all listened to the national anthem. That cake had thick white frosting and red, white and blue decorations. I ate two pieces every week. After the kidnapping, every time they rolled that cake out, I would see it, smell the frosting, and be immediately brought back to the kidnapping. My gut would clench up in some acrid, uncomfortable feeling which precipitated emotional recoil. I also somehow rolled Elton John's song "Philadelphia Freedom" into this weird concoction of pain as it was playing pretty much nonstop at that time too. To this day, if I hear that song, I immediately smell that white, almond-laced frosting and hear the screeching wheels of the metal table holding the cake being rolled over the gymnasium tiles. This never stopped me from eating my two pieces of cake, however, as my sweet tooth was always a giant chasm inside me.

In my childhood, I clocked and calendared my years in sections that were delineated by which man was living with my mother, sister, and I as the "man of the house." My 10th and 11th years were delineated as the years of Jim. My mother liked to have a relationship with "men," and I use this term lightly, who were much, much younger than her. Jim was 18 when he moved in with us, and he had just turned 20 in February 1976 when he was forced out by the next relationship time capsule in the form of Loni, another 20-year-old. You have to remember here that at this time my mother would have been 26 years old, a single mother of two, living with a 19-year-old as her sexual consort.

Jim was a very interesting character who, I am told later, went on to become a full-blown survivalist living somewhere in the upper Rocky Mountain region of Wyoming. In the fall of 1975, right around Thanksgiving, Jim got wind of the fact that my mother was getting ready to trade him in for a new liaison, and became very, very paranoid. I think paranoia was actually in his DNA anyway looking back at it now, but he became even more so. Jim had a gun cabinet in a cupboard at the bottom of the second story stairs, and kept it locked at all times. He kept drugs, guns, and a book of his connections for drug deals in there locked up. During that fall, as he became more and more convinced that my mother was shopping for a new lover, he changed the locks on the cabinet and ran phone wire into it while proclaiming that he needed a safe line for his drug dealings and that my mother's phone line could be compromised. When I would get a glimpse inside, I could see an avocado green wall phone in there with a tape machine attached. I knew better than to question Jim, and because I was so quiet with him, he seemed to think I was always "on his side," by way of me saying nothing. He would often talk to himself about his plans in front of me, I suppose just trusting that I was a kid and wouldn't understand anyway. We found out later that he had actually tapped our phone line through that closet, so that he could later listen to catch my mother in some deed of infidelity. He was a really paranoid 20-year-old with a drug problem and a lot of guns.

In late January, my mother was, indeed, obviously shopping around for a new love, and it was becoming more and more obvious by the raging, drug-fueled 2 a.m. brawls between my mother and Jim that Jim needed to go. The late-night screaming, fighting, and breaking of household items in a rage was escalating. Jim did not want to leave, however, and one February night after a particularly raucous party with my mom passed out, he killed a chicken out in our back barn, brought it stealthily to the bedroom, and spread blood and feathers all around the bedsheets where my mother was passed out. He then disposed of the chicken, crawled back into bed, woke my mom predawn to the bloody, feather-covered bedsheets. Needless to say, he tried to convince mom that someone had crawled into the bedroom unseen, and done this heinous deed while "they" slept in order to threaten her. He told her that she was in danger and that he could protect her and the "girls," and that she needed him. This would be so melodramatic as to be a fantastical horror movie, à la M. Night Shyamalan, except that it is true. It happened.

There was immediate screaming and fighting. Mason, one of my mom's many couch-dwelling druggy friends, came bounding up the narrow stairs to our rooms, pushing, more yelling, an extended exchange of voices crying, screaming, bedsheets being torn asunder, crashing, glass breaking, and doors coming off their hinges, all having to do with Jim's tall thin form being forced down the stairs amidst loud exclamations to "get rid of the bloody sheets, so as not to scare the girls."

There is an interesting point to be made here about drunk, drugged-out people, and that is that they always think they are being quiet. They always think they are in some alternate universe being quiet. They never, and I mean never, are.

At dawn there was a concerted effort by many sleeping partygoers, who had stayed over that Wednesday evening to escort Jim from the building with his guns, drugs, clothing, and all the general items that a 20-year-old paranoid dealer might be calling personal items out of our building. He was crying and begging while being physically forced out and asked to please not return under any circumstances. It must be that they were all too foggy headed to ask him for his house keys because it would be clear in the next 48 hours that he still had a set. All the while he was crying, yelling, fighting, and proclaiming that my sister and I were "his girls too" and that "he had a right to be with those girls too." Now, it is important for you, the reader, to understand that I was 11 and my sister was seven. Jim had just turned 20. Jim was 20! If he had not been a high school drop-out two years earlier, he and I would have been attending the same school together. Let that sink in.

Jim drove away, yelling out of his car window about how it was not over, and breakfast was made for all those in attendance who were hungover and, I guess, not working on a Thursday morning. Stephanie and I headed to school.

As I said, our elementary school was fully in swing with celebrating the Bicentennial. Sitting in the sixth grade on that morning, I can remember trying to process what had happened the night before. I kept thinking about Jim's maniacal face and the sheets with the chicken blood all over them. At that time, I did not understand even that it was chicken blood. I found that out much later, so it occurs to me now that I didn't know whose blood it was on those sheets and that was terrifying because it was a lot of blood. This story, like so many in my childhood, brings up the idea so heavily that I never felt safe as a child. That statement sounds so simple, and yet it is such a huge indicator of the impact on us later, I think, if we don't feel safe as children. It is only through so much work with Aralamb about the true nature of "safety" that I have overcome so much of the childhood terror that I felt.

I sat in my desk that next day listening to other kids talk about the Bicentennial and how it would be celebrated by their families, and I kept thinking, I wish I could learn to freeze and become invisible. If I was truly able to BE invisible, then I would also be safe and invincible. I also knew that if I could be invisible, I never would be because I could not and would not leave Stephanie in the terror that was our home life alone. I couldn't leave her.

This was about the time in my life when I began to understand, and I can't tell you how initially, that there was some kind of inner wellspring of existence deep inside me. I started to understand, at least theoretically, that biblical parable about "being in the world, but not of it." I started to look at objects, other people, animals, trees, music, just everything within our world that said, "Trees and animals don't care what we humans do." They exist in a parallel space in which all of the horrible things that humans do to themselves, and others don't affect them." I can't tell you if I made that distinction in a logical way, like I just described it, at that time. I do know though, that sitting there in my desk on that day, it hit me that "I" was a part of a kind of orchestra or Earth music and that I could tune myself in and out of any situation that I wished. I suppose, it was a sort of invisibility. I decided that day that I was no longer going to **take in** any of the "crazy" that my mother, my home life, and the abusive situations threw at me. I decided that I would be in this world for long enough to get through school and I would never be OF THAT WORLD. I knew that I had within me the ability to be like the trees, animals, music, sky, and just take my energy away from the negativity and abuse, thereby saving me for myself when I was grown. I would protect Stephanie as best as I could, and I would simply keep my true personage deeply held in safety until I could grow up enough to walk calmly away. On that day in the sixth grade, I went from being 11 to being 50 on the inside. I had no choice if I wanted to go on to my own soul's path. I don't know how I knew it, but I did, and I decided. I just decided. I would be an observer. I would comply, but I would keep my most sacred parts hidden and safe. It is only in the last 25 years or so with Aralamb's assistance that I have fully and finally begun to create my world, and feel safe enough to be **of it and in it** fully and joyfully.

Aralamb tells me that this "tool" for saving my soul as a child becomes unnecessary as an adult and this is where people get stuck. It's like as children souls put on an emotional safety lock, and then as adults they "forget" to unlatch the safety hook when it is no longer needed. In this way they don't learn the lessons, and block themselves from their true purpose in this lifetime. This is a really important piece to take from the difficult traumas of some people's childhoods. The tools you adopted to survive will, if not let go in adulthood, simply keep you from your best life later. That tool which kept you safe and separate emotionally does not serve you as an adult. It is so important to find that lock, break it loose if need be, and be "in your life, fully."

That following Thursday and Friday were high energy at home. Jim was gone and Mom was surrounded by her friends and cronies getting ready for the weekend, The Pioneer House Bar, and the hunt for a new man was on. As an adult, I can now see this all as a trend, a trend that would occur well into mom's thirties. As an 11-year-old, I looked at this as a mixture of fear and awe in a way. All of my mother's friends were on an average six to eight years younger than her, so I was at once watching the hair, makeup, "getting ready" to go out ritual with interest for when I was older, but also seeing the herculean amounts of booze, smoke, and often times diet pills, speed, crank, and cocaine being consumed with abject terror because this was a good time to expect any manner of terrifying shit to go on. Stephanie would often go to her gramma's house on these kinds of weekends. Martha was an amazing woman who, I think, had extrasensory perception when it came to my mother's debauchery and would pick us up often to stay with her. This weekend was not one of those times, and it had been decided that I would stay home with Stephanie and call down to The Pioneer House should anything happen at all.

At about 7:00 p.m. on that Friday, the whole menagerie headed down to The Pioneer House to kick off a weekend of crazy. After they left, I went to the front door and locked it. The bells on the front door made a muffled jangle as I shut it hard and locked it. I turned on the porch light and closed all of the heavy velvet curtains in the den and living room. Steph was sitting in the living room on the couch eating dry cereal and maple candies that were left over from Christmas. I had decided that we would sleep on the couch together until the party came home late in the night. I was a bit scared because our house was always a total open party place, and you never knew who might show up at any given time day or night. At about 8:00 p.m., I heard a car come down past the house and do a U-turn in front of the swinging bridge. School Street in our small-town dead-ended just past The Survey and our house with a large circular dirt parking lot butted up against a metal swinging walking bridge that gave access across the river to High Street on the hill above.

I ran to the window and tried to see who it was. The car had stopped past the house by the bridge entry where it was dark and I figured it was someone parked to smoke pot or do a drug deal, as that happened a lot in that spot. I can remember turning away from the window and seeing that Steph had fallen asleep watching American Bandstand. She had on light blue feet pajamas with pink flowers; I was wearing a matching pair. I walked back to the couch, got under the blanket with her, and started nibbling on the PBJ I had made. It was sticky with that thick purple jelly that had not one berry in it at all, but was sweet like nothing else and tasted like grape juice. I heard a key turn in the front door lock and the door swing open hard, brass bells jangling. I thought it was Mom with the party coming home early. Our living room was at one end of the house, and the front door was at the other. The reason for the loud brass bells on the front door was that if someone came in while you were doing drugs or smoking weed or whatever in the living room, you could stow away your drugs under the couch and not be easily snuck up on, as the door was not seen from that room at all. In that moment, I was very happy for the bells because I was 11, home alone with Steph, a bit nervous and hearing them come home was actually a relief. I got up, turned the corner into the kitchen and came face to face with Jim holding a shotgun in one hand and his keys in the other.

Jim had an interesting face. He had crystal blue eyes and a real Cheshire cat smile with one front tooth in silver. I am not kidding, he had one front tooth that was silver. He had that kind of wide smile that should have been attractive, but it had a definite scary quality that didn't make it all the way up to his eyes. When he smiled, you felt like you should be expecting something good, but your insides knew better. He was tall and slender with bright blue eyes. On this night, he looked as though he had been crying, and was now laughing and talking too fast. He seemed really, really unhinged. I stood in the kitchen as he came further into the dining room and started to babble to me about how much he loved Steph and I, how much he loved Mom, and how he was going to make things right. He pushed past me with the gun, moved through the living room, and went to his cupboard by the stairs.

On Thursday morning, when he had been forced out of the house, no one opened his closet, and Mom didn't want them to destroy the door and jam to get to his stuff. Now, he was opening the closet and handing me pistols, a sawed-off shotgun, and many boxes of ammunition. He grabbed his book and his tape machine. He pulled the phone of the wall with a jerk, and left all the wires hanging inside the closet. He headed for his car and jerked his head at me without even speaking. I figured it would be best to just follow him to the car with his stuff, and then he would leave. I was scared of the guns I was carrying because I was holding them like a bunch of kindling wood, and I didn't know if they were loaded. I would find out later that they were.

I was wearing big fuzzy blue slippers and it was February and cold outside. The snow and ground were frozen as I followed him in the dark across the parking lot. My feet weren't getting wet, but the bottom of the slippers was plastic, and it was like traversing an ice rink with an armload of heavy guns. I was afraid if I dropped one, it might go off and hit Jim who was walking fast in front of me. When we got to the car, he opened the trunk and started throwing everything in. I said, "Okay, I'm cold, I'm going to go back inside." It was dark, but I could see he was crying. There was one streetlight at the end of the road there by the entrance to the bridge and it was shining really green light on his face. Tears were running down his cheeks, but he was smiling, and I could see his silver tooth. I don't think I will ever forget that picture. Again, writing this now, it is hit home to me just how amazingly crazy some of our childhood was. Taking him in with both of us breathing out billows of frozen dark February air, it hit me that this was the time for me to be the 50-year-old. I understood in that one look at his face that I would need to really manage this situation in order for Steph and me not to get hurt. I knew it the way you know how long to stay underwater in a pool. At some point, your lungs and the need for air take over and your body uncontrollably starts shooting to the surface for life giving oxygen. There is no need to think about it, the action just happens in order that your cardiovascular system does not explode, killing you. This is the feeling that overcame me in the dark, under that street lamp, looking at his mental drug-addled face. There was no other choice.

I turned to run back into the house without seeming afraid. There were at least 120 yards between us and the front porch. I kept my jog really precise and not too hurried. I didn't want him to think I was fleeing from him. I could hear him following me without much care. I thought, "Lock the door, Melissa," only to remember immediately that he had the keys. Also, I was 11. There were no cell phones, there was no video surveillance on every street corner, no person who was going to come to the rescue, there was no help for us in that moment. We had no options. Even if I tried to outrun him to the front door and lock him out, he would overtake me before I even got to the porch. When I hit the porch and swung the front door open, the bells chimed hard. Steph was standing in the door to the living room awake now. She was holding a blanket around her, she was seven. When she saw Jim come back in behind me, she had a look of terror on her face like none that I have seen since, except maybe in those dogs gone bad videos you see of people being attacked on YouTube. I walked directly toward her and told her it was all right. "Jim is just picking up some of his stuff." I decided to just go back and get on the couch with Stephanie. I hoped that if we just acted totally normal, watching TV, munching snacks, and being under the blanket, he would do what he needed to and leave. That is what I hoped. I could hear Jim in the kitchen digging through Mom's stuff, he made a phone call to someone, and then it got quiet. I was relieved because I figured my plan had worked and he would just leave. After a few more quiet minutes, I heard him grab a glass from the kitchen and pour what I knew was something alcoholic. He sat down at the kitchen table. I could not see him from the living room, but I could hear him very well. Jim smoked Marlboros. He was one of those people who would light a cigarette and then every time he would take a drag, he would do it with that long sssssssssssss sound as the smoke went into his lungs. He would do the same with his exhale. A long sssssssssss followed by a short silence, followed by the sssssssssssssss exhale. It was like every exhale was a long sigh of relief. He did this with his front teeth together in the way people hiss when something hurts them. It really drew your eye to that silver tooth in the front.

I listened to him sit at the table, a second drink was poured, a third cigarette was smoked in succession with those long ssssss sounds. I knew he was thinking. He was mulling over whatever plan he had come up with. All of a sudden, I heard him get up and move toward the front door. My whole body shivered with relief, knowing that he was leaving. I stood up and crept to the doorway of the kitchen without being seen by him. As soon as he was at his car, I would creep to the phone, and call The Pioneer House to get help. Just as I was expecting to hear the front door bells jangle with his opening it, I heard instead the sound of him tearing mine and Stephanie's blue fur-lined snowmobile jackets out of the closet. They were polyester and bright orange on the inside. The jackets matched and had been a gift from our Grampa Vinnie that Christmas. Each jacket had a thick shaggy wreath of faux fur all around the hood. The sound of those jackets rubbing together was unmistakable. When the matching snow mobile boots were thrown out of the closet, all the blood ran out of my face. We were going with Jim....

Jim came around the corner with that big wide smile on his face, threw the jackets and boots on the floor in front of the couch, pointed at the pile, and said, "Come on, girls, we're going for a ride." I could smell the Crown Royal on his breath. Even at my young age, I could assess what kind of liquor a person was drinking by the smell on their breath. Crown Royal on Jim's breath was never a good thing. He was smiling so big, and his eyes were triumphant in a coldly frightening way. I just stayed under the blanket looking from him to the pile of winter jackets and boots. I said, "We better stay here and wait for Mom, she will be worried if we're not here when she gets back." He just said, "No, she won't." Jim reached down and grabbed Steph by the arm. He stood her up straight and began to put the snowmobile jacket on her. Steph stood like a rag doll just staring at him with wide, dark eyes. She started to cry, and he said, "Stop crying, be a good girl!" He said this in a harsh tone, which just made her cry harder. He looked at me, and said, "You need to shut her up, she is making my head hurt!" I jumped up and started to put Steph's coat on her. She was still crying, but more quietly. I zipped up her jacket, and stuffed the big boots on right over her feet pajamas. I kept crooning to her to "be quiet, it is fine, its ok." She just kept a low keen. Jim was now pacing back and forth in the kitchen with a cigarette in one hand and his shotgun in the other. I pulled my own jacket on and then my boots. I was so scared, but still trying to figure out a way to keep Jim from leaving the house with us. Steph and I stood in the kitchen with my arm around her. She was still crying, but really quietly. Jim scrawled a note to my mother on a paper plate, and stood back smoking, re-reading it, and thinking. We must have stood there in our coats and boots for a good 15 minutes in silence with only the sound of Jim's inhale phssssssssssssss, and exhale, phssssssssssssssssss of cigarette smoke punctuated by Steph's quiet crying. Jim held up the note and read it to me, "What do you think? Is this good?" He was drinking the Crown Royal out of bottle at this point. "Read it out loud," he said to me and jammed the paper plate against the front of my jacket.

The note said, "The girls are with me. They belong to me too. You can't take them from me this way. I love you. I know you will come to your senses. I am taking what's mine. These girls are mine. Jim." I read it out loud with no emotion at all like I was reading a grocery list. I shook my head in a silent yes and handed the paper plate back to him.

Jim was happy with his note, and I guess with my reading of it. He put it on the counter, grabbed Steph's left hand in his right, and half-walked half-dragged her out the front door. He was holding his shotgun in his left hand and yelled for me to keep up. Stephanie began to cry in earnest at this point. As I headed out the front door into the dark after them, I glanced at the clock on the wall, 10:30 p.m. The bar would not close for another four hours. I knew that no one would even miss us for at least that amount of time. I cannot tell you what my feelings were as I traversed the parking lot again behind Jim dragging Stephanie along with him. I knew that I could not cry, I could not fight him in any way because that would just expedite whatever he had in mind. He was really becoming agitated with Steph. I caught up with him and grabbed Steph's right hand in mine. Jim was trying to open his trunk again, so I said, "Here, let me get Steph in the back seat." He let go of her hand, and I pulled her into me for a full body hug. I said into her ear, "It's okay, Snuff, let's just go for a ride with Jim, and then we will come back and go to bed. Okay?" I said it like everything was just fine and normal. She shook her head, and I put her into the back seat. Snuff was my nickname for her. I don't remember why, but it was short for Snuffaluffagus. *Sesame Street* was a TV show that we both loved and Snuffaluffagus was one of the main characters. Jim had a sleeping bag in the back seat, which led me to believe that he put it there for Steph and had planned on coming for us. I got Steph in the sleeping bag, keeping her jacket and boots on as well. If we got a chance to get out of the car, I didn't want her to be barefoot. She looked at me with eyes so big and round like a deer in the headlights of an oncoming truck. I tucked her into the sleeping bag and held my finger against my own mouth in the silent symbol of "be quiet." She nodded her head, laid back, turned her face into the bench seat, and closed her eyes.

I got into the front seat at the same time Jim got in the driver's side. There was a large handgun on the seat between us. The car that Jim was driving actually belonged to his brother. It was a 1971 Chevelle. The car was loud and really fast. The front seat was a big bench, and it was cold. Jim's brother had added an eight-track tape player and an FM converter box to the Chevelle, so that the AM radio could play FM stations. Jim turned the key and lit another cigarette. He reached deep under the seat between his legs and grabbed another bottle of Crown Royal, this time unopened. It was a big bottle and had the soft purple bag with the gold tassels on it. He offered me a drink, and I waived it off. He threw the purple velvet bag to me and said, "Keep it." I actually did keep that bag for many years to come because it was a physical reminder that the night in question actually happened at all. Things I collected went into it. Pretty rocks, seashells from trips to Maine, and broken jewelry bits. Also, some amethyst stones I was given later. Jim took a long hard drink from the bottle and put it back under the seat. He did all this while holding his cigarette between his teeth. Jim talked often, moved fast, and kept doing whatever he was doing with the cigarette held between his teeth. He grabbed an eight-track from the box by my feet and plugged it into the player. Kansas's "Song for America" came blaring from the speakers. Backing up the Chevelle, Jim smiled at me and said, "This is going to be fun." As we passed the house, I could see that the front door was wide open to the freezing February night. The porch light was off, but light was flooding out from the open kitchen door. I could see the blue TV light glowing through the living room curtains as well. The house was wide open, and we were not in it. I was never a scared as I was right then. No one would know we were gone for a long time....

We headed south out of Chester without stopping. Twenty minutes later we were getting on I-91 heading south again at speeds that would have been frightening if not for the fact that Jim was talking, crying, drinking, and waving the handgun around like a wand in order to punctuate certain points in his speech, and that was truly frightening. It was like he was talking to himself, but occasionally he would look at me, point the hand-gun my way, and say, "You know what I mean?" I would shake my head yes and try to seem completely unfazed by his actions, which seemed to be growing more and more maniacal. "I love your mother, you know; I was just trying to prove to her that she needs me. You girls need me. I can keep you all safe." He kept telling me this over and over, all the while crying and wiping his nose on his sleeve. Then, he would laugh, light a cigarette, and get mad again, "She never understands. She needs me. You girls need me. This will make her understand." This rollercoaster of an emotional speech continued for about two hours as we wound our way toward Boston. I didn't know at the time that Boston was our destination, but it was. As a punctuation to his own loud hysterical musing, he would stop, get serious, stop crying, and ask me, "You aren't scared of me, right?" "Melissa, you aren't scared of me, right? You know I love you and your sister, right?" All of these questions were put to me by this person while he was holding a loaded handgun in the front seat of that Chevelle with Kansas blaring from the speakers at 80 miles an hour headed south on I-91 through the frozen New England night. I simply said, "No, I'm not scared of you."

As children, there are times, I think, at least in my experience, where you become clear on just exactly what you need to do in order to survive. There is a moment when you want to let your fear go and just pee your pants or vomit, but instead you look insanity right in the eyes, you corral your uncontrollable fear, marshal your face, soften your eyes, and lie. You just lie to the drunk crazy man with the loaded handgun because even at 11 years old, you know it's your only hope. That is what I did. I lied. I agreed with him. I shook my head in a very solid yes motion and said, "I know you love us. Mom will change her mind. She will let you come home. Yes, I will tell her to let you come home." Led Zeppelin's "Over the Hills and Far Away" was playing as we got off the exit which took us through Deerfield and Athol, Massachusetts, toward Boston. Stephanie woke up and started crying in earnest. Jim turned the music down and silently pulled into a gas station. He grabbed the handgun and the front of my jacket in one smooth move. The handgun was stuffed into the front of my jacket. "It's loaded so don't move around too much; it could go off." Jim got out, lit another cigarette, and started to pump gas. I didn't turn around to look at her, but I asked Steph to stop crying. "It's going to be fine. Jim is just taking us on a ride, and we will go home. Okay?" I heard but did not see the sleeping bag go back up over Steph's head and she stopped crying. I sat not moving, feeling the hard cold handgun against my chest and belly. He had told me not to move or it could go off and hurt me. I just sat there, staring straight ahead. I could smell the gas vapors as he filled the car. With the metallic slide of the cap going back on the filler pipe, Jim went into the store. He turned to look back at me and smiled as he threw his lit cigarette on the ground. I didn't move my hands or arms. The gun, tucked against my stomach, sat there like a terrifying guard dog letting me know not to make a move, so I just didn't move.

Jim came back to the car, threw a carton of Marlboros in the glove box and threw a handful of purple and red Giant Pixie Stix into the back seat at Steph. He held out 4 of them to me, and I didn't move. He remembered the gun and unceremoniously unzipped the front of my jacket, grabbing the gun by the barrel. After placing the gun back on the seat between us, he handed me the Pixie Stix like a bouquet of flowers and smiled. I took them and heard Steph's being pulled beneath the sleeping bag in the back seat. Jim said, "what do you say?" He kind of yelled it, and smiled at the same time. We both mumbled "thank you." It was surreal sitting there in the front seat with those 2-foot-long plastic tubes full of sugar. The idea that he would get us this candy was somehow more terrifying than if he had not. Pixie Stix, if you do not know, were a confection of sugar dust and citric acid which came in small straw like tubes, or, in 2-foot-long large plastic tubes which were striped in the varying flavors of what was inside. Jim reached across me and pulled a large Bouie Knife out of the glovebox and handed it to me so that I could I guess cut the ends off so that we could eat them. I unlocked the knife, and a 7-inch blade was now unfolded in my hand. It was a reassuring sound somehow as everyone's Grampa in the 70's in rural areas had one, so it was not uncommon to hear that metallic locking sound as the knife unfolded. I wish I could say that I thought about stabbing Jim, or somehow forcing him to pull over in the dark with the knife and let us out, but at 11, it never even crossed my mind. I simply cut off the end of the long tube I was holding and then did the same as two more of the sugar filled tubes were pushed at me from the back seat and then disappeared under the dark mass of the sleeping bag. For the next hour, Jim regaled me with stories of what our future as a family would be like as he cried and laughed intermittently. I sat quietly and listened, eating the delicious sugar and shaking my head in silent agreement. Jim told me what a "good little soldier I was turning out to be." He said that "I had the makings of a really good soldier." The Chevelle had a clock in the dash near the speedometer. I could see that it was 11:45 now and the bar would still not close for two hours. Then I remembered that we had left the front door open. Maybe someone passing by would see that, think it was strange and look for us. I knew this would not happen. I was alternately trying to think of what to do, if anything, and I was getting so tired. Jim was constantly talking, smoking, and driving.

After a time, I can't say how much for sure, I think I had dozed off, I came awake, and we were in a big city. Boston was all around us, and the clock in the dashboard was reading 1:30 a.m. We were in some kind of industrial area which was near both the harbor and Boston Logan Airport because I could smell ocean and hear planes. It was cold, but even through the closed windows, cigarette smoke, heat vents blowing and Crown Royal, I could smell the ocean. Jim pulled slowly past three or four alley's which were lined along buildings that were mostly dark on the interior and looked like warehouses. He asked me to slide down in the seat a bit so that he could see back into each one. I did so. We passed one on our right and Jim reversed deep into the alley. I am not sure how far he backed in, but the main street was at least a block away and there were very few doors, windows or openings that I could see on either side as we backed into the alley. Jim stopped the car, looked around, rolled the window down, threw out his lit cigarette, and looked at me as if he were trying to figure out what to do. Finally, he picked up the handgun, and again pulled at the front of my jacket, unzipped it, and put the gun down the front. I started to protest, "I won't go anywhere, I don't need the gun." He didn't listen and placed it back in my jacket, this time against my chest. He zipped up my jacket and said, "just sit still. It's cold and I am going to leave the car running. I will be right back out. I have some business to do. Don't move around, that gun is loaded." From inside the car, he popped the trunk, got out and left the car running, the heater roaring and Pretzel Logic by Steely Dan playing softly in the 8-track. I saw him in my peripheral vision disappear behind the car. Jim passed by my door moments later in a dark outline of a large bag on the right side and a shotgun held in the other. He disappeared to my right into a dark spot on the side of the building.

When Jim left the car, it was 1:48 a.m. on the dash clock. I sat motion-less in the front seat. The heater was making me sweat in my jacket and it was blowing so hot on my right boot that it was actually kind of burning my foot, but I was too scared to move with that big gun in my jacket tight against my chest. I sat there not moving, staring straight ahead down the alley toward the main street. Jim had turned off the headlights and the only light was from the dash, radio, and the glowing green of the streetlight on the snow far away in front of us. I sat and hoped Steph would keep sleeping. I was 11 and I was so far out of my element, even for me, that I could not make sense of what was going on. I was so afraid and so tired that I had moved past the initial fear and on to some kind of numb disassociation. I was trying to figure out how this was going to end. I wanted to go home. I wanted this kind of life not to be mine. I sat there daydreaming about other kids' homes. I especially liked the safeness of those homes. I thought of my Gramma Patty. In my mind, I reached out to her house. She would be asleep and warm in her bed. I loved her. I thought of her perfume and how good it smelled, like roses, and I felt better. The 8-track clicked over, and I woke up. I was slumping on the gun a bit and the fact that I had fallen asleep on it made my fear very real again. Maybe I could just unzip my coat and pull it out. Maybe it wouldn't go off? No, I would not move. I was too scared. I looked again at the clock, and it was now 2:50 a.m. We had been there for over an hour with the car running. 2:50 a.m.! Mom knows we are gone. She has come home from the bar; she got the note. The police will have been called and they will be looking for us. A rush of adrenaline and relief bowled over my body and I thought for a moment that I would pee my pajama bottoms. I had to go to the bathroom, but I just held it. They would be looking for us. They would be looking for us and we would be ok. Just at that moment, the trunk of the car slammed shut, Steph woke up with a kind of muffled cry, and Jim threw the sawed-off shotgun into the front seat as he jumped into the car. We began moving out of the alley at a really high speed and Jim was raging at the top of his lungs. As we hit the main street, Jim turned right hard without even stopping. I was thrown off balance toward him and was sure the handgun in my jacket was going to go off. It didn't, but I started crying and so did Stephanie. Jim was swearing, "fucking assholes, fuckers, they are going to pay for this!" "I had the money, I had the dope, and they try to fucking double fucking cross me, well see now, they have no money, they have a few less teeth, and they have no dope, fuck, fuck me!" "Ok, ok, I gotta think, I gotta think, you two need to shut the fuck up! I can't think with all this fucking crying! Shut the fuck up, Melissa, shut her the fuck up!" We were careening through intersections and making small, hard turns here and there like a scared animal running for its life from tree to tree. Jim grabbed my jacket with his right hand and ripped the zipper down in one hard yank while he was still driving with this left. The handgun fell out, hit the middle of the bench seat, ricochet off of the sawed-off rifle laying there, made a harsh metallic sound falling to the floorboards between my feet. Jim even looked amazed that it had not gone off, and I turned to Steph in the back seat and asked her to stop crying, but I was crying loudly myself, and it made it worse. Jim was screaming and ordered me to get in the back seat with Steph, I did so immediately diving over the back of the bench seat into the darkness. I got under the sleeping bag with Stephanie, and we huddled together. I put my face close to hers and put my finger up to my lips to say "quiet." Tears were running down my face, and my neck hurt a bit where Jim had torn at my jacket, but I made no sound and peed my pajamas. I just laid there and soaked my pajamas and the seat beneath me...

I could hear Jim's muffled angry conversation with himself through the sleeping bag, but I dozed. Occasionally I would start to wake up, but then just doze back off. At one point I was having a dream that I had fallen asleep in the back seat of the car with my cousins coming home from a drive in Movie. The drive inn near Bellows Falls was open in the summer, and falling asleep in the back seat on the way home was an always event. All of us jammed into blankets and on top of each other like a pack of puppies with my uncle Bob driving the car. Warm, quiet and just the car engine keeping you lulled to sleep.....

The car engine stopped. I came awake, still in the dark, a quick look around let me know that we were not home. Jim had parked the car close to a dumpster at the back of a parking lot near a diner. We were still on the outskirts of Boston from what I could tell. I didn't recognize where we were at all. The back door opened before I even realized that Jim was not in the car. He leaned into the car, sat Steph up and put a dark bag of some kind down the front of her jacket. She said nothing and then he turned to me. Jim had all of his "dope" in bags that were about half the size of pillow cases, and he started pushing the final 4 bags down the front of my jacket. I didn't even protest. Steph and I sat there and let him do it like two victims of coma who just came out of that deep world after 10 years. He pulled Steph out of the back seat, and I followed. He was chattering in a really fast tight voice. He was acting happy, and kept saying, "everything is going to be ok. We are just going to get some breakfast, and I am going to figure out what to do next, I just need to think." He kept this mantra up like a nervous, weirdly happy bird cackling all the way across the parking lot to the front of the diner. We entered the diner and sat in a booth. The booth was central to the big room and near a free-standing telephone booth in the middle. It was the kind that diners had back then where you could go inside and close the glass doors and make a call. We sat and the waitress brought Jim black coffee. Jim ordered orange juice and pancakes for Steph and I without looking at the waitress. He lit a cigarette and we all sat there in silence while he thought and smoked in his hissing way. The diner was mostly empty except for a few other people who were obviously drunks coming from last calls at local barrooms. The big clock on the wall said 5:30 a.m. Steph was sitting on the inside of the booth across from me and next to Jim. I sat looking at the both of them. Steph was playing with her straw and pulled it on and out of the cup of juice that the waitress had left. Jim started talking to us low. "Now listen, I am going to go over to the phone booth there and call your mother. She is going to understand, and we will all go home. We are a family, and she will understand." Steph needed to go to the bathroom. Jim took her to the bathroom and told me to sit very still because I had all that dope in my jacket, and I would get in big trouble if it fell out here. I watched him walk away holding Steph's hand and I thought, "I would go to jail. If anyone knows I have all this in my jacket I will go to jail." In my 11-year-old mind, I was just as guilty as Jim if I was caught with all that weed in my coat. Jim and Steph came back to the booth, and Jim told us to stay put. There were small booth sized jukeboxes in each booth. There was a nob on top and you could turn it to see what songs the box would play. Jim put a big handful of quarters in the top of it and told Steph to pick songs. He looked at me and said, "I am going to the phone booth to call your mom. I am going to talk to her. You have to sit here with your sister, don't get up because you have all that dope in your jacket. It's safe in there, no one will suspect a little girl of holding that much dope." He smiled that big nervous smile and went to the phone booth with his cigarettes and the matches he got from the waitress. I saw him enter the phone booth. He turned and looked back at me with another big, weird, nervous smile. I was so tired that I just stared at him. I kept my eyes on him the whole time, I was trying to read his face and see what mom might be saying to him. I didn't want her to make him mad. I was terrified that she would make him mad, and he would hurt us. Steph was playing an assortment of random songs from the juke box, ABBA, Doobie Brothers, Elton John, Kansas, The Rolling Stones... I didn't say anything to her, I just kept staring at Jim in the glass phone booth. The waitress brought our pancakes and we both had a few bites, all the time I kept looking at Jim through the glass of the booth. I could not hear what he was saying, but he was on his second cigarette, and he was furiously putting more change into the phone. Once I saw him get mad and act as if he was going to break the hand set on the glass, his jaw was tight, and his face was white. He looked so mad, he was shaking his head and I could see him saying "no, no, no!" Movement to my right dragged my eyes away from Jim in the phone booth and two blue uniformed MASS cops sat in a booth about 15 feet away. They glanced up at me as they sat, but Stephanie's head didn't come above the booth's back and they didn't see her, I think. They only gave a cursory glance over at Jim in the phone booth, and went back to ordering. I sat frozen looking from my plate of cold pancakes to the phone booth where Jim was still obviously arguing with our mother. He was crying now, and I willed him to please stop crying and look at me because I did not want to have those two cops take me to jail for having all that dope in my jacket. I moved a bit because the plastic of the bags down the front of my jacket was hot, and I reached to tighten the waist tie that was on the inside to keep snow out when in the weather. Jim had tightened it himself, but now I was terrified of having it come loose and spill all the weed out in front of those cops. "He had said, no one will suspect a little girl of having all that dope in her jacket." I hoped that was true. I pulled the drawstring as tight as it would go and when I did, a draft of air that smelled like weed and dried pee came up and out of the opening at my collar. With the smell, I thought I would start crying, but Jim must have finally seen the two cops so close to us and he was suddenly there across from me. He had obviously been crying hard, but he seemed like a balloon with all the air out of it. He said, "she loves, me. It's all going to be ok. We can go home. We are a family, and she understands why I had to take you girls. She loves, me." I could not speak right then from a mixture of terror and relief. Jim asked the waitress for the check as she passed by us on her way to the cop's booth with their food. She took it out of her pocket and handed it over. In one long smooth move, like a pro, Jim handed her a twenty, put his cigarettes in his pocket, grabbed Steph's hand, did a kind of bow to me, I got up, walked toward the door with Jim behind me pulling Steph along. I passed the cops booth without looking up at them at all and heard Jim right behind me say, "officers," in that same kind of formal, bowing way as the three of us just passed on by them and out into the cold.

As an adult, it occurs to me that Jim was so diabolical that he knew better than to leave the massive amounts of drugs he had in the car along with his cash. He knew that the absolute safest way to not get himself caught for kidnapping, drug dealing, illegal gun carry and a multitude of other charges for which he would get at least 25 years in prison, was to place all of the responsibility actually on the bodies of an 11- and 7-year-old child. He was so smooth about it. He was right, it worked flawlessly. I wish now that I could talk to those two MASS cops and just ask, "what would you think if you had known that this happened right under your noses?"

Out in the parking lot Jim was a changed man. He unloaded our jackets of all the weed while we stood behind the car right into the trunk. He took his shot gun from the front seat and placed it in the trunk with the dope, but kept the handgun in his waist band as he did this. Steph and I were placed again into the back seat. Jim got in, started up the Chevelle, and lit a cigarette. He was looking for radio stations, crying, smoking, drinking Crown Royal, and talking out loud about how "it was all going to be all right. We are a family; we are going to stay a family." I was sitting in the back and saw on the clock that it was 6:09 a.m., it was February, and the sky was just turning the pink of dawn around the edges as we headed home. I lay down sideways around Steph with my feet still on the floor-boards and became unconscious.

WCFR was the big station to listen to in 1976 in Southern Vermont. If you were lucky at night, you might get some of the bigger Boston or even New York stations like WBZ or WAXQ. WCFR was, however, the big station for our rural part of upper New England. My aunt was dating the station manager at WCFR, Mike Robbins. Mike was a big guy with a great smile and a really winning kind of personality. He was always so good to Stephanie and me. He was like a rock star in my mind, and I loved him. He was the morning DJ Tuesdays through Saturdays, and it was like having our very own uncle talking on the radio and playing songs we loved every morning. It was to his voice that I came suddenly awake in the back seat. I was stiff from being in a half-sitting, half-laying position in the back seat and the smell of urine was coming up through the opening of my jacket at my neck. Stephanie was asleep next to me on the seat. The sun was up and I could hear Mike Robbins on the radio exclaiming happily that it was a beautiful, sunny but cold February Saturday morning in the Green Mountain State. The sun was bright, and the morning was beautiful. I sat dazed looking out the back V-shaped window as the stark winter scenery sped by. As Jim Croce came on the radio, I realized we were almost back to Chester. Jim had been crying, laughing, sobbing, smoking, drinking, and professing his love for our mother and us when we left Boston in the dark earlier, but was now quiet and smoking. The only sound from him was the inhaled and exhaled hiss. It was completely surreal to me, even as an 11-year-old to be riding north on Main Street, with the bright sun, Seals and Crofts' "Summer Breeze" on the radio. We passed Gould's Market and there were cars in the parking lot. I looked at the dash clock, 8:17 a.m. Jim caught my eye in the rearview mirror, those crystal blue eyes still looking crazy, but weirdly happy. "Were almost home, sunshine, wake up your sister." He acted as if everything was just fine and kidnapping us in the middle of the night at gunpoint was no big deal at all. As we took the left onto School Street, passing the Green, I felt like my whole head was caving in with relief, fear, shock and something else that I would later, as an adult, know as a feeling of pure adrenaline-laced happiness at the realization that you had survived something you did not expect to.

Pulling to the end of the street past our house, we made the long curving U-turn at the swinging bridge, the very same we had made the night before when we left the house. Sliding up to the front porch this time, and parking, I was suddenly very aware that there were no police cars in our yard. There were only a few cars, and one car that I did not recognize. There was nothing to make anyone believe that children had been abducted or that a crime had been committed. The whole scene was bright and sunny. Fear hit me and I grabbed Steph's hand and pulled her out of the back seat behind me. As we stood on the far side of the Chevelle, I didn't move. It was brisk cold but the sun was shocking and yellow. I knew in my well trained 11-year-old guts that something was not right and that something bad was about to happen. The front door opened, and our mother came out in her nightgown and slippers. She had her arms open like Jim had taken us on a well-planned out camping trip. Again, in my mind somewhere I thought, "Oh, the cops are inside, and this was just a ploy to get Jim to bring us back unharmed." That is when I met Lonnie for the first time. Out the front door came a 20-year-old with a beard and longish hair. He came down off the porch and before Jim could even react started hitting him in the face. Lonnie was hitting Jim over and over. I started to drag Steph to the porch, but the fight was between us and the house. Finally, Jim was not fighting, he was crying, and he kept saying through his bloody, broken face that he loved her. He was letting Lonnie hit him in the face while looking up at my mother the whole time, pleading with her. He was crying, bleeding, and saying "You lied to me?" "You lied to me to get me to bring them back?" The look in his eyes was terrifying, not because of the blood or the fact that he was a monster but because he was a broken person, pleading to be let back home. A second young man came out of the house as we passed by the form of Lonnie, pounding Jim's face on the ground. As we came up on the porch, Mark pulled Lonnie off of the not-moving form of Jim and told him, "Enough!" Lonnie kept jumping around like a prize fighter and kicking dirt onto Jim who was on his back on the walkway, and blood had spattered everywhere. Mark bent down, pulled Jim up, and put him in the car. Blood was pouring from open gashes across Jim's nose, chin, and bottom lip as he fired up his engine and screeched away garbling, "This isn't over."

We had been watching this with our mother on the front porch in the sun. "Well, I am so glad you are home." She turned us both, pulling us into the kitchen. "Here, sit, and I will make you some pancakes." She sat us at the table in our jackets. I started to peal mine off and Steph did the same. Some of my mother's friends were there too, obviously having spent the night. Lonnie came in without speaking to Steph or me and sat at the table drinking coffee with a few of the others. It looked like everyone was going to have pancakes. Someone lit a joint, and it was being passed around the kitchen. The incident, the blood on the pavers in front of our house, the fact that we had been taken in the night, the pee, which was now dried in my pajamas, the crusted dried pixie stick powder that was dried on Steph's face mixed with the millions of terrified tears she had cried in the 12 hours before were never spoken of again. We sat in our horrified state at the kitchen table without one mention of what had happened. What we had been through, were we okay, were we terrified, what had we seen, nothing. Pancakes were served to me on a plate, and I sat there eating them with thick real maple syrup that my Grampa Vincent made in his sugar house up on the hill above town. Lonnie was eating his pancakes and had not even bothered to wash Jim's blood off his hands and knuckles. I can remember that I could not understand why he would want to eat his breakfast with that much blood on his hands. I could actually smell the blood as I was sitting next to him all coppery and new.

They had come home, found the door wide open, found the note Jim had written on the paper plate, and they had not called the police. The whole time we were with Jim, no police had been called. They had drugs, people, and illicit shit going on at our house, and those things and being caught outweighed the idea that a maniac had her children and could easily kill them, leave them out to die in the night, set them on fire in the car, and call it done. She did not call the police. She did not call the police. When I say it now, as a mother myself, and far from perfect, I would not be able to NOT call the fucking police. This episode was never spoken of at all ever from that point forward. It was as if it never happened. Lonnie moved in that very day, and it was never spoken of. The police were never called. I believe that incident was when I started looking at my mother and knowing that she was never going to truly protect either Stephanie or I from anything at all, ever. The terror of that fact at 11 was a crushing weight in my chest. I had to protect myself, somehow, in some way, I would have to save me.

Aralamb:

I specifically wanted Melissa to share this event from her early childhood because it illustrates what souls do when they find themselves in a situation where there is no safety, and how that need to feel safe can manifest itself later in unhealthy ways. I will not break down every turning point in this timeline of events, but I would like to touch on a few. If a child is pushed to the edge of survival in this way, a protection mechanism will kick into place on a soul level, which literally supersedes that need for that soul to still be within the lifetime. To explain a bit deeper, when a child senses that it may be extinguished from its life, the fully grown soul will intervene in such a way as to keep that child's lifetime moving forward even in very treacherous circumstances. Melissa did this within this experience by "becoming" the sane mind in the event. She understood at a soul level that Jim was not in his right mind, and that in order to survive, she would need to comply while still being unshaken. Within this plan of action was the obvious decision to try to be 50.

In manifesting this survival mode, however, often the children of difficult circumstances will keep this particular tool as something that they then go on to apply in their adult lives as a daily practice. Using this "separation" or "seeing from above" emotional tool, they are cutting themselves off from what they were meant to do within the lifetime. Once a trauma is over, and a soul is apart from the crisis, there is no need for the tools of control, fear, within the lifetime. The optimal situation for a soul within a child's body is to have an environment of support in order, so that the lifetime which has been entered can be manifested in a learning and experiential way. This is the optimal situation, which, obviously, particularly in your time period upon the Earth, is not the norm. Many of you reading this will have come from very difficult, treacherous, and abusive childhood situations. On some level, you would have chosen your parents and situations in order to learn specific lessons about forgiveness, flexibility, inherent soul gifts, and a myriad of other soul talents. This all being said, however, the larger lesson that a soul will and should glean from surviving a difficult or abusive childhood is the idea that you are not only meant to survive the difficult childhood, but you are also meant to survive, integrate, forgive, and overcome such events by way of bringing them into realistic focus as a part of the whole of your soul's experience and not the "definition" of the soul's lifetime.

This idea of making your survival of an abusive or terrifying childhood the "definition" of the lifetime is the most important lesson. If you as a soul survived a very difficult or terrifying childhood, you are not meant to wear it as a badge of honor; you are supposed to feel it fully and integrate it into only one aspect of who you ARE and not fully what you ARE. There is a very fine line of difference between the two, yet the differentiation of the two is monumental in the experience, release, forgiveness, and integration of the experiences.

For example, Melissa moved forward from the time of this experience, using her tool of control, and "being like a 50-year-old." By using this tool all the way through and up until her mid-20s, she was able to protect herself from the terror that she knew was waiting for her on the other side of the experience. The protective tool helped her get through the remainder of her childhood, but it also removed her from some of the aspects of growth that the young soul needs in order to fulfill its chosen life's purpose.

During her mid and late 20s, through our relationship, Melissa began to purposefully examine, feel, and release the control and safety issues that she was still using in her everyday life, which were wonderful and kept her safe as a child, but were now, after the traumatic time had passed, not serving her. Melissa, now at 58, has more access to her completely innocent, joyful, and creative child soul than she ever had when she was a child. This is very important to understand. You must, if you are interested in being the full-blown creative Earth soul that you came here to be, go back and be sure that you are not using some latent, long-forgotten protection tool from your childhood. Until you revisit the why of these tools, they cannot be disengaged from your attitudes about your life.

Every soul needs to examine the ingrained tools that they put into place as children, especially those that were protective in nature. These tools must be addressed and released in adulthood if you want to progress and live the lifetime that you are in to its fullest potential. This process can be harrowing and frightening. If you were abused physically by a parent or some other adult in your childhood, and you survived the event, you may still be living with those parameters as an adult. Twenty or thirty years later, you can be looking at and responding to your life events through the lenses of that childhood victim without even knowing it. What do you fear in your adulthood? Where does that fear come from? If you are standing in a supermarket and the man in front of you uses a certain kind of clothes soap and it reminds you of some childhood abuser, how does that affect the rest of your day? The man in line is no threat to you. You are not in any danger. He is a total stranger whose wife just happens to use a certain kind of laundry soap. Do you relive the fear immediately? Does your stomach tighten just a bit? Do you want to put your groceries down and leave without paying? How are you negatively affected by the smell of that laundry soap on this stranger? This is an ingrained tool from your childhood which is still trying to keep you safe, but it is no longer needed, and it will cripple your attempts to grow into your life fully as a soul.

Melissa points out above that by her 11th year of life, she could determine which kind of alcohol was on a person's breath, and whether to be afraid of the coming incidents simply by being able to discern whether that person was drinking beer or whiskey. This was a tool in her childhood which served her well. This tool allowed her to become invisible and hide when her home was going to become dangerous. This tool in adulthood will not necessarily be needed. What if one of her major life possibilities was going to be possibly accessed in a social situation where there was going to be socially responsible alcohol in the mix, and she would miss the opportunity specifically because she had trained herself to know or understand as a child that any smell of whiskey in the air meant that "the shit was going to hit the fan in a really bad way." Melissa might actually avoid the very situation that her soul had set up for her in this lifetime in order to "stay safe," even though there was no danger at all.

What if the tool she employed at 11 to "be a 50-year-old" made her seem aloof or "above it all" in later life. How does that affect her chances later of connecting with the opportunities and crossroads that require her to connect with others fully with no fear at all? It will affect her negatively until she looks at the reasons why she adopted the survival tool and purposefully releasing the tool. If a grown soul does not look at these tools put into place by themselves as children, the full potential cannot be met. You will continue to look at your whole life through the lenses of the survival tool. It is best to begin to examine your ingrained childhood tools in order to release those that are not working for your life now.

CHAPTER 13
Death of the Body

Melissa

So, this is the part where Aralamb is going to speak about the single thing that is one of the deepest fears a lot of humans experience. I mean, let's face it, no one wants to think about his or her own death. The big unknown. That place where, for whatever the reason, your body stops doing what you go about your business every day just taking for granted will continue to happen, and just stops. Dead. The one cool thing, for me at least right now, is the fact that many scientists, healers, mystics, and just regular people are studying, returning from, and having some input on what death of the body is, and what it really means for us as souls. I, for one, through my relationship with Aralamb, have much less fear about physical death. It's not the death I fear anymore, it's the "leaving." I don't want to leave all of the amazing people and experiences that I have in my life, so that is where my fear lies. I don't believe that we are all just a wink in time, and then there is nothing. This girl has seen too much to believe that anymore! So, for me, it's not the death of my body someday, it's the leaving the amazing loves and experiences of my life that I fear. Either way, fearing "death" is a serious waste of time! Don't get me wrong, I am not saying anyone should seek out death or look forward to it, but certainly fearing death is not nec-essary. Aralamb will explain more about how it works and what happens next. That is the greatest part, there is a "next," we aren't just worm food in the end! Our physical body does go back to dust, be WE, ourselves, in the big awesome sense go on, and on, and on. That is good news!

Aralamb

Your human body, just as with other species on other worlds, is simply a very highly evolved vessel in which your soul can reside. Within your body lays your brain. You brain evolved in order to allow your soul to connect with your faith tether, third eye, and consciousness. Your brain works as a fully integrated organic informational sonic wave tuner as well as the bridge between fully electromagnetic information coming in from the Universal codes, which is then transmuted into full physical being at the lowest levels of frequency by the tether and the DMF. Your brain is an organically derived "computer" system, by which all input from Earth's energetic plain and the Universal Creation Plane are combined in order to facilitate your free will within a lifetime. Your body is the one arena for all information at your fingertips to converge, allowing you to live, breath, BE within your life.

Your brain has at its subconscious levels, full access to all informa-tion that is available throughout the Universe. However, at this time on your planet, humans are not using or accessing the full potential of that information. Species on your planet and on many others have many levels of access to this information, which is always evolving, hopefully upward. Put simply, there are species who are further down on the ladder of brain evolution, and many, many more who are much higher on the levels of brain evolution. Your brain, as it sits, is fully capable of evolving up the lad-der of sense and understanding. At this time in Earth's history, the upgrade of your brain circuits is fully underway. This upgrade, however, is also a free will issue so there is never a forcing of such information. You, as a soul and human at this time, are simply being given the road signs to read or not read at your own pace and insistence.

The reason that I give you this information about your brain is in order to speak with you about an issue of importance to humanity: physical death of the body.

How a death happens is fully within the control of the incoming soul prior to its birth. By this statement, I literally mean that every soul prior to its birth onto the Earth plane will have chosen, and obviously "forgotten," two or three possible intersections where death could occur. The final time of death would also be chosen. Let me explain. During a lifetime, a soul can build into that life some or the other hardship which may result in the death of that body and the end of that lifetime. In the lifetime, the soul also has the ability to choose to fight and stay in the lifetime. By placing these intersections into a lifetime, a soul gives itself great opportunities for growth. A perfect lifetime, after all, would not impart many lessons. Souls deciding to incarnate for a lifetime usually choose to have great learning potential placed within that coming lifetime.

A soul may place intersections of illness, accident, choice, or difficulty to learn the lessons of healing, manifestation, strength of character, strength of will, etc. I mean to say that during difficult or life-threatening events, souls often overcome those odds or experiences and live long happy lives, changed by those difficulties for the better. Now, there is no judgment assessed if a soul leaves during one of these possible death scenarios; it would just be a decision of free will. Should a soul determine to survive a difficult patch and not choose death, then the lessons learned would be added to their experience as a soul and not need to be addressed in future lifetimes.

Into each lifetime a predetermined birth and death are situated. A soul will be born, and if that soul chooses to learn and survive any mid-life crises that it decided to place into a life, then a final exit or death will be in place to finish the lifetime. Keep in mind that there is no set rule that says multiple crises must be placed within a lifetime; it is just an option. Some souls after particularly difficult physical lives will choose to reincarnate into much less challenging lives and place no divergent death possibilities for themselves. This is also fine and not judged in any way.

So, let us, for example's sake, assume that the soul of "Maddie" had a long successful life as the wife of a beet farmer in Alabama. Maddie had four children and is now living with one of her daughters in the same town she raised her family in. Maddie is 94, still a member of her Baptist church. Maddie can just walk with a cane and still helps with Sunday dinner, but gets tired in the afternoons and likes to sit in her chair near the open window and doze while she thinks about Harlan, her husband of 50 years who died 10 years ago in the very house she and her kids still live in. Maddie has a lot of knee pain, but she is happy. She daydreams, or maybe she is sleeping, she is not sure anymore. Sometimes her dreams drift into her daytime and she can hear Harlan in the kitchen making coffee for them or smell his cologne as he bends to kiss her velvety 94-year-old cheek. There is a pond out the window where she sits, and she can see Harlan coming up the lane for supper. Harlan is tall and handsome. Maddie blushes now even thinking about the day that they had been married for two months and she was pretty sure that she is pregnant. Maddie sees him coming closer up the path, sees the sun in his dark red hair, and hopes that their baby has his hair. A breeze moves the surface of the pond, he looks up and sees her through the window. Smiling, he picks up pace towards the house. She loves him so much that it hurts her heart. She fears if God would ever take him. He is half of her. She wipes her hands on her apron.

"Momma, it's time for supper, Momma." "Oh, I must have been napping. Maddie glances out the window and the surface of the pond is rippling in the sun like stars. She lets Sylvia help her up to her walker and smiles as she looks at her daughter's slightly graying red hair. Sylvia is her first baby and has Harlan's hair.

After lunch, Maddie is tired, and Sylvia gently walks her back to her chair by the window. The chair is old but big and overstuffed. Sylvia and the other kids had it reupholstered in 1990 for Harlan. The chair had been his mother's and sat in her parlor when they first started dating. It was actually a huge, overstuffed loveseat that had been in the family since 1910 or so. That loveseat had been shipped down from Chicago on a horse-drawn wagon and handmade by an Italian furniture maker. It had been her and Harlan's prized possession, and Harlan sat in it every evening to watch the birds and deer visit the pond below the house. The big chair had been upholstered in a beautiful smoke gray fabric with giant white and pink peonies in the shades of sunset all interwoven with deep green grape vines. Sylvia had found the fabric at a fine restoration place in Los Angeles, and it was from the original pattern of the loveseat.

Maddie had not eaten much lunch. She felt fine, but so, so tired. It was October, and the windows in the house were all open and fresh fall air was coming in. It was cool, and as she looked out toward the pond she could see her great granddaughter Madeline, named after her, pulling at her three-year-old son Chase's hand to get him further away from the edge of the water. Maddie smiled and closed her eyes, or did she? The time for Maddie to leave and join Harlan had drawn near, she knew. Harlan would visit her in her naps and her night-time dreams more and more now. She knew that he would be meeting her soon. She could not tell anyone how she knew, but she could feel the presence of her mother, Harlan, and some of her cousins who had passed over before her. She had the feeling that she was about to return to a place that was truly her home somehow. When she was a child, in the summer, her whole family would ride on horseback out to Lake Willoughby and camp for days on end. She loved the feeling of the whole house packing up for the long ride through the wilderness to get to the lake. Maddie loved to ride on ahead with her brother Justin, and be the first two at the shore to set up camp. Every time they broke through the trees and the first glints of the lake sparkling in the sun came through the pine boughs, she felt at home. Maddie had that same feeling now. She knew she was about to go home again.

Maddie died that afternoon sitting in that chair. She fell asleep in the chair. Maddie's soul simply "let go" of her body. This is the first stage of a physical death which takes place in this manner at the end of a lifetime. The body and soul simply let go of each other, much in the same way that a ship in the harbor moves when the tether anchoring it is disconnected from its mooring. There is usually a small whooshing sound heard by the soul accompanying this "letting go." This is literally the sound of the soul departing the vessel of the body. In Maddie's case, for example, she was sitting, and she was already noticing on many levels the idea that she would be leaving very soon. This is very often the case with souls whose bodies are old, infirm, wracked with illness, in a paralyzed or catatonic state. Those bodies, who are at the end of a lifetime, and the soul are fully aware of the end of organic life. In these kinds of situations, the soul becomes more and more connected to The Lobby, and less and less connected with the Earth plane and the physical body. A soul will often even speak about "seeing" or sensing some other place or people who have passed on to the surviving souls around them. In Maddie's case, she was seeing and sensing Harlan, who was ready in The Lobby to meet her when she crossed back over. Because Maddie's soul was becoming disconnected from her organic body, she was beginning to sense and see many more of the energy levels between the Earth plane and The Lobby. She was literally beginning to "see" where she was going.

During this process, Maddie's soul will have popped suddenly out of her body, been fully aware of the process, and been standing, if you will, beside Harlan looking at her elderly body sitting in the chair empty of her soul energy. This process is never frightening to the soul who has just died because there is sudden and complete memory of who they actually ARE and what is really going on. At that point, Maddie would have quickly scanned the energy of her family and risen to the place of her arrival back in The Lobby. Maddie is met by her guide/teachers, family members, other souls in her learning pod who have returned before her, and any other souls who wanted to greet her upon her return.

In the period where Maddie was sitting in her chair and still alive in her body with her heart beating, her soul and faith tether began to disengage from her third eye and brain stem. This is always the case in this kind of dying experience. As her soul and faith tether begin to disconnect from her physical brain stem, her "mooring" to this world weakens and those connections to The Lobby grow more in number and stronger. At the point where her soul energy is more connected to The Lobby and The Creation, she will leave her body fully. The organic body, organs, and electromagnetic brain systems will not function without at least 35 percent of the soul engaged in keeping the body running. In near-death experiences, although the breathing, heartbeat, and functional body may seem to be dead, the soul will still be engaged energetically to the 35 percent mark, while that soul is 65 percent connected with The Lobby. Because of this, often, when a soul chooses to re-engage in the lifetime, the body can be brought back with organic medical intervention. The truth is, if that soul truly decided to leave the life at that time, and pulled out that final 35 percent of energetic involvement, the body would die no matter what was done to it by medical intervention. During the near-death experience, the soul is likely to be watching the medical team trying to resuscitate the body and decides with the help of family or guides to stay or go home to The Lobby fully.

Within both of these death scenarios, there is no physical pain. The act of dying itself is not painful. The seconds just prior to the soul leaving the body can be painful, of course, but once the soul is out of the organic body, there is no pain.

Should the death experience be fast and unexpected, the exact same rules apply. Should a body find itself in an accident where it is suddenly damaged, the soul will pop out instantly from the organic body. This soul may be confused momentarily about what has happened, and be very suddenly outside of the organic body looking on. These kinds of deaths are usually planned by the soul prior to birth for learning purposes, and a guide will be present for that soul to assimilate the death. Again, a soul may or may not choose to follow the body for a decision to stay or move on. This process is not fear-based in any way. In this situation as well, the second that the soul is "outside" of the organic body, there is no pain sensation at all. Pain is only felt by a soul when it still resides within the body. Your body, while an amazing and blessed kind of vessel with a Universally brilliant and holy brain sensory computation unit attached to it, is still just your vessel. You should care for it, treat it well, and honor it, but it is not YOU. You are a soul. YOU are all of your combined works, thoughts, accomplishments, lessons, hardships, loves, etc. Those experiences make up your soul over lifetimes and lifetimes. Your body is very simply your vessel and home for a lifetime.

After you have departed your body, there is *no one correct way* for the body that has been left behind to be dealt with. Your old body can be buried in a box, embalmed, burned, cremated, spread as ashes in any location, taxidermized, eaten in pie by family members in remembrance (these latter two suggestions were made by Melissa to add humor to what she calls "a heavy subject"), buried under a tree, shot into space, sunk in the ocean, built into a home's foundation, and on and on. My point here is that to The Creator/God, organic bodies of any kind are simply a very elegant and functional invention meant to encompass souls throughout lifetimes on Earth and an uncountable number of other planets and levels of existence in this Universe. Period. The Creator/God does not care how you adorn, tattoo, pierce, or decorate your body as long as you don't prematurely destroy your connection with it by free will choice to leave the playing field of your life (suicide, see chapter 4). Period. All and any religious doctrine rules about what the correct way to deal with the body after death are rules made by mankind to comfort itself after the loss of that soul who left. That's it on the empty body vessel after death.

After your soul has left your body, you will be free to move toward The Lobby. You are, after meeting with your guide, given many options for your next moves. As a soul, you are given the opportunity to look in on those who are left behind in the life you just left. You will be given the chance to spend those days looking in on your family, the funeral, the conversations, the celebrations, or lack of celebrations of your lifetime. You will be able to hear and see the inner conversations of those left behind you. This is offered to all souls directly after death and almost all souls returning from Earth engage in them. In very rare cases, a soul will return and the whole of his or her soul pod will have been already back in The Lobby. This would be a case where the returning soul chose to be an anchor, so to speak, for a whole group of souls and be the holder of a final lifetime where there were literally no remaining family members or close contacts, and that soul will not need to view the souls left behind. This is quite rare and 96 percent of the time, a soul will view everything happening regarding his or her death for the month or so after that death in Earth time.

After the soul is done with any viewing, they get to decide if they need a kind of rest time for rejuvenation, or maybe they travel out into The Creation levels of The Lobby and spend eons of time with their kindred soul pod. If the soul is on a very active and joyous learning curve, he or she may decide to take a short time of rest and relaxation, only to decide to jump right back into a new lifetime on the Earth plane in order to continue the schooling that is life. It is the practice of many souls to reincarnate back into the same soul group who is still living on Earth as a new grandchild or great grandchild in order to continue to learn themselves and facilitate the learning situations of those still within that family lifetime. This is a great tool that is used to help raise up whole soul family groups within short periods of time.

The structure would be that if the whole soul pod group needs to learn about forgiveness, then they might keep incarnating together over and over until every soul in their group has had to learn forgiveness from the viewpoint of the "forgiven" and the "forgiver." It's the most literal way to learn "the other persons shoes" and "do unto others" rules.

I share with you these details because from the point of view of your soul, the natural death of the body is like a graduation of sorts. You return home from the Earth school and get your grades for that lifetime, visit all of the souls you missed while you were gone, have a vacation, and then decide if you choose to return and work at another level of knowledge. From your soul's vantage point, death of the body is simply a glorious graduation and the opportunity to, as Melissa so aptly states, "saddle up and ride again! Whoo!"

I would tell you that fearing natural death is to waste the beauty of your trip worrying about getting back home. You will get home, so you should really take each breathtaking moment in. This is why your soul chose to come and inhabit your body in the first place. It is the experience that you came for, not the fear of those experiences ending. Death is not the end; it is just another chance to begin again.

CHAPTER 14

SHAME

Melissa/Aralamb
Melissa

When I was nine, in July 1973, I learned that all "homes" were not like mine. There was a certain amount of shame in that. I was at a friend's house, which was located about three blocks from my house. We lived in a small New England town as you know, and so, the elementary school was small, and there were not thousands of kids, but only 30 or so kids in my whole class. All the kids knew each other, and so did their parents. Most of the families with kids were extensions of families that had been in town generations before. Most of the family names were the same ones that had put down roots there before the revolutionary war.

I was at my friend Tonya's house, and I can remember standing in her living room waiting while she asked her mom in the kitchen if she could come stay over at my house. I was so excited because honestly, I could not remember a time before that when anyone, other than cousins, had come to stay over at my house. Most of my friends just always had me stay over at their houses. I stood there playing with the crochet tassels hanging over the arm of the couch in her living room. Her Gramma Stanley made crochet stuff, and I loved how it felt rolling between my fingers. It was summer and her mom had closed all the shades, so the house was cool and smelled like zucchini bread baking.

It was taking a long time, so I sidled over to the door casing to listen to the conversation between Tonya and her mom, just out of sight. "No, Tonya, you can't go over and stay at Melissa's." "But why? Come on, Mom." "No, that's it. There are too many goings-on over there. Daddy and I don't feel like it's safe. Melissa can stay over here if you want her to."

And there it was. "The goings-on." At nine years old, I had not really put words to what my home life was like. "Goings-on" would be with me for the rest of my life as the best way to describe what "home" was like during my childhood. I knew that Tonya's house was different, I knew that the bulk of my friends' houses were very different. I could notice things. Small things, really, but they seemed to make all the difference for some reason. Like the absence of so many people who seemed not to have anywhere to live, unless they were living on the floors, couches. or porch of our house. The absence of "crazy" in general. The smells and lack of garbage piling up and stinking in the "garbage room." The absence of "fear." Sometimes what you notice as a child is the absence of certain things in your friends' houses. Now, as an adult, I understand that there is no perfectly safe place to grow up, but there is certainly a wide swath of living styles that are somewhere in the middle. My home was not even close to that middle normal ground.

And there, on that hot July day, with the smell of baking zucchini bread drifting into the room, I felt the burning, stinging edge of embarrassment and overwhelming shame. Shame is a strange emotion. Shame will make you do and say things that are completely untrue. Shame will make you want to hide in full sight or remove yourself from the physical world buzzing around you at any given moment. Shame hit me on that day like a truck loaded with bricks. Shame made me run out of that house and up the street before Tonya even got out of that kitchen. Shame made me see in the eyes of the parents of so many of my friends a "wishing," a "regret," a silent "those poor kids." Shame was what propelled me to look at the floor when I was sent up to the corner grocery store with a list of items and not enough money. The wonderful lady at the counter always sent me home with all of the items, but I knew it was out of pity that she did it. It was a hard, sour, poisonous taste in my nine-year-old mouth, and it took many, many years to finally spit that out.

As I ran out of their yard on that day, I only had about half a mile to walk, and I would be in full view of my house. It was a Thursday evening, 6:45 in the hazy pink summer. I stopped before I got within sight of the house, and sat down on the cement stairs of the Survey Building. I could hear Tonya's mom over and over in my head and her words, "dangerous" and "goings-on." I knew what she meant, I had never really put those words on my home life, but there I sat, at nine years old, alone, not wanting to go home, and knowing that there was a full evening of "goings-on" getting fired up at my house even as I sat there. Drugs, guns, drunkenness, fighting, sex, constant debauchery, and general disorder were always the special of the day.

The National Survey was the business that my grandfather owned. It was at that time one of the biggest employers in Chester. The National Survey had been started by my grandfather's father, Lawton, and his brother, Henry, during the first part of the 19th century and grew to its most prolific state during the Second World War doing top-secret mapping for the United States Government. The Survey was just on the other side of School Street, and ever present in our lives. My mother worked there her whole life, and I don't believe ever held another job. Sally did not ever hold a driver's license, and so walking across the street to her "job" was a good deal for her. Her world was very small, and she seemed to like it that way.

At nine, I still loved my mother in some of the ways that young kids do, or I should say I was still trying hard to. Sitting there on the steps on the back side of the Survey that afternoon, I could not make my stomach stop burning from shame.

I did not know, then, even what shame was. Shame is, and quoted here from Webster's Dictionary: "A painful emotion caused by the consciousness of guilt, shortcoming, or impropriety," and "a condition of humiliation or disgrace." I could not have told you then on that hot summer evening what shame was, but it was nonetheless eating up my insides and clamping down my resolve. I felt guilty about my home. I knew on some level that to the rest of the general public; my home was not right; it was not even generally within the boundaries of what was considered safe and/or good for children. Shame is a particularly acrid pill for a nine-year-old. I think it was then that I "decided" that if my mother and her lifestyle were going to make me feel this way, no one would see it. I would never let any person again "see" my shame. Shame is a very lonely world to live in for a kid. I would BE something different, I would just not take it in. "I" was not her story, "I" was my own story. I would find out that the "stories" that we come from are not so easy to lay down or put away. Some stories will just keep coming back at you again and again until you decide to look at them, love them for what they give you in lessons, and walk away peacefully. The "peacefully" part is the absolute hardest part to grasp. I certainly did not grasp that at nine, and as a grown woman, I still have to choose to grasp that lesson peacefully. There is nothing peaceful about shame. The other issue is that through our lifetimes and reincarnations, if shame is not addressed we will keep piling up more and more diversionary issues in order to NOT look at it and peaceably release it. It is one of the most deep-seated and difficult lessons to work through.

Shame would become a visceral part of my insides

My mother really liked men, she especially loved men who were much younger than her. This would have been of no consequence really, except that some/most of them in the early days, were barely, and sometimes not quite, above the legal age of consent. Often after I had my own son, I would think back to those "daddies, men, breadwinners, dudes," and feel literally and physically sick thinking of my son. What would I say to him if *he* came home at 17 and said,

"Hey, I have found a mentally unstable, alcoholic, drug addict woman who has two small daughters, and I love her, and oh yeah, she's 32, I am going to quit school, work full-time to support them. Don't worry, Mom, I got a full-time job, I am super happy about it. I mean, I'm a senior next year anyway!" Even writing this now makes me feel just, well, shitty for those parents, and sick to my stomach, and there were literally a few sets of them. I know that in the same situation I would have put a stop to it for my own son. I can't believe in retrospect that there were no charges filed or at least an irate mother and father showing up with a shotgun to retrieve their young man from our home. Even as a 9-, 12- or 14-year-old child, I knew that it was not right. I also knew that our house was a perpetual party, which made it all the worse because from the standpoint of a completely sober nine-year-old, they were there for the drugs, freedom, and lack of anything even resembling a normal environment, which would seem pretty shiny and amazing to the average 17–25-year-old male in 1975. For me, as a small kid, that made the shame and heartbreak even more devastating because Sally would share with me her love life, her unabashed belief that "this one really loves me," and it fed the shame. I wanted her to be happy and I wanted her to be sane, but neither of those things was true and it destroyed me inside. Even at nine, I felt 340 years old. I felt broken on the inside because I knew. I knew too much about her sex life, I knew too much about her addictions, I knew too much about her unstable mind. I actually knew that I had more sense and emotional stability than this woman who was my mother and knowing that was terrifying. Perfectly and 24 hours a day, seven days a week, terrifying. The inmates were in control of the prison, the person least qualified was driving the bus. Terrifying!

Aralamb on the subject of SHAME:

Shame is a human emotional construct that was designed by The Creator/ God as a very specific tool by which a soul can make a direly needed correction. Shame in and of itself has nothing to do with the soul before that soul comes into a life. Shame is something that can be freely given from one soul to another when incarnate in the body. Shame can be bestowed upon a soul/person by a society, group, family group, or singular person or event but is usually incorporated by the soul itself. Shame, as you will see, is also completely avoidable as long as it is not attached to a particular event which the soul has perpetrated itself. If a soul/person goes on a robbery spree, ends up in jail, and then joins a gang within the jail and does nothing to address the actions and its repercussions on the souls/persons upon which it has perpetrated, then "shame" is and will continue to reside within the soul's/person's energy body for as long as it takes to come to the truth of its actions.

By the same mechanism, at any point during this time if the soul/ person begins to truly see, experience, and address the negativity of the behaviors and their effects on the souls perpetrated upon, then shame will begin to dissipate and be cleared. Interestingly, shame, unlike having a conscience, cannot be dislocated. Throughout human history, there have been those humans who are so dislocated from their souls that they seem to "have no conscience." While it is true that a soul can dislocate from that energy form which humans would call "the conscience" to a very large degree, "shame" is a part of The Creator's/God's lesson tool box that cannot be fully eradicated in a soul/person who is refusing to learn and grow in a positive direction. Shame will remain in the depths of even the most seemingly hardened criminal types of souls/persons. These soul/persons will deny having any kind of shame for their actions, but on the inside the shame will reside as a constant reminder of a path negatively chosen. There is no escape from that kind of shame. Until the soul/person addresses its actions, the shame remains.

Shame is, on the other side of it, an emotional body which with much inner truth-seeking can be eradicated and released. Upon releasing shame, the soul/person can, and will without very much strife begin to drop away the "old stories," as Melissa calls them. As the "old lesson stories" begin to fall away, the soul/person is freed from the shame. This change is exponential in nature and continues to build upon itself. Shame, which is closely linked with fear, anger, anxiety, jealousy, rage, and a myriad of other "negative" emotional states, is one of the main cogs in the progression of the soul upon the Earth. There are species which have advanced beyond the need to have "shame" as a tool of growth.

Shame is a mechanism by which the soul can, as in Melissa's case, "decide" to extricate or change direction in order to put actual physical, emotion, and or spiritual distance between oneself and the object/person/ soul that is causing the painful physical and spiritual feelings of shame. Shame is a lesson on acceptance, judgment, release, and eventually love and peace.

Once the decision has been made at any age, to "see" and begin to distance the soul/person emotionally from the object, person, or behavior that is causing the soul shame, the next step is *acceptance.* It is often very difficult for a soul/person to differentiate themselves from the person or situation that is causing the feelings of shame. If the shame is felt due to the activities of another soul/person who is close to you, that is, parent, loved one, partner, child, there is so much love mixed with the shame that for the soul/person to accept the situation for what it actually is can be painful at best, and untenable emotionally at the worst. Even so, accepting intellectually, emotionally, and spiritually that the soul/person or situation is shameful, whether you are responsible, or another is, must be truthfully addressed and accepted before the next step—judgment—can be attained. One cannot openly judge a situation until acceptance has happened fully and in a way by which the soul/person cannot slide back into denial or, in some cases, active participation in the relationship or activity which is causing the shame. The truth of the situation must be fully accepted by the soul/person.

Judgment of where the "shame" is coming from is a necessary hurdle and healing cannot happen until this step is taken. When I use the word judgment, I do not mean in the large sense of passing judgment, I simply mean that until a soul/person can openly judge where the "shame is coming from" and judge whether this shameful situation/behavior is that of the soul or an outside soul/person, healing cannot happen.

As a soul/person, you need to be able to judge without anger or hatred where the shame is coming from, and who or what is causing it, even if you yourself are the cause. For example, if you were abused as a child, then the shame that you feel could come from that situation and in order to heal from it, you will need to look and judge very honestly how much of the shame you feel from that situation is your own, and how much is actually due to the actions of your parents or whoever the perpetrator of the abuse was. If you go on to abuse your own children, you will need to look at your own behavior toward them and "see" and "judge" honestly your own misdoings and judge the shame that you feel from your actions, correct those actions, seek forgiveness, and change your behaviors immediately. Finding and judging the roots of your shame is the beginning of soul growth.

Often, as Melissa described in her memory above, shame is held close to the soul and the decision is made to hold that shame close and hard inside of the body in order to never "feel" that shame again. So many adult souls are holding childhood shame deep inside of them, and it colors everything in their life. The issue with this kind of protection tool is that shame often comes from the actions or circumstances of those adults who were in charge of your upbringing. So, when judged very honestly and openly, that shame is not the child's at all. A child should not and cannot be held responsible for the actions of the parent or those around them. Because of this propensity for children to internalize and take full "responsibility" for the shame of the parents or other adults around them, they are literally taking on emotional lessons and hurdles that they themselves did not commit.

A child who is sexually abused by a parent, adult, or family member usually carries the shame and responsibility for that within themselves into adulthood. From a completely energetic point of view, how can this responsibility be their own? Even if the child found some comfort, safety, or powerful sensation in that abusive situation, there should still be no shame for that child as the care for that child's soul was firmly in the hands of the surrounding and/or abusing adult in the room.

Moving into adulthood with this kind of victim shame is one of the most destructive and difficult lessons for a soul to see, learn from, release, incorporate, and overcome. The release of shame, however, is also one of the most vibrant and major milestones in growing the soul from lifetime to lifetime. For the soul of an adult to truly release ALL shame from childhood and release any responsibility for the idea that those around them were behaving in less-than-optimal ways, especially if the child was drawn into those same activities, is the most powerful growth decision that a soul can make. The freedom that is gained from releasing unwarranted shame from the soul's past is immeasurable in nature.

Once freed from the shame, which usually resides in the solar and root chakras of the human energy system, that soul body can and naturally will begin to stand in the light of its own gifts, opportunities, and lifetimes without the shackles and filters of the unwarranted shame energy.

Shame in the human energy field was initially implemented by The Creator/God in order to be a satellite emotional trigger to fear, so that that early humans begin to learn "self-sentience" and survival skills. As humanity moved forward in its evolution and was eventually seeded by off-world species, the shame emotion was diverted to a multilevel situation by the newly burgeoning brain synapses and began to play a larger and unintended role in human interaction. This is why shame can be felt at such a deep level by children for the actions of others. A child inherently knows when actions are socially or personally less than optimal for healthy survival. This is where the unintended shame can come fully into play. That child's brain does not have the ability to fully separate themselves evolutionarily from the shame that *should be felt* by the adults around them, and when not corrected by those adults, children will take that on themselves. It is simple, and yet once that shame is internalized and unchecked, it will go on to color those lives into adulthood and block the full joy of the journey that the soul incarnated to experience.

If your shame stems from "actual" wrongdoings that you, the soul, perpetrated upon yourself or others, then you need to make full amends for those behaviors and actions immediately, so that you can grow, release, and move forward. That would be the balanced and true performance of the tool of shame. Any other type of shame stemming from childhood is not and never was meant to be the spiritual hurdle that man has incorporated it with. From the standpoint of shame that is buried deep within us from our childhoods, adults do and will incorporate that shame "being" upon their own children without fail, unless they root it out from their own psyches. Shame of this kind must be put under the light of the soul and released in order to free subsequent generations from the burden of that internalized shame. Simply put, if you carry childhood shame within you, you will impart that to your own children in some way. You will need to release and heal that shame. You must feel it to do that in entirety.

Finally, it is imperative that any awakening soul determine to let go of any shame they are most likely holding within themselves from their own childhoods. Any "perceived wrongdoing" that was perpetrated to, by, or in front of the child or surrounding adults, that caused the shame must be looked at, felt fully, and taken apart intellectually in order to be completely released. Once this occurs, the soul can move forward without the anchor of shame. There is no need to suffer from the tendrils of shame coloring your lifetime journey. As children, you are never guilty by association with your parents or the adults around you. You are not able to remove yourself, and the shame which should be felt by those adults should not be transferred to you. If you were made to steal toilet paper as a child by your parent in order to keep enough money for cigarettes, booze, and weed, that is not your burden to shoulder in the way of shame. You would have had no choice in the matter and choice is the major issue with shame. As a soul grows into adulthood, the idea of choice becomes pivotal to shame and who should take on its burden. If you find yourself at 16, 18, or 20 robbing a liquor store, that shame is your own and your own responsibility. To understand the difference in those two situations is the lesson.

Melissa

As I became an adult and had my son at the age of 21, I would look at him and wonder how I was to be even an acceptable mother to him in any way. I knew that I loved him in a way that literally made me the second chair in my own life. Suddenly there was something in the world that I loved more than me. I also knew that I had so much shame from my own childhood that was at that time not even fully finished. At 21, I was heading down a road that would ultimately be a probable carbon copy of the woman who I was at the same time so ashamed of. My own mother's life. I was on the path to repeating it with all of its emotional destruction, substance abuse, and maniacal uncertainty. I was looking into the mirror of my own childhood and all of its abuse and shame within the tiny face of my newly born son.

One thought began to run through my mind, and it was this. I never want him to feel the sick, dark, poisonous ball of emotion that was sitting at that very moment in my belly. I never wanted him to look upon me as a 2-, 4-, 7-, 9- or 16-year-old and hope against all odds that someone would not know that I was his mother. I did not want him to feel afraid that I was not mentally well enough to keep him loved, safe, fed, and clean. Looking down into his small pink perfect face on that day, it occurred to me that I did not want him ever to feel any misplaced shame because of me. I did not know how I was going to accomplish that, but I knew what my own shame was doing to me in my life, and I drew a hard line in the sand in order to stop my own shame from coloring his world in any way. I was going to try at least to make sure that he never ran from a friend's house in order to escape a tsunami-sized wave of the shame that overtakes a child when they are isolated from their peer group because of the "goings-on" at home, and all of the debauchery that is inherent in the statement. Hunter gave me the gift of at least seeing the problem with shame. Seeing the shame within for what it truly is, is more than half the battle to begin the healing. Once you can see your shame sitting on the ledge of the gate to freedom deep inside you like a coiling, hissing snake, you can surely begin to know that you need to get it up and out of you. Even if you don't know in the beginning "how" to get that painful hissing thing up and out of your insides, you have seen it and that is so much of the battle won. Once you know it's there inside you, it cannot be unseen, and you will begin to heal without fail.

CHAPTER 15

Addiction and the holes within us

Melissa & Aralamb

I have lived with, grown up with, and wrestled with addictions of many kinds in this lifetime along with friends, family, and acquaintances. Food, alcohol, the need for acceptance, drugs of all kinds, electronics, pornography, entertainment, sugar, discord, hurtful relationships, adrenaline, and victimhood. All of these situations, experiences, substances, and *emotional stances* can be and often are addictive. I myself have often felt completely outside of my ability to control one or more of these addictions, mine being sugar, alcohol, and victimhood. Aralamb will speak about them all, and I want you to remember that you, the soul, living within your body have complete control to overcome all of these issues. Even on that day when it seems impossible to be victorious over that addiction, whatever it is, it is possible. I want to honor both of my parents with this chapter. Sally Crocker and Charlie Gates were kind enough to teach me many, many lessons on addiction within their short lifetimes, and I am thankful for that and them. I dedicate the following chapter to them, their struggles, their triumphs, and tragedy. The love they gave me, which was all-engulfing, and the journey they shared with me, for better worse and every possibility in between.

Addiction: *Devotion to, dedication to, obsession with, infatuation with, passion for, love of, mania for, enslavement to, powerlessness in the face of no matter the consequence; an activity which is to the detriment of the person's life, health, and emotional wellbeing.* —*Websters*

Melissa

This chapter, above all others, has been the hardest for me to write. I have avoided even starting it for months now. I have found every possible reason to "not" sit down and write this chapter. Some of the reasons are as follows: doing the dishes, cleaning, "show holing" multiple dramas on Netflix while eating mass quantities of any kind of sugar I could jam into my mouth, overscheduling myself to the point of exhaustion with a myriad of less important issues, activities, and needs of myself and others. I have been practicing all of these avoidance and procrastination skills in order to "not find out" what Aralamb is going to say about addiction, and in order "not to feel" whatever is going to come up for me around this subject. You might ask yourself why at this late juncture I, even with my relationship with Aralamb, am still able to practice this kind of wasting of time. Well, it's the free will, my friends. Free will allows us all, me included, to engage in minutes, days, weeks, years and even whole lifetimes of unbroken "time wastery" while avoiding the growth, healing, and fear of just choosing differently, going through the pain of the lesson, and coming out the other side of the issue with a fully healed heart, body, and soul. It's really that simple, you cannot and will never be forced to grow. You must decide to grow and choose that path of your own free will.

For whatever reason, I, like everyone else, have spent some time in the tail-chasing activity of avoidance and procrastination. I certainly know better, but still don't do better sometimes. So, for the last couple, or to be honest, three months I have been seeking out 324 reasons why I can't or don't have time to sit down and get the hell on with it already!

When I think of all of the stupid energy it has taken out of me to just keep avoiding the writing of this chapter, I could have had it done two-and-a-half months ago for frig sake! If you can give me a few more seconds of your precious time, I will tell you that to write this chapter lays open some of the most difficult places in me, tears off some of my oldest scars, and really just lays bare a lot of what my lessons for this lifetime have been. I know that so many millions of fellow humans are wrestling with these issues right now, and so I will share my experiences, and Aralamb's thoughts on the subject, so that maybe one more person can shake off the shackles of addiction. Or conversely, at least understand someone they love who wrestles it. Aralamb tells me it is fully a choice, and that if you allow your soul to have complete control of your decision-making process, addictions will have no power over you. Period. I understand this in theory, and I know intellectually at least that it's true, but for me personally, that knowledge often does not stop me from eating one more doughnut behind a closed door at a party when I have already had four or finishing the cheesecake of a stranger at a party because I could not seem to stop eating it. In the words of a fine young friend of mine, "You can't not eat that shit!"

My addiction

When I was a young girl, maybe six, I was so terrified all of the time that I began to use sugar, and food in general, as a way to feel okay. I was not even looking for a way to feel great, I just began to understand that when I was eating anything very sweet, very sour, very salty, I was able to just feel okay. Somehow when I was eating food, usually alone, it was like a cat licking itself over and over. You will see a cat purring, licking itself in a preening, soothing way. If you really watch a cat do this, you get the feeling that it is meditating on itself and in its own world, it's so soothing. Eating for me became like this. I knew that if I was alone, in front of the TV, in my room, hiding in a closet with a jar of grape jelly and a spoon, I could self-sooth with whatever food I was eating. This activity had no nutritional value at all, not then and not now. I have never met a person who emotionally self-sooths with a bowl of broccoli. Please correct via email if I am wrong, but cake crumbled over ice cream and washed down with a Coke is more like it for me!

The eating of any food at that age was really not about hunger for me, it was about survival and feeling good, safe, happy, and loved. I learned much later into my adult life that sugar in particular acts upon your dopamine in the same way alcohol and cocaine does. There are plenty of great books now written on the science of dopamine, sugar, heroin, opioids, alcohol, and addiction, so I am not going to extrapolate here. (There is an appendix at the end of this book with some great books on the addiction to sugar.) I know this now, and it explains why I could secretly eat a whole cake when no one was looking. Once started, I could not stop. I can remember one incident when I was about 10.

Pickles

In 1974, I was 10 years old. By this time, the communal drug and alcohol party was in full swing at home with my mom and her ever-present entourage of partygoers. On weekends I would often visit my dad, who lived just a few miles away in the same township. My dad had remarried and was really digging into his alcohol issues to the tune of a 12-pack of Miller High Life every day. It was July and there was to be a birthday party and BBQ for one of my younger siblings by my stepmother Becky. I loved Becky because she was beautiful and very, very different from my own mother. I did, however, feel strangely out of place within that family unit when I was young, probably because honestly, I didn't remember ever having a family unit. I was just very uncomfortable and completely self-conscious about how I was supposed to fit in. Because of that and the close proximity of my Gramma Patty's house, and my cousins living with dirt bike range of my dad's house, I rarely stayed at my dad's in those years. I would get dropped off with my weekend bag, leave it in my room, and immediately head out to Gramma Patty's or cousins' house, not to return to my dad's often until Sunday when it was time to go back to my mom's. Looking back now, it really wasn't my dad or Becky, it was me; I just couldn't feel comfortable.

On that particular weekend with the party planned I was to stay at my dad's. I was really nervous about having to stay and not go to my gramma's or cousins' house for the night. I woke up in the middle of the night and went to the fridge. The whole house was quiet and dark. I don't know what exactly I was looking for, but what I found was a huge jar of dill pickles. I knew that they were for the party the next day and that I should not open them, but I did. I remember distinctly standing in the dim glow of the fridge light looking at the oversized barrel shape of the pickle jar. The glass was made to look like a big barrel with a white screw lid. I got them open and to this day I can still smell the vinegar. It smelled like heaven to me. I took two pickles and put the jar back. I quietly took them to my bed where I slept at the front of the house and ate them in the dark under the blanket. In the next hour, I returned to the fridge over and over, eating all but two of those pickles. As I was returning and grabbing more, I knew on some level that the jar was getting empty, but I kept talking to myself about the reasons why no one would notice. I kept on arguing in my mind why it was not a big deal, just one more, a couple more won't be missed. My last visit to the jar found me cracking one pickle in half, and leaving two-and-a-half pickles in a huge empty jar which originally held 30 pickles.

I looked at the jar as I put it back in the fridge and realized that I had eaten all of the pickles which were for the birthday party, my stomach was full, and if anyone knew what I had done, I would get in trouble. I didn't know what had compelled me to eat them all, in secret, alone in the middle of the night. At 10 years old, I don't think I could make any kind of sense of it at all, but I knew it was wrong, I knew that I felt shame about it. I knew that I felt out of control about eating that whole jar of pickles. I also knew that for some reason I could not stop eating them. After I ate 30 pickles in the middle of the night, alone under a blanket, I went back and ate 12 frozen ice pops as well. I could not stop. That food was love, it was security, and it beat back the demon of fear that I had, even at the age of 10, been living with coiled in my stomach like a viper. When that snake of fear gripped my insides, sugar, food, mastication would somehow calm it. The viper would lay back and stop biting at my insides, or at least calm down and go back to sleep for some indefinite amount of time. Sugar did this for me. Sugar calmed the monster waiting to swallow me whole. I was a child. I needed to be okay. I needed to just be okay. I was never okay. Food made it okay, at least for a while.

Kool Aid and the Special Paste

In 1978, I was 14. I had plenty of alcoholics in my life, but I was not a drinker myself. This was kind of a miracle because both of my parents would have been at least generally skilled in the art of cocktails by the time they were 14 or 15. I did, however, have an addictive ritual with a certain food that would carry on well into my early 30s and 40s. When I was particularly stressed, which was most of the time, I would engage in what I now can only describe as a chemical and ritual addiction.

Kool-Aid drink mix at that time was a container of basically sugar. Sugar in its most violent and poisonous form. A canister of sugar powered with citric acid, flavors, and red coloring. This drink mix came in a large can. The idea obviously was to dilute it with water and make gallons and gallons of bright colored sugary drinks that were to be enjoyed over a long period of time by many members of a family. It was all very wholesome. I do not remember the first time I mixed up a batch of the bright red paste, but it was as glorious to me as I think that first bump of heroin or that first shot of vodka is to an addict. I took a coffee mug and put four big scoops of the powder into it. I think I was going to just eat the powder, but it occurred to me to put a few drops of water into it and eat it like a paste off the spoon. The first time I ever did this the sharp smell of the concentrated flavoring along with the granular feel of it in my mouth was the best thing I had ever tasted. My mouth waters as I write this, remembering the smell. I began to eat the thick, wet, granular mush off the spoon. It was an immediate and high-octane flavor with a sugar kick to my brain. The color, the smell, the taste of that paste overpowered every lingering sense of pain, fear, worry, and emotional discomfort. The dopamine rush from that intense concentration of sugar was a drug, and it became my go-to. Who needed alcohol when this was available, cheap, and food, right? It was just food.

I cannot count the number of movies I have watched in my lifetime sitting transfixed while eating a brightly colored sugar paste from a spoon. Many times, I would go through two or three batches until my tongue was sore and my stomach felt sick. As I moved into adulthood, I would use this self-soothing addiction any time life got stressful, which it often did. I always felt guilt, shame, and embarrassment about eating the paste. I could not stop eating it once I started, and would often eat it till it was gone or I felt ill. I became a connoisseur of just the right consistency of the mixture. The paste had to be a bit rough with just the right amount of water. Too much water and the paste lost its granular mouth feel. Too little water and it was dry. There was a perfect balance and I would work at the mixture each time till it was perfect. This was part of my ritual.

My favorite drink powder was Cherry Kool-Aid, but it would leave my mouth very red, and it was very acidic. Later on, I found that Tang was a great alternative, it was a bit milder, sweeter even, and after all, Tang has vitamin C, right? It's good for you. I believe in my 20s I was eating three canisters a week, which would add up to about 1,560 canisters of sugar in my 20s alone. I must have eaten 10,000 pounds of sugar paste over that time.

In my late 20s, my father had died of heart-related alcoholism problems, and I decided that my Kool-Aid/Tang addiction HAD to stop. I would be in the grocery store, and come to the drink mix isle feeling like an addict on a street corner trying to score heroine. I would often walk on by and not put a canister of the sweet powder in my cart, only to get out of line at the register and go back to get one. I was so ashamed of this behavior, yet because I was just grocery shopping, no one knew what I was really doing with the powder, or how much I was actually eating. My feelings every time I failed at giving up this addiction were the same: shame, pain, self-loathing, and relief that I would have my substance one more day. Even writing this now is making my stomach tighten up. By the time I was 32, I had decided that I could not keep on with my addiction, so I stopped buying the canisters of colored drink mix completely. As any good addict will, though, I found a work-around. I would buy large bags of table sugar and make sure that I had lemon juice in the fridge. At least once a week I would, when alone, pour table sugar into a cup and squeeze lemon juice into it. I was not eating a spoonful of sugar; I was mixing up a full baking cup of sugar and eating it. I would often go back for a second full cup. I would then make the paste and eat it. It was not as good as Tang or Kool-Aid, but it would do in a pinch. I would pour white bleached table sugar into small bowl, about two cups worth. Lemon juice would then be added until the paste was just the right consistency to be eaten off a spoon.

The very last time that I consumed this addictive substance was when I had first moved out West in 2007. My friend committed suicide, I moved apartments, and I found myself at the grocery store staring at a can of Tang powder. I bought it, went back to my little apartment, and literally ate half the can mixed as paste. I ate so much that my tongue was actually raw and hurt for days afterward. It was horrible and it was the last time I ate the sugar paste. It has been 16 years since that time and I will not go back to it. I actually think of it sometimes, but I will not go back to it.

I wanted to share my incredibly embarrassing addiction with you because you could switch out the words, Tang, paste, sugar, and Kool-Aid anywhere in my telling of the story above, and **replace** those words with crack, vodka, cocaine, heroin, Vicodin, porn, sex, gambling, getting hit, getting abused, victimhood, gaming, candle eating, scab picking, cutting, and a myriad of other repeated and uncontrollable obsessions with the story remaining the same. Addiction....

So why the hell is there such a self-involved issue at the base of addiction? Most addictive intakes or behaviors ultimately end up something that a person finds themselves doing alone. I, for one, always preferred to eat the sugar paste alone. It was MY ritual, and I would not have done it in front of another person either because they would have seen it as weird or inappropriate like the person who can't stop eating candles or the person who keeps on smelling the cats' head or the woman who spent her life obsessed with feeling the shape of her own knees. There is no good reason to do the activity except that it makes you feel better somehow. These activities are self-soothing like masturbating to fall asleep, or a baby sucking its thumb. The behaviors become a problem when they can't be stopped for physical, emotional, psychological, or biological reasons. Addiction is, I think, at its core a repeated activity which gives the false sense of being safe, secure, and happy which one can give to themselves. Addiction is a complete giving away of my own power in my own time. Giving yourself over to any addiction is giving yourself to something that does not care about you. Addictions become our closest friends and lovers who will never leave us, yet the addiction cares nothing of our demise. It sounds obvious to anyone, but an addiction is not our lover or our friend, it is a hole with no end into which your soul falls to be broken. It was heartbreaking to come to this realization for myself and my loved ones. It is, however, the only way to break the addictions, see them and know that you can walk away. To this end, Aralamb would like to speak on the subject.

Aralamb on addictions and the human soul

Addiction is at its most basic energetic system a decision. A choice. Humanity on your planet at this time is trying to abdicate the choice and free will aspects of addiction in order to classify addiction as something that a human is a "victim" of. Humanity is not a victim to any emotional, physical, psychological, or chemical addiction. Addiction is within the full use of a human's free will right to choose to direct the soul's energy fully into a practice which supports a constant negative outcome for that soul. Choice is at the base of all addictive behaviors which are negative in nature.

All addictive behaviors that The Creator/God would deem as having a negative effect on a soul's forward progress are engaged in so that the soul avoids painful lesson experiences. By way of the addiction, the soul literally "chases its tail" for whole lifetimes in some cases in order to avoid the very lessons the soul came into the lifetime to experience.

I am in no way negating the organic fact that a human body can and will become chemically dependent upon substances and behaviors. I am stating, however, that this fact does not negate the all-powerful tool of choice. Positive free will rendered consistently over time will, without fail, kill and eradicate any and all negative addictions and compulsions. This rule is in place concerning chemical, physical, psychological, compulsive, and all other addictive behaviors which become negative to the soul and its growth during the lifetime.

Melissa listed above a large group of substances, activities, and behaviors which can become additive to the body and mind of a human. There are an uncountable number of activities which can become addictive to humans within The Creation. Any substance, activity, or emotional stance can become negative when and if that activity is repeated and is given importance to the mind and soul above all else within the lifetime.

Addiction and the Masking Emotions

Masking emotions are any or all of the negative emotional conditions within the human spectrum in which a human will engage in addictively to mask or avoid the most basic negative emotion in the human lexicon, which is fear. Fear in its most basic form is the emotion that all other destructive emotional addictions rest upon or seek to mask.

Emotions within the human experience are powerful in daily life because the power which is resonated with those emotions interacts directly with the DMF. Negative emotional states, when addictively adhered to, will manifest more of themselves within the DMF just as positive emotional states will also manifest. A human's future possibility arcs will be affected by those negative addiction emotional models as well through the DMF. If a human is addictively recreating real or imagined situations in his or her mind which give them a constant stream of negative emotions, that human is literally manifesting those outcomes through the DMF field and they will experience a self-fulfilling loop of those negative outcomes. Because the human emotional field is so powerful, to become addicted to anger, jealousy, victimhood, shame, hatred, sorrow, and fear will begin to manifest in very destructive ways. The negative "charge," if you will, becomes not only an addiction but also a reality in the life of that human.

Obsessive revisiting of negative emotions will not only become addictive chemically in the brain of the human, but will also impact the gravity field in the DMF around that human within the field, thus beginning to manifest and create actual matter within your lifetime. At the time that this negative and destructive emotional loop is closed and self-sustaining, that human soul will begin to see and feel the self-prophetic manifestations within his or her life. That human will have created the very sort of situations or life experiences that were within the negative emotional fields that they obsessively feared, raged against, or compulsively thought of and felt. The human mind in conjunction with the faith tether is capable of creating in the physical plane very difficult and challenging realities.

Be aware, however, that all of the negative and painful emotions that humans "feel" are simply masking a deeper emotional stance which, as I said, is fear.

Anger

Anger is one of the frontline emotions when it comes to masking fear. As a human, you can cover fear with any number of angry stances. Within human relationships, anger is used as a kind of mallet of control. If your loved one is not doing what you think they should be doing, you become angry. You can become angry because of another's action as well as inaction. Humanity uses anger as a sword of "correctness" as well. If you perceive that another person is incorrect in any issue, or opposes your view on that issue, you will become angry. Anger can be used in any situation. Some examples:

Dan is angry because he gets cut off by a stranger in his morning commute. Dan holds on to that anger for the rest of the day, taking the random act of a stranger personally and lets it bleed into his daily interactions with others.

Marla is angry because her husband just had an affair with his secretary and she can't believe he put the whole family in this situation. She is heartbroken and angry.

Thomas is angry because he is getting overlooked at his job again for promotion; the guy who got the promotion is 25 years younger than Thomas and has a lot less experience. He is angry, he is always overlooked; it's just the way things go.

Beth is angry because her brother is always the favorite in her family. He is the charming one, the funny one, the smart one. Beth is so angry at him and her parents for not seeing all of her great qualities in the same way. She is angry, bitter, and always feels like an outsider.

Seth is angry because his son died of leukemia. Seth cannot see why any God would allow this kind of loss to happen. Seth is angry with his folks for being so goddamned Catholic. Seth is so angry that he can't look at his wife and her grief anymore. Seth has checked out of his life.

Sherry is angry because she is so short. Why can't she just be beautiful and tall like some of the other girls in school? She hates the way she looks and is just pissed down to her bones. She doesn't need to be friends with any of them anyway. She is better off without friends. Even her little sister is taller than her.

Roger is angry because he never got a chance in life. Roger's family was poor, and he never got the help other people get. He is working in an entry-level customer service job, and he is angry. Roger is angry every day at his station in life and his prospects. Anger drives his every decision.

Cassie is angry because she gave up her whole life for her kids and they couldn't care less. Now in her 70s, she is bitter and angry because she never did the things in this lifetime that she really wanted to do. Anger has been her companion for most of her life, simmering just below the surface. She feels out of time and cannot enjoy any of her children's successes because she is angry and bitter about her own choices.

Samuel lives with anger every day. Samuel is angry with himself because his wife had told him every day that she loved him for 20 years. Samuel was never comfortable with that kind of mushy talk so when she told him she loved him, he would just smile at her. When she died last year, Samuel tried to tell her that he loved her while she lay in her hospital bed, but she was already gone. Samuel prays every day that she knew how much he loved her. Samuel is angry at himself for letting his ego get in the way of his love for his wife.

These kinds of scenarios could be listed in infinity for billions of souls in billions of lifetimes. The point I make here is that every one of these situations can be changed at any moment. Remaining in anger is a choice. Remaining in bitterness is a choice. To remain in these states of being over lifetimes becomes a habit, an addiction to those feelings, that energy, those chemicals coursing through your body. To be freed from the powerful emotion of anger is a choice. You can free yourself by choice alone. In the end, anger is a masking emotion for what is just underneath, FEAR.

If your "go-to" response to situations large and small which do not go your way is anger, you are masking fear. Fear of not being enough. Fear of being left behind. Fear of being victimized. Fear of not being as good as the soul next to you. Fear of being weak. Fear of being alone. Fear of losing what you have. Fear of being unworthy. Fear that others will reject you. Fear of being deemed less than. Fear of letting go. Fear of losing your identity. Fear of being taken advantage of. All of these fears are at the base of the destructive emotion of anger.

I am not intimating that you should never feel anger. I am, however, pointing out that anger in its most useful form is something that is used only in immediate or dangerous situations that can be or need to be rectified immediately. Anger is not a state that a soul is meant to linger in for more than a few moments or days at the longest. If someone steals your car, by all means, be angry for a short amount of time. After that short amount of time, you will need to quickly move out of anger and begin to put your experience into a more useful framework in order to move forward and continue your life without letting that one situation set the course of years of your life. Humans also tend to have a large area of anger where they store up all of the situations, or experiences that made them angry into one large reservoir of anger which they can feed upon exponentially over a lifetime. This is a complete waste of a lifetime, and becomes a completely addictive situation. You will become addicted to the adrenaline of anger and fear. You will be allowed via free will to conduct this type of lifetime if you wish, but why would you if you can choose and learn differently.

This exponential buildup of the anger reservoir might look like this. In the 10th grade you fell during a soccer game and had to sit out the State Championship games. Your leg healed well, but when you were 20 you wrecked your mom's new car and had to work a summer to pay off the repairs. You earned a college degree in education, but decided after two years of teaching that it wasn't for you. You have a large student loan for a career that you aren't in, and because of that you cannot move to Hawaii like you wanted to become an organic farmer and you are now 30, way too old to start a new life. You are a middle manager at a telecommunications company and play fantasy football on the weekends while your girlfriend scans FB and basically ignores you. You are angry for all the bad breaks and wasted time. In your mind you have no options, and you are just so angry about it all. Some people get all the breaks, and you aren't one of those people. It all started with missing those friggin State Championships in 10th grade and you are simmering and angry about it all. Nothing is going to change, and you shut down.

This kind of anger reservoir is what so many souls have and keep adding to. In any or all of these situations, choice is the one change that could have and can have a life-changing effect on the soul. As a human soul, you never need to accept any situation, as all situations are within your powers to change or adapt to as you see fit. That is the Universal Law of The Creator. There are no exceptions to this rule. It is your right as a soul. Adding to and keeping close to your energy field all of this anger becomes a lifetime addiction, and it will become a self-fulfilling prophecy which will dampen or kill all that you dream of being or doing in a lifetime. Choice is at that core of the situation in every moment of your lifetime. Choose to move past and free anger. Anger feeds fear which feeds addictions.

Grief and Sadness

Grief and sadness are real and difficult emotions. Human souls will feel grief and sadness usually when there is a loss of someone, something, some situation, some want or perceived need. Grief and sadness are the body and mind's mechanism for paying attention to and paying tribute to what was lost, damaged, or changed. This is a natural emotional process. When the grief and sadness process is worked through correctly, a human will move from the sadness to the brief stay in anger and on to gratitude for the lessons, experiences, and positive memories of that person, place, thing, or situation that was lost or damaged. To stay within the grief and sadness emotional process for extended amounts of time is masking fear. Grief, sadness, and anger are movement emotions that are meant to be worked through and transmuted to gratitude.

Losing a loved one to death or change is one of a human's most challenging emotional lessons. Losing a partner in love, children, parents, beloved pets, friends, colleagues is a shock to the physical, energetic, spiritual, and emotional body. There is no way around the process of grief and sadness in these cases. A human soul must work through these emotions and eventually come to that healing and release place of gratitude for what was experienced and knowledge that nothing and no one is actually lost. I want you to remember that I am framing all of this information on emotions, addiction, and the holes within you in the framework of The Lobby. When you lose a person, pet, or any other sentient being, they will have moved on to The Lobby where you will actually and literally meet again. This fact is not mythology. This fact is written in the energetic signature of this Universe. If you have lost a loved one, pets included, you will have the opportunity to be reunited. This Earth School is, at its most basic, an opportunity for you to grow and learn through blessings and challenges to the point where you see even the challenges as blessings in your journey.

Grief and sadness are not to be added to your reservoir of anger. Moving through these emotions is true growth. When you have a loss, you will feel pain, anger, sadness, grief, and fear. You are meant to feel all of those things, and any other emotions that come along with them, and then you are meant to turn your attention to everything joyful and positive that you got from the person, pet, or life situation that is gone from the Earth School. You are meant to understand that no ending is forever and that the actual law is that everything has no ending. Every soul is timeless and, therefore, will be reunited with those who share a frequency together.

Understand that every soul you come into contact with in the lifetime you are living will be made whole to you again at the time of your crossing to The Lobby. All of the unattended emotions and experiences will be addressed at that time between you and your loved one, pets included. You will be able to make it right with exes, loved ones, pets, perceived wrongdoers, and enemies alike. The idea is that during your time upon Earth, you learn the lessons these interactions teach you, forgive, release, and move forward. Addictions keep you, as a soul, from this very important phase of learning. Addictions keep you in a closed loop of experiencing the fear, anger, guilt, sadness around those learning situations, while the addiction itself poses as a way to escape those very lessons. Addiction is not your ally.

Addiction is the place where souls go to avoid the growth they came into a lifetime to experience.

Upon your arrival to The Lobby, you will have an opportunity to see and feel your addictions as well as those around you in perfect peace and truth. You will know both sides of the story in perfect truth. If you or a loved one is dealing with any kind of physical, mental, emotional, psychological, or chemical addiction, it is imperative to get assistance in getting out of that loop. I will have Melissa list many books in the end of this one, which I would encourage souls to read.

I would close this chapter with the idea that addiction is not insurmountable no matter what you may believe. Free will is the overriding principle in a soul's lifetime, and with choice will come freedom. You can choose to leave the loop of addiction and self-sacrifice. No incarnate human soul is meant to spend a lifetime addicted and blocked to the true nature of themselves.

CHAPTER 16

Sally's Goodbye

Melissa

By the time my mother was diagnosed with breast cancer in 2001, I had been in contact and working with Aralamb for about 12 years. Mom knew nothing about my connection with Aralamb or any of the work we had done with people. I had never shared it with her. I was terrified of sharing it with her. She knew that I was sensitive in a psychic way, but she did not have any idea who I really was as a grown person, and she certainly did not have any idea that I was working and writing with a channel named Aralamb. I think that the one true regret I have as far as my relationship with my mother goes is that she never truly knew me. I could not let her see who I truly was in this lifetime because she was just brutal and judgmental about so many things, or I perceived her to be. She was not stable, and it was just never something that I felt I could divulge to her. My relationship with her was, for the most part, what I still refer to as "tap dancing." I only let her see what she could handle, or maybe what I could handle. You might say that I was making that decision for her, but trust me, at that time, if I breached her line of comfort, she would let me know immediately. This was just the reality of her. Now, years later, I have to take some responsibility for her not knowing me. I was a coward, and I should have just been who I was with her, and I didn't. I was just too scared of her. Even as a grown-ass woman, I was just scared of her.

With Sally, as long as you did the interpersonal dance that she expected to see from you, with no curves or changes, you might be okay for an interaction or two. She could not and would not brook any kind of free thinking, free will, or boundaries from my sister and I even into full adulthood. I was trained to be hypervigilant to her needs at a very, very young age. In order to survive, you had to be able to know what was going on with her emotionally at all times. She absolutely refused to respect any kind of emotional, physical, or intellectual boundary. To this very day, I struggle with having healthy boundaries. We were not allowed to have any thoughts, feelings, emotions, or movements to ourselves where she was concerned. You just were not allowed to have any emotion or thought even begin to creep its way onto your face or into your body language that she was not reading, judging, and digging at, real or imagined on her part. It was exhausting. As a result of all that, as an adult, I really never went down School Street to visit her unless there was some holiday, party, or event at which my absence would have been noted. I was a diligent daughter in that I did not leave her fully alone, but I would not engage her if I didn't have to. It was just too damn exhausting and because I was grown, and a mother myself, I did not have the ability or energy to tap dance correctly for her anymore. She knew it, I knew it, and somehow it made us both sad. It was, I think, like the very end of a long marriage where the combatants love each other but they can't care anymore about trying to make it right by one another. That is where I was emotionally in 2001. I loved mom, but I just could not "do it" with her anymore. I couldn't. The Creator/God hears these things as they run through your mind.... You know, the "God hears everything" sentiment, from my experience, is truth.

Mom called me at work one afternoon in late spring of 2001. It was late May, I think, because I can remember the smell in the air of moist damp earth and pending greenery. She wanted me to come have a drink with her after work. I had not seen her in a while even though we lived in the same small town. She kind of begged me to come down "for just a couple." She sounded different than usual, which made me say "sure, I'll stop after work" much faster than I normally would have. She had divorced Bill at this point, and was living with a man 20 years younger than she, who had gone to school with my sister. To this day, I believe that she knew she had cancer, and threw her whole life away in order to sort of "sow some wild oats." She felt she was running out of time.

Later that afternoon, I arrived at mom's house after work, and she was mixing drinks. Coffee brandy, milk and vodka. Two shots of coffee brandy, two shots of vodka, and a splash of milk shaken in big green glasses. I walked into the kitchen, and she was standing on the far side of the counter. I think it was a Tuesday, and she was dressed and ready like it was a Friday night from 1979. She always liked to dress up a bit, but she was wearing skinny jeans, a lot of jewelry, makeup, and her hair was done. She looked good in that "cougar" kind of way that people refer to. She was overdressed for drinks with me on a Tuesday, and I had not really ever seen the look that greeted me on her face before. I was a professional at "reading" her mood, but this face I could not read other than to say it was not good. She seemed, for the first time in decades, like an eight-year-old girl who was really scared. She seemed fragile, helpless, and vulnerable. I was totally unaccustomed to seeing or feeling this from her. As was my training from childhood, I was trying to determine via body language, energy, eye movements, and a myriad of other things just what her mood was. Aralamb tells me that this "hypervigilance" learned in my childhood was actually some good, if not painful, training for later being able to hear him for channeling. I guess it was a kind of boot camp for psychic awareness. I know now that there are many less painful methods of training your senses. Before I could fully figure out what was going on with her, we both took a big, long pull from those (double, might I add,) White Russians she had mixed up. That alcohol hit the back of my throat and I have to admit, it tasted so sweet and good. It was the taste of home for me. It was the taste of mom. To this very day, if I really want to remember what I can carve out as good from my mother, I will have a snifter of Allen's Coffee Brandy. I just sit, drink it, and listen to the ice clink in the glass. I don't even put milk in it, I just drink it straight. That experience, even now, makes me so melancholy for her presence even though her presence was so often painful. It is a very strange sensation to miss a person who was so brutal to you most of the time....

I was just enjoying that sensation when she said, "Melissa, I have something on my chest that I want you to look at." Without hesitation, I got up from the kitchen counter and followed her to the bathroom.

In the bathroom, she pulled her right shoulder out of her low-cut top and exposed her upper breast and collar bone. What I saw was sort of indescribable and was, what the oncologist would later describe as, "only seen textbook photos from the late 1800s."

My mother stood there looking up at me while I looked down at a silver dollar-sized open wound on her chest. The wound was somewhat concave and looked as though there was living molten lava on the inside. It was as if there was some kind of growth that was not skin, not bone, not fatty, or muscle tissue. The growth on the inside almost looked crystalized in some way. The spot was oozing and glistening. It smelled a bit like hamburger that was going bad after a bit too long in a broken refrigerator. I had a hard time not gagging or making the face people make when they are horrified and beyond words. It was a big as a small plum, and it had broken the skin on her upper chest. It was like something from a movie. It was large and she had been keeping a bandage on it to keep the oozing under control. On some level, I knew physically that I was looking at cancer which had been left to its own devices and had broken the skin in an eruption. For the first time since I had held her head in my hands when I was 10 while she cried about a lost love, my heart broke for her. I looked at her, looking up at me. She wanted me to tell her that it was a rash. She wanted me to tell her that it was just a weird patch of skin. She wanted me to tell her that it was going to be okay. Mom wanted me to be the parent that she had never had. She wanted me to tell her we would get it fixed up, no problem. The problem was I knew better right down to the core of my bones. I knew that this was not going to just go away. Tears started to roll down her face and I held her. I asked her how long it had been there and how it started.

She said, "Well, it started as just a little bump under the skin, like a pencil lead or a grain of rice." "How long ago did you find the little bump, mom?" She replied, "About three years ago." I wanted to scream at her! Three years ago?!?! Are you fucking kidding me??? You have watched this grow into your body and break the surface for three fucking years?!?! But I didn't say any of that. I knew it was too late for that. I just held her and stroked her head like a little child. Something inside of me finally broke for this woman. I heard and felt something inside me break. I can't tell you what it was, but I know that it broke and would never be the same again.

There is something so visceral about love. For a million reasons, I knew I should not give a shit about this woman who had abused me. She had been miserable, mean, brutal to me for most of my life. Alcoholism, mental illness, meanness, craziness, controlling, bipolar, and raging with strange jealousy, but she had also loved me in some way. And in that moment, looking into her eyes, I was so hurt for her. She was such a broken human. She was my human, and she was so damn broken. The other issue for me was that Aralamb had told me so many times that we choose our parents in order to learn lessons from each other. I held her, we cried. I told her that it was going to be okay, and that we need to call Sissy, and we need to get it looked at. That's all, we just need to get it looked at. We called my sister. Mom couldn't talk to her, so I did. Mom sat at the kitchen table drinking her White Russian while Stephanie and I made plans for her to come to Chester right away. Sally sat at the kitchen table looking out into space past the front porch on out toward the swinging foot bridge which spanned the Williams River. I told Steph I would call her when I got home. I told her I loved her. I told her I would see her in the morning. Mom's boyfriend came home from work, and we finished our drinks as if nothing had happened.

The next morning, I called the last doctor that my mother had seen about five years earlier for a throat infection. The doctor was a really nice lady, who had a clinic in Springfield about 10 miles away from Chester. She agreed to see mom at 1:00 p.m. that day. Steph was on her way over from New Hampshire and was going to meet us there. When I picked mom up, she was kind of overdressed again. It made me so sad to see her dressed up too much. I think it made her feel like she had her armor on, like she was in control. I was driving a really old Land Rover at that time. We drove the 10 miles without talking much at all. Mom was scared, I could see that she was, but she was being very quiet and almost angry that she had to rely upon me in this way. Sally had never gotten her license. She had, for my whole life, been completely dependent upon others to get around. When we first pulled into the clinic, she would not get out of the truck. She just sat there. Looking back now, I wish that I could have been more loving and softer with her, but I was just so jaded to her insanity that I could not make sense of her suddenly "needing" me. I was being good to her, but in the way you might be good to a wild animal that you find on the side of the road who had been injured. You want to help, but you are also scared to be bitten. When she finally got out of the car, she was visibly terrified. Sally did not ever go to doctors. She literally had sworn them off years earlier.

We sat in the waiting room, and I filled out her paperwork for her on the clipboard while she directed me. Because this was just a preliminary family clinic, the waiting room was full of tiny children and pregnant women. This was not any kind of specialized office. This was literally just "strep throat" kind of place. Finally, when Sally's name was called, we stood up and went into Dr. Stearns's office. She was glad to see mom and said, "Sally! I am so glad to see you, it's been too long." She then said, "Okay, let's see this rash you have." When Dr. Stearns pulled the pad off of the wound on mom's chest, the look on her face was something way outside of professional. She said, "Sally, I wish you had called me sooner." She looked up at

276   Melissa Gates-Perry

me accusingly, and I said, "Mom just showed this to me yesterday for the first time." "Well, Sally, I, uh, I am going to need to have you see Dr. Kuraht later today. He is a specialist in this kind of thing, and this is just past what my specialty is." My mother looked at her and said, "It's a rash, I just need some cream." Dr. Stearns was so sweet she grabbed Mom's hand, "Sally, you know this is not a rash. You need a specialist for this. You should have come in sooner." She ushered us out to the front desk and made a phone call herself. At that very moment, Steph walked in with her two little baby girls. All of our eyes came together at once. Dr. Stearns was on hold waiting to speak with Dr. Kuraht. I could hear her almost yelling at his secretary, "No, I need to speak with him now! I am sending my patient to his office in the next five minutes, and she needs to be seen today. Please let him know that and have him call me as soon as he gets out of his appointment." She hung up the phone and hugged mom. "You will like Dr. Kuraht, Sally. Do as he recommends. Please." She hugged mom, Sister and I. "Melissa, keep me in the loop please." "I will, Dr. Stearns." I will never forget the look of complete pity that she had on her face as she watched the three of us with those two little girls leave the waiting room.

When we got to the parking lot, it was warm bright spring sunlight everywhere, and mom broke into tears. "I am not going to that doctor, he is an oncologist, I don't need to see him." She was getting pissed. Steph, mom, and I sat down on a picnic table that was across the parking lot on the lawn and sat. Mom cried and finally I said, "Mom, it won't hurt to go see the doctor." Steph's two little girls were playing in the grass while we sat there. Steph was crying and holding mom, and I was literally trying to come up with what the strategy was going to be for getting mom two miles down the road to the oncologist's office. It felt to me like having a tiger in the back seat of a Volkswagen Bug, trying to figure out how to get it down the road and to the vet without getting killed. We all sat in silence together for minutes, a long time, I can't tell you how long now. Finally, I said, "Mom, let's just go see the doctor, chances are it's not a big deal." She agreed. I think that at that point, Steph and I were both so emotionally sideswiped by the sudden emotional turn that our relationship to this woman, our mother, was taking. Mom was so mad. She climbed up into my old truck, and we rode the few miles down the road in silence toward Dr. Kuraht's office. Sister followed in her car with the little ones.

Dr. Kuraht's office was clean, quiet, and filled with people who were there for various levels of cancer treatment. On the way into his office Mom was muttering about how "she did not need to be here with these people." I just ignored her and told the nice lady at the front desk that Dr. Stearns had sent us. I will never forget the woman behind the desk, she was a girl that I had gone to school with some years earlier and the look she gave me as she scanned between me, mom, and Steph was what I can only assume is the face that the women who were loaded onto the boats to escape the Titanic gave to their men they were leaving behind. If pity and sorrow have a definitive face, that was it. I hoped that Mom did not see it.

Dr. Kuraht was from India. He was just about mom's age, I think. He was probably 53 at the time. Mom and I followed him into a small room where he just looked at the both of us. He said, "Sally, I am glad that you are here, but I talked to Dr. Stearns, and I am not sure what, if anything, I can do for you at this time." I looked at him and thought that was the worst bedside manner that I had ever seen in my life. Mom stood up, and was ready to leave. "Wait," I said, "don't you want to see it?" Mom was standing and tears were running down her face. It was so terribly surreal. The doctor was like, "You're screwed, you're done, I don't need to see it, go home, you stupid woman." He didn't say that right out but that was the gist of his speech.

He looked at both of us, looked up at mom, and I could read on his face that he was mad at her. He said, "Sally, let's have a look at what you have here. You have children, yes?" He began to unwrap the bandage, while talking to her all the while about how he could not understand why she did not see a doctor when she first found the tiny bump. He talked to her about her children. He told her that he knew that she was a smart woman, and he could not understand why she had waited so long to get the wound looked at.

All the while, he was taking one of those wooden sticks that doctors use to poke at a skin tumor or a wart to be removed, and poked at the wound. As he was poking it, the outer skin of the concave growth was breaking open a bit and it basically smelled like rotten, dead meat. It did not seem to hurt mom, and she was not answering his questions, but simply looking past him out of the window. I will never forget that because it was like she was seeing something amazing out that window, even though it was frosted completely over for privacy. I did something then that would become the only thing I knew how to do from that point onward, I grabbed her hand and gripped it firmly. I just held her hand, well past the point of it being awkward. I held it well past the time when I think she wanted me to. From that day forward, Steph and I just started holding her hand whenever things got really rough or really scary or just plain unmanageable, and they did and often.

Dr. Kuraht broke my mom's stare when he said, "I need to biopsy this, and I am going to do it now." She immediately started crying and protesting. I squeezed her hand tighter and said, "Mom, it won't be a big deal. It will be fast, over, just like that." She looked at me, angry, aggressive and then resigned. "I want you to come in with me." She looked at the doctor and said, "I want Melissa to come in with me." He agreed and we went back out to the waiting room.

About 10 minutes later, the nurse came back out and led us to a room at the other end of the building. It was a small operating theatre, but the tools were all still from I would say the late 1970s. Clean, serviceable, shiny, and sharp. The operating table had that shiny black covering that dentist chairs had in the 1960s. It looked like a movie scene in a way, and although it was post 2000, I could not help but think it looked scarier than it needed to.

Mom was physically shaking with fear, she would not take off any of her clothes except her shirt, which Dr. Kuraht did not like, but agreed to. He laid mom on her back and began to lay cover and tape all around the outside edge of the wound. He applied a strong spotlight to the area and then began swabbing acrid-smelling bright orange Bacterize all over the site. I was holding mom's hand and sitting on a stool directly across from the doctor. It occurred to me that I might faint, or dry heave, but I didn't. I kept my face devoid of emotions. I realized that mom was looking directly at me, and I needed to hold that face so that she would be okay for the biopsy. I was holding the kind of face that civil war nurses gave a soldier right before the morphine kicks in as a doctor saws off a limb. It is a totally fake expression of happy non-concern, but the face holder and the expression receiver does not care as it is meant to keep a calm façade in the face of pain and horror.

Dr. Kuraht picked up a three-inch scalpel, brushed it with Bactrian, and began to cut away in raisin-sized bites at the growth. Mom started to silently cry and then she began to moan in a low keen, which finally ended in an open weeping. I held her hand and cooed at her like she was a small child. I kept telling her he was almost done. After what seemed like a chasm of time, he said, "Okay, Sally, I need one more sample and we will be done. You are doing great; I know this is painful." I have never seen anything like the tissue that he was removing from her body. Later this doctor would pull me aside after a surgery to remove the growth from mom's right breast and say: "You know, Melissa, most people have not seen this kind of cancer break the skin and grow since the late 1800s. I had not seen this in 25 years of practice since my med school days in books, and the only reason that they showed us these photos was on the odd but slim chance we would see it in person. I wish your mother had come in sooner. I found a lot of metastases in her lymph and lung. We will talk later about that when she is awake."

After the day of the biopsy, mom only gave permission to have the lump removed. She would not agree to any other treatment of the cancer that had been growing in her body for more than four years. We would find later that she had cancer in her lungs, brain, breasts, and spine. She was offered treatment, which the doctors told her would give her 10-plus years from her time of diagnosis, but she declined. She was 53 years old and decided that she was not going to have any treatment at all. Those next three-and-a-half years were filled with a strange knowledge that she was dying, but we were not allowed to have any opinion on the lack of treatment. She acted as if nothing were wrong with her and that included going back to her same old emotional and alcoholic issues. She never had any kind of epiphany that Sister or I saw. My sister and I just agreed between ourselves that is she was going to decide to leave the Earth in this way, we would just stand and hold the space for her to do so. She was brutal to be around on many days and it was exhausting. We held her space anyway, and simply waited with her as she drank, smoked and emotionally wrestled her way toward her own end. She leaned into her addictions and with her diagnosis had yet another reason to do so.

For the next three-and-a-half years, my sister and I did our best to respect mom's wishes. After she had the growth removed from her chest wall, she did not want to talk about the cancer at all. She absolutely would not talk about any of it. In the days just after the surgery, I received a barrage of calls from various doctors and medical professionals who wanted to know why she was not going to get treatment, saying, "She is so young and has so much to live for." After a month or so, those calls stopped and life with mom went back to the general modus operandi that it had always been. She would become violent if anyone even asked her, "How are you feeling?" In my case, I felt like at least once a month I should ask her if she wanted to at least talk about treatment or options maybe. She was not interested in speaking about the situation at all. Looking back now, I think that her life had been so fearful and painful that the diagnosis was almost a relief to her in some strange way. I think it was her way of saying, "Well, this is where I get to get off this fucked-up ride." The mental illness, alcoholism, and ruined relationships, I think, had become too much for her.

She spent her life, I think, trying to seem "normal" when she was strug-gling every day. The cancer was her out.

So, as the months passed, Steph and I did our best to just "pretend" that everything was normal. She would have it no other way, but in doing that, she was, I think, sort of "let loose" to behave even more badly than was her normal boundary. She became so out-of-control emotionally abusive on certain days that it was hard to be around her at all. It was a brutal situa-tion. Over those three years, the cancer spread completely unabated by any kind of intervention and due to that, certain facial features and physical aspects manifested. I know that for me one of the hardest to see was that mom's left eye seemed to change shape and become a bit protruded. She acted as if nothing had changed, and just applied more makeup, which was so, so difficult to watch. Steph and I were always expected to "see" her in the light that she expected, but now her need for us to confirm that she was "looking good" or "really sexy" was just so heartbreaking. Her breathing was becoming very labored in that last year as well, and she would just keep saying that she had bronchitis. She would make us go through whole conversations about how, "My bronchitis is bad today, Melissa, I think you should pick me up some cough syrup for it." If I did not confirm for her wholeheartedly that she had bronchitis, she would become enraged. Finally, in the winter of 2004, I was worn out by it, and I just didn't see her much between March and May. I could not hide the fact anymore that she was obviously just growing sicker and sicker without wanting to comfort her in some way, and she would have none of that. So, I stayed away for a few months until her live-in boyfriend at the time came to me at work early in the morning and said, "I think you should call your mom, she didn't get out of bed today. She says she has the flu from her bronchitis." It was 7:30 in the morning on June 20, 2004. I was in the process of planning my son's graduation from high school party for that coming Saturday night, and I had been thinking about taking that coming Friday off from work. I picked up the phone which hung in the production room of the salsa company I worked at and called her.

When she answered, I could tell that something in her had shifted hard. She was abnormally out of breath, even for her, and she said, "Melissa, I think I have picked up a flu bug which is making my bronchitis worse." I asked her if she needed me to bring her anything from the store. "Yes," she said, "I would like some Wonton soup and ginger ale." Wonton soup and ginger ale were always our families go-to for any kind of illness, hangover, or just comfort, so I said, "I will bring it to you at lunch. Do you want me to come hang out with you for the afternoon?" I asked her this very carefully because usually if I showed any sort of concern about her, she would get mad. On this day she said, "Yeah, that would be nice." "Okay, I will be over at lunch. We can watch some TV if you want." When I hung up the phone, I knew that something had changed for her, and I knew that the life clock that we all live by was suddenly moving its big hand for her. My stomach knotted, and I just stood there with my hand hanging on the phone. I picked the telephone receiver back up and called my sister.

When I arrived at mom's house, I had to let myself in. She was lying on the couch coughing hard. I walked in with the groceries, dropped them on the kitchen counter, and studied my facial expression in the mirror before I walked into the living room. She looked so much worse than I had remembered from seeing her weeks earlier. She had lost more weight, and her facial structure had changed even more around her eye. I cheerfully said, "Hey, I will make you some soup." She said great and went back to watching TV. We sat on the couch for some time, her coughing hard and drinking and eating a bit. It was Monday afternoon by now and I was not sure what to do. I felt like I should stay there with her overnight although she had not asked me to and I knew better than to bring it up. At about 5:00 p.m., she said "Melissa, I think I want to go back up to bed for a rest." I helped her up to bed and said, "Hey, why don't I stay tonight in case this flu gets you up in the night, then we won't have to bother Billy?" Billy was her live-in boyfriend with whom I worked at the salsa company. She looked at my face as if she was searching for even a hint of sympathy or worry in my expression. When she saw none, she said, "Yeah, that might be good, if you don't mind." "Of course not," I said. "I will see about getting some dinner." That was the first time I had seen my mother not have a drink in the evening, and it was pretty much the last time she ever got up out of her bed again in that little 1786 house on School Street.

During the following five days, over 75 people came to that little house on School Street in Chester, Vermont, to say goodbye to my mother. Sally had a million and one friends throughout her life. In those final days, they all came through to say goodbye to her and she presided over the celebration, for the most part, from her bed as the grand dame of the occasion of her leaving the planet. The whole week-long party was facilitated by my sister, myself, our Grandmother Peggy, and my dear lifelong friend Linda, accompanied by a large bottle of cherry-flavored liquid morphine. People stopped by day and night to sit at mom's bedside and talk about whatever their life connection was and had been with her. Flowers, food, bottles of booze, candles, plants, cards, letters, and jewelry were all brought as what seemed like offerings to a kind of queen. The truth is, although Sally could be brutal, crazy, angry, out of her mind, and a very difficult person as a parent, she was at the very same time, dazzling, artistic, loving, charming, terrifyingly psychic, and empathetic when she wanted to be. She was the glowing commune leader, she was the life of the party, she was, I assume from the long list of lovers past and present who showed up to pay homage, a memorable lover, as well as having a pirate's ability to drink anyone under the table. She had accumulated a large cast of family, friends, ex-husbands, partygoers, sycophants, and believers who all wanted to hold her hand and say goodbye. It was truly a five-day procession of and celebration of a truly complicated and gorgeous soul's imminent departure.

My sister and I played the consummate hosts to this final week-long party as we had always done in our lives for mom. The procession lasted well into Friday night of that week, and then on Saturday morning, it trickled to just the final few family who would be there on the "train platform" to see her off.

Throughout the whole week, I had been talking with Aralamb about her final leaving of her body. I wanted to know if he was going to alert me when the time was upon us. He told me that in her leaving I was going to be witnessing something that would later be written into this very book that you are reading. I trusted that he would let me know what was happening with her. Sister and I had been sleeping on the couch together for that whole week, and it was hard. Mom was upstairs in her little room, taking long raspy breaths, and we were getting up every two hours to give her more morphine for pain. I could not tell you what part of her was actually hurting, but by the end of her life, we knew that the cancer had moved to her brain, bones, spine, lungs, and facial structure, so I assume she just hurt all over.

At about 3:45 a.m., on the 27th of June 2004, my sister and I laid on the couch in the dark downstairs. We were both unable to sleep and talked about how hard it was to sleep now as adults in mom's house. This was the same house that we had grown up in, but there were so many really terrifying memories there that it was even still hard to sleep there. We talked, cried, and held hands until maybe 4:45 just pre-dawn, when my mom's boyfriend came downstairs and said, "You girls might want to come up and check on your mother, she is breathing pretty badly." We both jumped up in a kind of exhausted stupor in the pre-dawn light and headed upstairs.

When we entered the room, Aralamb said, "It's just about time for her to fully come over. I am going to let you see some parts of it, and when I tell you to let go of her hand, you must do as I say. It is not your time, Melissa, so you must let go of her hand when I direct you to." I silently agreed. Mom was lying in the dark with a small night light on, and some light starting to peek grey into the room from the window at the end. Sister laid down on her right side, and I laid down on her left. We all three lay on our back. Mom's breath was very labored, and her breaths were coming very slowly and with long intervals in between. She did not speak to us, or open her eyes at all. We all lay there on our backs. For a moment, I caught Steph's eyes and we both silently cried and grabbed each other's free hands over mom's body. I mouthed the words, "It's okay, it's okay" a couple of times to Steph and we lay there. The two of us, mom between us.

Laying there in the pre-dawn light, Aralamb came to me and said, "Her soul is going to be leaving over the next 20 minutes or so and I want you to see it happening. I am going to let you see it, but when I tell you to, you must let go of her hand. It is not your time to leave and although you may feel compelled to, you cannot follow her." I agreed again. I will not lie; I was stunned in so many ways at what was going on. My heart was breaking and opening for her all at the same time. In the next 20 minutes, as my sister dozed on the right side of Mom, I witnessed the following:

Directly above the bed and encompassing the whole roof, a dark blue, white, and opal swirl of energy began to open. It looked something like a reverse vortex of water going up into a drain. All around the edges, fuzzy (almost watercolor painting)-looking beings in long robes began to appear all around the edges. Each of them was holding out their hands and holding on to the next, creating a circle all around the outside of the vortex. Aralamb told me that there were 35 or 40 of them. These beings were called healing soul transfer facilitators. He said that because mom had lived such a difficult journey in this life, she would need to have a comforting rest time for her soul when she passed over. These "facilitators" were constructing a kind of "soul cocoon" for her when she arrived. I think I must have been holding Mom's hand a bit hard because I was stunned at what I was seeing and feeling. There was an indescribable feeling of reverence for these beings and the energy they were emitting. Mom's breathing was becoming more labored beside me, and just as I noticed this, a thin, blue, white sparkling line of energy began to float like some kind of electrical web from her breastbone up into the energy vortex above the room. It was as if this silver chord was being sucked up into the vortex slowly and rhythmically emptying her body. Aralamb said, "You are witnessing her soul leaving her body and being safely caught in her rest space."

Tears were rolling down my face in rivers, and it was not just from the loss of mom but from the profound energy coming from the beings catching her soul energy. As her soul continued to move upward, the vortex of the cocoon changed colors and radiated with what looked like the soft pink heat lightening you can see when it's humid in the summer sky. At some point, I realized that the cocoon seemed to be holding more of the light of mom than was left within her body. I heard her breath soften and slow markedly. I turned to her and could "see" physically that she was almost gone. The energy light that makes a person "them" was almost gone. As I looked back up at the energy vortex above us, the beings were sort of beginning to pull the cocoon around the edges like a sack being pulled shut. I could feel the tug of the pull myself, in my body in my own soul. Aralamb said, "Let go of her hand, Melissa." I couldn't at first, it was like being a little child when your parent or grandparent has your hand crossing the street. You sort of can't let go of the safety of that feeling. It's like a lock, you know you are loved and safe. Again, Aralamb said, "Melissa, you need to let go of her. She needs to go and it's not your time." As he said it, the beings turned just for a moment and looked at me. They actually looked directly at me, and I felt nothing but the vast expanse of love that is at the core of our Universe. As they looked away, I let go of mom's hand. At that very moment, the whole of the energy vortex opening began to pull its way above the bed and disappear. At the same time, the sun had come up outside the little window on School Street, and as I turned my head toward mom, I could see and feel that she was gone. When I say gone, I mean that everything that had made Sally Ann Crocker light up in this world and "be" was gone. I touched my sister's arm on the other side of mom and her eyes opened. We held hands over mom's body while she took about 15 more long labored breaths in her final 10 minutes. She was gone and the memory of her soul leaving this world would change my view of it for the rest of my life. I believe now that her most precious gift to me was letting me see her soul leave the planet. I had literally been allowed to see and feel her go.

Aralamb tells me that when a soul leaves a human body to cross over to The Lobby, or back home from where we come, that soul can leave in a number of different ways. In my mother's case, she needed to have a rest period. She had lived through a painful death and had endured a life of emotional, psychological, addiction, and psychic pain as well. She was received in a way that was comforting and restful for her soul. At the time of her departure from this Earth plane, she needed some energetic care, almost in the way a person might go to the ER at a hospital. Her soul was literally "tired out" from the painful learning journey she had been in within this lifetime. From that day forward in my life, I was no longer afraid of death in the same way. I am in no hurry to have this life end, but I am not in any kind of fear about what happens when it's time to go. Aralamb has always said that the whole crux of The Creator/God's Earth School is about how well you live your life, learn your lessons, and then cross back over. My mother's soul stayed in that protective cocoon for about four Earth years after her death. I would often check in with Aralamb about her progress with the healing. With that experience, I learned that birth and death are just gateways back and forth for our souls to grow, learn, and experience love. There is no actual end to any of us. I am forever indebted to this lovely, brutal, gorgeous, terrifying soul who was my mother for letting me "see" this in the most concrete sense. Her passing freed me from one of the most visceral fears that humans deal with—the fear of death. Now, I am sharing her experience with you. Fear not, you are a loved soul.

CHAPTER 17
Choice/Decisions/Victimhood/Reaction

Melissa-Aralamb

This chapter is the shittiest in my opinion because it fully and completely spells out the fact that everything in your lifetime is actually in your power to control. Yup, that's what I said. All the things you experience every day are within your control. Yes, that means everything, and personally as a real human living here on this planet that information scares the crap outta me. Mostly it scares the crap outta me because it means any time I am being a victim to my own Cowboy Hat self-talk, all of the can'ts, shoulds, have tos, don't want tos, I'm screwed, you're screwed, I will never get outta this, I'm done, I'm dead, I'm too stupid, you name it, all of that is fully within my power to *choose* around. Say I am sealed in an underwater cavern and sure I will die at any moment, or at least in the next week from any manner of bad shit, (including but not limited to: stinging eels, cave bugs, starvation and caffeine withdrawals, exposure, and on and on), it is still within my power to decide how I want to feel about it, thus changing my experience of said disaster. It sounds so simple, and in theory, it is, but let's face it, scary, often painful things happen to us all, and it's a hard concept to grasp when you are waist-deep in the proverbial shitter, that you are in full control of how you feel and what you do in response to said "shitter".

Being stranded on a desert island with just enough water and coconuts to keep you alive for the rest of your life can be either a living hell without end, or a very long and fruitful meditative retreat where you teach yourself the art of minimalistic survival and shelter-building, simply depending upon your choice, emotions, and decision-making process about that situation.

Hell, with enough time and the right mindset, you could build a watertight boat out of palm fronds and sail to South America, write a book about the experience, get a movie deal, and build a meditation center on that same island to retire. Blessing, right? Or you can sit down in the sand and wait to die of thirst, sunburn, and the acceptance of certain death. That's it. And from what Aralamb tells me, it is all your responsibility to decide how you are affected, feel, and what you do about it. If you had broken your ankle on that same island and died a long death from exposure, still, how you leave the planet in that situation is really up to you.

Terrifyingly then from what Aralamb says, you are truly and fully in control of your experience here on the planet. You are responsible. There is no one, no situation, no event to blame. The amount of joy or challenge you feel by everything, and every person around you is YOUR choice. What?!?!?! That has to be bullshit right? I can't do anything about people getting cancer or being hit by a bus and ending up in a wheelchair. I can't solve the world peace problem, and so many good people get killed, maimed, or abused every day. Don't even get me started on animal rights or global warming, pandemics, it's overwhelming.... I am not in control of any of that horrible crap....

Aralamb

Melissa is using humor to describe to you what she calls the "scariest, shittiest Universal rule." That rule is the sister to the Rule of Free Will, which is choice/decision/victimhood. Choice/decision/victimhood are the implements, the tools which The Creator/God gave us all to work through lifetimes. Without the full ability to understand choice/decision/victimhood and free will together, you are not fully able to use these tools. Simply having free will is not enough to keep you stable and learning through challenging life lessons. The true power is in the choice/decision/victimhood side of the free will rule.

As you know, free will is the Universal right given to all sentient lifeforms by The Creator/God of this Universe. This is the way in which no sentient being possessing a soul can truly be subjugated by another. Every soul has the inbuilt ability to use or not use free will.

You may wonder how I can make this statement of fact when there is a long history of slavery, physical abuse, and tyranny on a grand scale upon Earth throughout its past eons and even now. Souls on the planet have been and still are enslaved by the color of their skin, their ethnic belief systems, religious systems, and economic and gender labels. Humans have been in one form of a slave mentality from their seeding to this time. The simple way to look at this issue is that the treatment that you receive from any person, institution, religious body, governmental body, corporate body, state, or group, should it be negative, is fully within your control to respond and react to regardless of how direly you perceive that situation.

If you see, envision, and feel emotionally that you are a victim, you will be a victim. A person who is held captive, tortured, maimed, and eventually whose body is killed is still in the most organic way possible attached to and in control of how the mind, soul, and energetic body reacts to and gives over to the fear of that situation. I use this very difficult and fearful example only to make you understand that any situation, no matter how challenging, is meant to be a learning and growth experience for the soul who is experiencing that challenge. Every situation you will ever face, up to and including the death of your body, is there for you to be a learning experience within the lifetime. You are meant to learn and understand your own power to choose how you experience and react to all situations. This lesson is powerful. The action of simply choosing your emotional and intellectual response gives you the power to create.

Beatrice

Beatrice was the most beautiful baby pretty much anyone had ever seen when she was born. Unlike a lot of babies who looked like "shriveled spider monkeys," as her father would say, Beatrice was just perfect. Carl and Cindy had tried to have children for years and Cindy was quickly coming to what she was considering her last chances to conceive as she approached the age of 41.

Carl had already imagined that he and Cindy would adopt the next year if they did not conceive. Carl loved his wife dearly, and it did not matter to him whether they conceived a child together or not as long as they raised a family together.

In November of Cindy's 40th year, and three months before her 41st birthday, they found themselves once again sitting together in the fertility clinic for a final IVF treatment. Cindy and Carl had three eggs left to try insemination one last time. They were, at this point, not really hopeful, but felt that they owed it to themselves to use this one last try and then move on to adoption. Cindy knew that the odds were very low of conceiving at this point, but she wanted to carry her own child if she could. As usual, sitting in the tan outer office, looking at magazines and trying hard not to be nervous, tears started streaming down her face. Carl squeezed her hand and said, "You wanna go? You don't have to do this, Cin, it's okay." She loved him so much, he was her heart. "No, I am good, just emotional, it's our last shot, babe." They smiled at each other through tears as the nurse came and announced they were ready.

Nine months later, Cindy gave birth to two beautiful babies. Beatrice and Adan were not identical twins but were clearly brother and sister. Both babies were born naturally and with no complications. They were a miracle for Cindy and Carl from the moment they found out they had conceived. By age three, they looked so much alike that people often asked if they were identical twins. Both children had a beautiful combination of the features of their mother's South African family, and Carl's German heritage, beautiful brown complexions with hazel green eyes and striking chestnut hair. Cindy had quit her job as a nurse to be a stay-at-home, mom while Carl remained in his position as an IT manager with Cal Med.

When the children were about to turn four, Beatrice began to show signs of what Cindy thought might be a nagging and recurring flu or cold bug. Adan seemed fine and never contracted the cold. Six months later, the pediatrician was suggesting that Beatrice might have a blood disorder which she was immediately tested for. Beatrice tested positive for this disease, Adan did not. In the next year and a half, Beatrice became more and more ill while Adan thrived.

Five months before Beatrice's sixth birthday, Cindy and Carl sat by her bedside in the Children's ICU at Cal Tech Medical Center and watched their beloved baby draw her last breaths. Beatrice died with her parents holding her hands. Cindy and Carl had lost their baby girl after trying so, so hard to have her.

Aralamb

In this painful example of what seems like an untenable situation, there are still choices/reactions/victimhood issues to decide upon. It is understood that the initial phase of grief is to be experienced and worked through. However, the amount of time that the soul stays in that phase is in the end up to them. Does the family fall apart? Does the loss of Beatrice put a wedge between Cindy and Carl? Does the loss of Beatrice become an unspoken emotional wall for Adan to deal with? Does this family unit heal? Do Cindy and Carl begin to self-medicate to "deal with" the pain?

Or, do they try to understand that Beatrice may have agreed to come into the lifetime with them and die in this way, in order to help them learn lessons about love, acceptance, faith, perceptions of failure, family, helping others through tragic events, acceptance, gratitude, release of fear and anger, self-control, and healing? If Cindy and Carl were to transition at one point from fear, pain, and victimhood to choice/reaction, the painful situation can and would be transposed into something of great joy, gratitude, and growth for them and Adan. This is a very hard transition to make, but it is what the system of choice/reaction/victimhood is all about.

Through that process, all things in your life that you perceive as good, bad, immovable, unchangeable, impossible, or untenable can and will be traversed with grace and wisdom. The fact is that through free will and choice/reaction/victimhood you always have the power to choose what you think, feel, and do in any given situation. There is no caveat to this powerful rule. No matter what you face within the lifetime, you and you alone have full control of how you will react.

Lottery

Stan, his wife Molly, his daughter Lora and her 10-year-old son Jayden all lived in a six- room trailer outside of Cheyenne, Wyoming. Stan drove a truck for a large grocery chain and was on the road five days a week all over the Rocky Mountain West. Stan's wife worked part-time at the local Methodist Church as an office administrator. Stan was well past retirement, but Lora could not live on her own, and Jayden needed them. Lora was struggling with a methamphetamine problem. She was 26, could not hold a job, and needed help caring for Jayden. Lora started her drug use in high school and Stan often felt guilty that he had been on the road so much. Lora had run pretty wild and now she was often in trouble with the law. Stan and Molly had put Lora into rehab facilities in Denver two times, but she never stayed the whole time and would be back in Wyoming, crashing on some other meth head's couch. Jayden had a learning disability and needed special care. Stan lived for his grandson and so he kept on driving to support them all. He and Molly often talked about the fact that they were probably enabling Lora to continue her drug use, but frankly they didn't know what else to do except love her and hope she saw the light eventually.

On Tuesday afternoon, Molly came home at 3:30 to find Jayden sitting next to his unconscious mother on the couch watching TV. Molly knew that something was going to have to happen for Lora. Lora's drug use was ramping up again, and it broke her heart to see Jayden staring at a TV while his drug-addled mother was passed out next to him. Molly had been, up to this time, unable to get through to Lora; she was never good at confrontation and Lora had always been able to just run over her, even when she was young. Molly's cell phone vibrated in her pocket; it was Stan. "Hello, my lovely wife!" Stan always called her his lovely wife. It still made her smile. Even now at 67, she was still lovely to him. "Where are you, baby? Are you gonna be home early tonight?" "Yes, I am going to stop in town, pick up a lotto ticket, and some pops for Jayden. I love you, Mol." "I love you, see you soon."

At 8:15 a sheriff's car pulled into the yard. Bob Denisen was an old family friend. Molly immediately thought he was there because of something Lora had done. Luckily, she was still passed out on the couch and would not make a scene no matter what. Molly met Bob on the front steps to the trailer and smiled, "What's brought you out, Bob?" Bob held out his hands and drew hers in, "Molly I'm so sorry there has been an accident."

One month later, the services for the only man she had ever loved were over and done. He had been cremated and buried in the small plot they had procured for themselves years earlier. Molly was barely able to keep herself in an upright position and had not gone to work for the last few weeks at all either. Molly was strong and healthy, but this was the most painful loss she had ever known. Stan had been the rock for all of them. From what she was told by the Sherriff's Department, Stan had stopped at the Seven Eleven just five miles from home, turned his pickup towards their place, and been t-boned by an oncoming oil transport tanker. Stan was killed instantly and pinned in the truck. The Sheriff's Office had given her a box of what the EMS people had cut off him, his wallet, some of the items from the glove box, and one shoe. Molly had not gone through this box, but had read its contents from the side which had been listed in a blue Sharpie Marker. She had been unable to stop thinking about where Stan's missing shoe was and had sobbed the day she realized that the missing shoe was not going to be found.

Lora had disappeared after the funeral and Molly and Jayden had not heard from her in four weeks or so. Molly had never felt so helpless in her life, and that didn't even begin to cover the huge hole looming in her chest after her husband's loss. The coffee pot in the kitchen hissed as Molly carried the box to the kitchen table and sat down placing it in front of her. Taking a paring knife, she slowly cut the tape and began to open the box. Stan's red and black flannel overshirt came into view first. It was torn and had dark stains, which Molly knew were most likely dried blood. She pulled the shirt to her face and breathed in the smell of her husband. Tears large and hot fell from her eyes and into the shirt. She knew it was no good, but she inhaled again and sobbed into the ruined fabric. She pulled out the contents of the box, and pulled out Stan's wallet last. That wallet had survived so many winters, flat tires, and miles. She opened it and smiled at the photos of them on the motorcycle, them at 30 smiling out on their future. They had so much fun and so much love. There was a picture of Lora and Jayden on one of Lora's good days. Behind the photo of them on their honeymoon in San Francisco was the lottery ticket that Stan had purchased just before he was in the accident.

Molly threw it down on the table and shook her head, wiping tears away. Stan was a dreamer, always a dreamer. The next day she drove into town to get groceries. She had not been sleeping much, and she needed to figure out what she was going to do. The trailer was paid for, but she was 67 and Jayden was most likely going to need help for the rest of his life. She was not able to work full-time, and Lora was still not back from wherever she had run off too.

Molly pushed her cart out of the grocery store and at the last minute grabbed the lottery list of the past three months' winning numbers. Jamming it down into her purse, she headed home. Lora came home that night, thin, gaunt, and out of her mind. Molly drew her a bath and made her some dinner. Molly knew that she could not start in on Lora when she first came home, or she would just run off again. Molly felt helpless and trapped without Stan there.

After Jayden and Lora were both in bed asleep, she sat in Stan's chair and pulled out his wallet which she kept in her purse. She loved to look at the pictures and know that she was holding the wallet which he had kept close to his body every day for over 40 years. It was a connection. Molly knew that his soul lived on somewhere and he knew how much she loved him. She flipped through the photos and came to the lottery ticket. She pulled the winning numbers' list from her purse and began to seek out the dates on the ticket Stan had bought. Molly sat in Stan's chair and cried quietly as she read the numbers to herself over and over. 12-5-18-37-9-24-1.

Ten years later, Lora stood with Jayden and many members of the Methodist Church while the minister said prayers over her mother's grave. Lora had enlarged the photo of her mother and father on the motorcycle which her dad had carried in his wallet all those years. That beautiful photo was now standing on an easel near the graveside. Lora could not remember what happened those years ago when her father had died in the accident, she had been too messed up. She had run away and not returned for a month at least. Lora would never know what led her mother to make so many decisions after she found that lottery ticket. For whatever reason, her mother just started changing everything about how their lives had been lived up to that time.

Lora remembered first that she had been ushered to a one-year program which she was unable to leave in San Francisco. She had gone kicking and screaming like some harridan, but her mother forced her with a steely will Lora did not know she possessed. She sat with Lora while she signed herself into the program with the caveat that she would be on lock-down for a full year by her own hand. Jayden and her mother came to visit every other week until she began to get clearheaded. The three of them would cry and look at photos of them all together. Lora was so angry at her mother initially for "growing a set," and she was so mean to her in those first months. Molly had just quietly and powerfully ignored her threats and horrible name-calling on those visits and continued to be strong in the face of Lora's addiction.

After six months, things started to change for her in rehab. It was as if she finally got clean enough to forget what was wrong and begin to see what was right. After rehab, her mother and Jayden had rented out the trailer in Wyoming and the three of them moved to a small house in Scottsdale, so that she could enroll in college. Lora wanted to become a veterinarian and Arizona State had a great program. Molly took care of Jayden and enrolled him in school while they lived there for her school-ing. After her graduation from the veterinary program in Arizona, Lora took an internship at a large animal hospital in Davis, California, attached to U.C. Berkley's extension. Lora had met her husband, Owen, there and Molly had loved him. Owen knew all about her meth problems and had been a really big support for her to stay clean. All of this was possible for her and Jayden because her mother had kept that news of winning the lot-tery from her and put into place all of the safeguards needed to allow her to get the help she needed and heal. Lora pulled Jayden closer to her and sent a prayer up to her mother and father in thanks. Lora had only a hazy drug-riddled memory of that time 10 years earlier, but she knew that her mother had decided that Lora was going to survive and thrive no matter what, and Lora could never thank her enough for that.

The morning after Molly found that the lottery ticket was a winner, she went into town without waking Lora and Jayden up. She quietly walked into her church, it was Saturday morning, and the church was quiet except for the alter area of the main chamber where she knew she would find Pastor Christian in meditation. Sitting down next to him, he smiled at her and they both sat in total silence for a good long while. Finally, Molly told Pastor Christian that she had found the lottery ticket and believed that the ticket was a winner worth $17 million. She told him that she felt horrible guilt because Stan had died to get that ticket and she didn't know what to do with it. She didn't want Lora to know about it because that kind of money would surely kill her. Pastor Christian took her hand and said, "You know, Molly, this is a blessing and what you might do is think about what you can do for your family and thank Stan for his part in what could change Lora's and Jayden's lives for the better. You will have to be careful, get some assistance, and don't tell anyone for now. I have the number of an attorney who can help you to set things up for you and your family. This can be a blessing for you."

From that day forward, Molly began to look at this as a blessing and do everything that she thought Stan would do if he were still alive to heal and help their family. For the first year of Lora's rehab, she didn't even tell her daughter how the money had come to them. She told no one except for her lawyer and Pastor Christian. She lived her life as it had been in order to take that time to decide what she should do, how to help her family the most. Because she was deciding to move forward in honor of Stan, she felt closer to him and knew that he would be proud of her. Getting Lora clean, educated, and on to a good life was her only mission. She took joy in that mission and the results of choosing wisely and having faith was paying off.

After the funeral was over, Lora, Oliver, and Jayden decided to leave that old trailer as it was and continue to rent it out. The place was a good reminder of the hard times, the losses, but also the idea that her mother had grown, changed, and moved forward from her father's death and that people can change. She had changed. She had become the person she was supposed to be. She would never begin to be able to make it up to her mother, but she would be a good mother herself. Lora put her hand on her flat belly and smiled at Oliver. She was pregnant with her and Oliver's first child. Ten years had changed so much in her life. As they drove away, she mouthed the words "I love you, mom and dad."

Aralamb

Molly had two options. The first would be to spend the next 10 years of her life mourning Stan and letting her life fall to pieces because he was gone. Within this time, the money could have been squandered away in meth, purchases made to fill the void of Stan's death, junk for Jayden, and anything that Molly could throw at Lora to try to fill the hole the addiction held within her. Molly could have let Stan's death become enshrined in the pain of his loss and the complete destruction of her family unit as it was left. Molly could have chosen/reacted and continued her perceived victimhood until her death and most likely Lora's early death. Now, I am not suggesting that Molly losing Stan was not one of the most monumental and painful life lessons that she would encounter. Loss of a loved one to illness, accident, or any of the other myriad of ways to experience loss, is painful and often debilitating. I am stating, however, that the Free Will Rule allows the human soul to use the choice/reaction/victimhood tools to either stay in the pain forever or, in Molly's case, decide to make a change of direction in reaction to that pain and loss. This is a truly good example of the whole of the learning process in action for the human soul. Molly suffered a near fatal loss emotionally and chose to feel the pain and react in a way that fully extinguished her victimhood option. In her choice to leave victimhood behind, she changed her daughter's and grandson's life as well. They learned the lesson through her valiant choices.

I would encourage you to look at your own life. Try to see the areas in your life where you are currently giving yourself over to victimhood and reaction. You are most likely giving your power away to any number of situations, people, addictions, choices, and living situations which you could transmute into powerful learning tools if you could just begin to see those situations within the choice/reaction/victimhood framework. What you think, feel, and react to *is your choice*. Period. Be mindful of what you are creating in your life by ignoring or using these tools.

CHAPTER 18
Three-Minute Rule (TMR)

Aralamb

The three-minute rule is something that I coined as a term for Melissa when we were talking about the purpose that a soul may come into a lifetime with. Every soul comes into lifetimes with something that I refer to as the Three-Minute Rule in place. As a soul begins to put together a plan for an upcoming life while in The Lobby, there are many obstacles, talents, experiences, both painful and joyful, that can be added to the lifetime possibility arc. There is always free will, so the possibility arc is similar to a general guideline which will offer opportunities for growth, both ecstatically happy and painfully challenging. The opportunities can be taken one after another by the soul within a lifetime, or that soul can completely ignore the possibilities as they come and live fully apart from the possibility arc for that lifetime. Most souls will combine a mixture of both engaging with the predetermined possibilities and, using their free will, ignore others. The soul is in complete control of the experience of that lifetime. For example, a soul may set up the possibility of becoming a doctor of medicine, curing a major disease, but after being within the lifetime decide to become an organic farmer, raising a large family, and living a loving life. Both of these opportunities are valid and have no consequences to the soul at the life meeting after death, other than lessons learned and experienced. The soul simply chose to ignore the possibility arc of the first and forge his or her own path. This is the beauty of The Creator's/God's system of free will.

That being said, there is the Three-Minute Rule. The TMR, as I will call it, is for lack of a better analogy, a specific point in time that a soul will place within its coming lifetime a three-minute *special* time which affects not only the soul but other souls around it. The TMR is an opportunity to exert an exponentially large amount of positive energy into the fabric of humanity, and the soul does not know when the TMR opportunity is to happen. You could almost liken it to a bonus symbol in a video game. The TMR is a fully faith-induced situation by which a soul can gain many levels of growth and foster exponential growth for others around them. Because a soul does not know "when" in its lifetime the TMR opportunity event is to happen, it is imperative that the soul stay within the lifetime to its natural end, whatever that might be. If a soul chooses through self-harm of the physical body to "leave" the lifetime, that soul may be missing the TMR opportunity event that the soul placed within that lifetime. In this way, the TMR which is not fulfilled will have wave-like energetic ramifications for the souls who were to be assisted by that TMR event. Every soul comes into lifetimes with the TMR event options in place. No soul knows within its lifetime, which "three minutes" might be the most important in the life's timeline. You do not know which three minutes *you* literally came onto the Earth plane to engage with for your growth and that of others. You do not know what the impact of your three-minute event may have. This is another reason why souls should also grow and exercise the intuitive and faith components of the soul within a lifetime. The examples below will explain the TMR further.

Example 1

Joe

Joe is a janitor at University of Miami Hospital. Joe works the evening shift six days a week from Wednesday to Monday. Joe is 32 years old and has a wife and three small children. Joe is very depressed, and for the last few weeks has been concocting a plan to kill his wife and children, and then himself. Joe cannot seem to make ends meet, and he has not had enough sleep in months. To save money, his wife, who he loves, works days and he is at home with the kids during the day catching naps when he can. At night, his wife comes home, and he comes to work at the hospital. This schedule has been in place for three years and Joe cannot see any reason to continue. Joe cannot see any way that his life will change. Joe's depression is blocking him from seeing any way out of the overwork, overtired, underpaid situation he finds himself in, and his depression has now gotten so bad that he feels that taking his family and himself out is the only answer. He feels that if they all "leave" together, they can all be at rest.

At 4:30 a.m. on a warm Thursday morning in July, Joe is about to punch out and go home. He knows he will not be back again to this job or this place. He has made his decision and today will be the day they will all leave this world. Joe is resigned to this plan of action. As he has a few minutes left on his shift, he decides to go through the 5th floor lobby and up to the roof to see the city before he leaves for home and smoke a cigarette. He gets off the elevator on the 5th floor and heads for the stairs to the roof, moving silently through the geriatric unit. As he nears the door to the roof stairs, he hears a voice coming from the last room of the hallway. "Young man, young man, can you help me?" The voice is so, so soft and barely audible that Joe considers ignoring it, and then closing his eyes, his hand on the door to the stairwell, exhales in a deep sigh, and turns toward the room.

Artie is a 92-year-old ex-accountant with terminal cancer. He and his wife Ruth had lived in Miami since 1932 when they moved down from New York City just as the hardest years of the Depression were hitting.

Artie and Ruth already had three children when they arrived in Miami, and were to have five in total. Artie had been invited by his uncle that year to bring the kids down and be a "bean counter" for his uncle's investment company which had at least survived the initial hit of the 1929 fall. Artie packed up Ruth and the kids onto the train from Grand Central to Miami. They could not afford a cabin, so they all sat together sleeping, eating and holding on to each other through the long exhausting trip south.

Joe walked silently into room 596 and saw Artie propped up on the bed in a semi-sitting position. There was one small light shining next to the bed stand. Artie smiled at Joe and said, "Oh, thank you, young man. I am so thirsty, and I can't quite reach the water there on my table." Joe smiled at Artie and said, "No problem, man." He walked around the side of the bed and poured Artie a small cup of water. Artie could not quite hold the cup in his hand as his IV lines were numerous and strapped down at his side. Joe held the cup up to the old man's lips and he drank very deeply. Artie motioned him to get more, and Joe refilled the cup and helped Artie to drink again. "Thank you so much. Will you sit for a minute? I know you are not a nurse, and you don't have to, but I need to talk with someone for a bit, and I want to talk to another man." Joe thought of saying no, he thought of the cigarette that waited for him, then he thought, I will never be back here again, so what do a few minutes matter? Joe said, "Sure" and pulled the stool close to the bed. Artie relaxed and smiled a bit. He exhaled slowly and said, "I'm Artie, what's your name, son?"

Joe told Artie his name, and waited while the old man sat silent with his eyes closed for a minute. Joe figured he was asleep, and started to move as if to get up. Artie's hand moved just an inch and laid cool, surprisingly strong old fingers on his wrist. Joe sat back down. Artie's eyes opened and he said, "You know, Joe, I never really believed in all the religious hocus pocus that my Ruth did. Ruth, she always wanted me to believe, believe, have faith, she would say, God is good she would say, there is a plan, she would say. Well, I guess I did have faith in a way, I had faith in Ruth, and she had faith in God, so I guess that is where I left it. Artie laughed at his own joke and coughed, catching his breath with a long rasp. Thing is, Ruth was a beautiful woman, we were married for 70 years. Seventy years!" He almost yelled it, and Joe was a bit startled by the sudden sound coming from the old man. "Seventy years and five children. My God, I am not sure how Ruth ever put up with me for all that time. Ruth is gone now; she died 10 years ago from the cancer. Not the kind I have, but cancer. Sometimes when I wake early in the morning here, and at home when I was home, I could feel Ruth sitting on my bed. I could just see her, beautiful and young like she was when we were struggling for money and all the kids were young. And here I am, old and crusty, but still she would look at me just like I was then. Like as if she can come in and see me as a ghost and she is with me and still loves me." Joe wondered how long this was going to go on. He wanted to leave, and yet he didn't move. Artie had that hand laying on his arm.

Artie went on. "The thing is, Joe, I am leaving very soon from this world, and I have to tell someone about something that was in my mind at one time. I have carried the burden of this way of thinking, and I never told anybody. I have carried the shame of it, and I have to tell someone, a man, another man so that I can go meet Ruth and my maker with a free conscious. You know what I mean, Joe?" Joe wasn't quite sure what he meant, but he shook his head yes and continued to listen. Artie was staring past Joe and into space, in that looking-back-at-the-landscape-of-his life kind of way. It was as if Artie was looking back through the 92 years of his life and trying to narrow in on a specific time. "I was 25 when Ruth, Sadie, little Art, Lucas, and I arrived in Miami. We moved into a side room at my uncle's house, and I started work for him. He had a one-room accounts business in the neighborhood, and I was his first and only assistant. There was no money pretty much anywhere at that time, but my uncle kept saying that once the mess in New York was cleaned up, there would be money again, and we would be poised to be the people who could keep tabs on it. You have to understand, Joe, that in 1930 accounting as a trade was a kind of new thing, we were bean counters. We were so poor. I was working 15-hour days and basically not getting paid at all. I was just working for our room and board, which was a bedroom in my uncle's house. My Aunt Leyfa was a Russian Jew and she cooked nothing but cabbage and potatoes, both of which she grew in the backyard of the house. I got so stinking sick of cabbage and potatoes. To this day, I can't enjoy an eggroll because of Leyfa and her cabbage!" Artie laughed and squeezed Joe's hand, coughing and sputtering. Joe tried to give him more water, but he waived it off.

"You know I was a pain in the ass back then. I was always complaining to Ruth about how we worked and worked and there was no money. I was a real pain in the ass, Joe. Ruth would look at me and say, 'We have the cabbage, we have each other, and that is all we need, Art.' It turns out that she was right, Joe. Ruth was right. I loved Ruth because she always saw the big picture of life. Ruth had faith that things would always change and get better no matter what. That was my Ruth." Joe again made a move as if he would get up, and Artie again held his hand firm on Joe's arm. "So, the thing I want to say to you, Joe, is that in 1933, my son Lucas and my uncle got malaria or some kind of fever, and they both died. Many folks died that year in Miami from the flu. I will never forget those months following their services. We had no money and Ruth was so aggrieved by the loss of our son that she was not eating, and she was pregnant with Nora. My uncle had left me his house, and the care of his wife Leyfa who was a kind soul but lost by my uncle's death. Leyfa sat in her chair and stared at the garden in the backyard after my uncle's death for days not moving. I was going to the one-room office every day in the heat, alone, feeling the loss of my son, my uncle, and knowing that there was no way out of the horrible life in which we found ourselves. I began to think about how to get us all out of the situation together. I began to think we should all just leave this life together. In my misery, pain, and depression, I began to think about just ending it all for everyone in my home. I was a failure in my mind, and I could not take the feeling of loss anymore. You know, Joe, that time during the Great Depression, a lot of great men took their own lives, and many took their families with them. Hmm, great may be the wrong word, successful men maybe, yes, successful men." Artie had silent tears ebbing down his cheeks.

Joe was transfixed by the old man's painful stare into space. He sat staring at nothing as if he were watching a horrific movie in which he had played the lead role.

"Joe, I gathered the only thing we had on hand for free, and I began to plan to murder my whole starving family with rat poison in a cabbage stew." Artie began to cry in earnest now, and Joe wiped his face with tissues he pulled from the box on the side table. Joe was stunned and could not move. He did not even remember that he had wanted to go. He just sat and watched Artie as he continued. "I was going to put my whole family out of their misery, and I had a plan. My God, I almost did it, Joe. I planned to do it for weeks, crying and sobbing and deciding. I was lost in my own sense of failure and ego as a man. On the day I was going home to kill them, I stepped up onto the front porch and expected to see the very same thing as I had the day before, and every day before that, my family in misery, tired, and starving. Instead, I came face to face with my cousin Agnes and her husband Mel. They hugged me and said that the family in New York had decided that I might need help keeping things going for a bit, and they brought some money to hold us all over for a few months. Ruth was crying, Leyfa was crying, and I began to cry also. That one change, Joe, that one shift in my perception made everything different. I was sickened by what I had been thinking and I was thanking God for all of the trials which would lead me to the next place. I was thanking God that I did not do the horrible thing which I had been planning." Artie's tears had slowed, and he looked up at Joe. "I have never told anyone what I had been planning. Joe, thank you for listening to me. I did not want to go and meet Ruth with this on my heart." Joe realized that he was silently crying himself. Artie squeezed his hand again. "You know, Joe, our lives were not perfect, but our life together with our kids, grandkids, and great grandkids was full and so, so beautiful. I would not have missed it for the world, Joe." Joe stood to leave. Artie said, "You know, Joe, no one day is the whole of life. Every day builds upon the next day and altogether they combine to make a glorious life. Some days are bad, some stretches are bad, but the beauty is in living your whole life and finding the blessings! Ha! Now I sound like my Ruth. Thank you, son, I surely appreciate being able to talk with another man about this." Joe felt the urge to hug Artie suddenly and leaned in carefully to embrace the old man. Artie felt like a small bird in his arms. "Sleep, Artie, I will visit tomorrow night if you like." "Thank you, Joe." Artie winked at him as he left the room.

As Joe passed into the stairwell to the roof, he took the two flights of stairs two at a time in silence. The roof was deserted in the dawn light. Joe stepped to the rail and looked out toward the East where the sun was not quite broken over the ocean's horizon a couple of miles away. Lighting his cigarette, Joe suddenly broke down into a torrent of hard, bitter tears. The reality of his conversation with Artie hit him like a blow to his midsection. Joe lit a second cigarette and cried more, as his nose began to run freely. Joe had never believed in anything really, but at that moment he knew, somehow, that there was some kind of, what? Something. What the hell was he thinking for Christ's sake? This old man had lived through more than he had or probably ever would, and he didn't quit, he hadn't given up. The realization of what he had been thinking of doing hit him so hard that he stood for a long moment and just tried to stop the nausea that was rising up in his throat. Bending over, he threw up once, and then again, his stomach emptied there on the roof of the hospital. When the wave of nausea left him, he stood up and a bloom of cold sweat erupted down his back, soaking his work shirt. The sun started to burn its fine pink, orange line above the ocean surface and a beautiful glow lit Joe's face and the whole of the rooftop and the city beyond. Sunrise spread out there before him in all directions, the Atlantic coming alive before his eyes. Tears continued to run down his face, sliding into the collar of his shirt and down his chest. Joe did not bother to wipe them away. Grabbing his cell phone out of his pocket, he hit his sister's number and waited while the phone rang and rang.

The sleepy voice of his sister Maria in Texas responded, "Joe? Joe, is that you? Is everything okay? It's early, are you all right?" "I'm fine, I am sorry it's early. Hey, I want to take you up on your offer. I want to come work in the restaurant with you guys. I would like to put Chandra and the kids on a bus tomorrow and follow them in two weeks after I get paid. Would that be all right?" "Of course, Joe, oh, Tom is going to be thrilled! Of course, let me know when Chandra and the kids will be arriving. And don't worry about anything, we will get you all set up when you get here. I love you, Joe, I am thrilled!" "I love you too, Maria. I will call you later, go back to sleep."

As Joe hung up the phone, he felt all the weight he had been carrying shift, and he cried for 10 minutes more. He determined to go home, hug Chandra, and put her and the kids on a bus today. He could sell their stuff in the apartment, and give his two weeks' notice. He could cash in vacation time and have plenty of money to get them set up after a few months in Texas with Maria. He marveled at Artie's story and how his perception had been changed by that one conversation with a stranger in the middle of the night.

The next day toward the end of his shift at the hospital, Joe went to see Artie and thank him for sharing his story. When he entered, the room was empty, and the nurse was readying the room for a new patient. Joe asked where Artie was, and she said, "Oh, such a sweet old man, he died in his sleep at around 6: a.m. today. We will miss him." Joe left the room and decided then and there that he would be for some other man what Artie had been for him.

Aralamb:

Within this story lies the mechanical workings of, and the truth of, the TMR. This intersection of two lives in a seemingly random way was, for both souls, a huge point of change and physical positive reinforcement. Artie was at the end of his life and engaged in his TMR with Joe, thereby saving Joe and all of his family. By engaging Joe in his TMR moment, he forwarded the positive impact that Joe and his family may have on other souls within the lifetime. Artie had to wait till he was 92 to engage in his

Three-Minute Rule moments. Joe was 32 and experiencing his. Joe may go on to be involved in the facilitation of many other people's TMR moments as Artie did for him.

The idea of calling these important energetic intersections Three-Minute Rule moments is simple. When a soul comes into a lifetime, that soul has no idea which "three minutes of their lives" might be the most important three minutes. Because of this, a soul needs to stay in the life path, and at least understand that everything that you make others feel could be a pivotal "three minutes of time." This is not about being a perfect human on the planet. It is about the idea that you want your general impact on the planet to be a positive one. Small, negative actions, words, deeds, and thoughts can have a huge impact on those around us, just as small, positive actions, words, deed and thoughts can have a huge impact. If Joe had just ignored Artie's small cry for help, he and Artie would have missed the moments they spent which facilitated them both healing and changing for the better. In the three minutes that it took Artie to call out for help from Joe, and the three minutes that it took Joe to decide to turn and go help Artie, both of their lives were changed in immense ways.

It may be likened a bit to the "butterfly effect" by where a butterfly's wing stoke on one side of the planet can and does affect the whole of the weather pattern on the other side of the planet. The energetic footprint of the "three-minute rule" is much the same. As a soul you will have built into your life possibilities, one or more of these energetic intersections with other souls. You will not know when these are, and just how important they are. You are meant to look at your whole life as sacred and do your very best to treat others as such.

Example 2:

Megan hated her fucking job! I mean, for fuck's sake. The commute alone from Simi Valley to Thousand Oaks was brutal. Megan had worked for Miller Communications for 15 years and in that time, she had taken only one vacation and two sick days when her mother died, and she had to go back to Kansas for the funeral. Megan was the HR Manager for Miller, which at least allowed her an office with a window looking out on the 101 freeway. The view was not great, but at least she got sunlight in her office, which was so much better than the interior of the cubicle farm on the inside of the building. The big sunny window allowed her to have plants in her office which she loved as she had a massive green thumb. In the winter months her office was filled with the sweet smell of the potted Gardenia bush she had on her desk. Megan was 42, divorced, and the mother of two daughters, Chase, 12, and Kendall, 17. Kendall's father Sam had been in the Air Force and died in an auto accident when Megan was six months pregnant with Kendall. The Air Force had given Megan a small settlement at that time because the auto accident had happened during exercises at Edwards. Megan was not told the details of the incidents and was to overcome with loss, feeling alone, and young in age to press for them. Megan took the whole of the settlement from the Air Force and bought a small house so that she had a place to stay while she grieved Sam's death. Sam had been her first love and a larger-than-life personality with a huge smile and a loud infectious laugh. They were just starting out life together and the loss of him was still a hole within her all of these years later. Chase's father had been the friend of a friend she was set up with after a Super Bowl party in Simi Valley at her good friend Judy's house. Gary owned three car dealerships spread out over Simi Valley and made a good living. He was 15 years older than her at the time, but was a good guy and seemed like such a safe haven for her and Kendall. She moved in with him and they were married after six months when she became pregnant with Chase. Gary had urged her to sell the little house she and Kendall had been living in, but she could not as it was one of the only connections she still had with Sam and decided to rent it out instead. Gary wanted to just sell it, but Megan had insisted that she keep it in Kendall's name along with hers as a possible college fund later. Gary agreed and for 10 years, it was rented out to a variety of people with the money going to the upkeep and savings for Kendall's college education. Looking back at it now, Megan was so amazed that she had stuck to her guns on keeping the house, as she would move back into it when the girls were still quite young. Gary was not a bad guy, he just liked younger women and when Megan became a 30-something mother, he was no longer interested in staying in the marriage.

Megan would often lie in bed at night in the small three-bedroom house that Sam's death had gotten them and marveled at the idea that for once in her life, she had made a great decision by keeping the place. Gary tried many times to get her to sell that "money pit," but she just wouldn't. Now, for the past few years, it had once again been a haven for her and her girls. Gary paid child support and all, but the house was their place, it was hers. It was the one time in her life that she could remember making a decision that was not just a reaction to someone else's expectations of her, and in that one moment, she had, without even knowing it at the time, kept an important life raft for her and the girls. Laying there in the predawn light, she could just see the outline of the photo that was framed on her dresser of her and Sam when they were dating. She knew that it would go to Kendall at some point, but now it made her feel safe and secure in her life with the girls. It would stay.

Megan hit the alarm clock just before it went off, 5:27 a.m. At least it was Friday, and that meant two days off, nowhere to go, beautiful California sunshine, and all to herself. Kendall was going camping with her best friend's family for three days, and it was Gary's weekend to pick up Chase. Chase didn't like Gary's new wife Julie, who was literally 20 years his junior, pregnant, and a yoga instructor to boot. Chase was a beautiful young 12-year-old who loved books and couldn't care less about yoga or green energy drinks. Julie was a good person, just a cliché in Chase's eyes. Either way, both girls had places to be this weekend and thus Megan would have 48 hours of unadulterated alone time. Because all of her friends at work were constantly trying to find her a man, she had already garnered several invites to parties, strip clubs, the beach, shopping, and drinks as well as a variety of other "meant to find you a man" destinations. Megan had turned every one of them down. Garrett nuzzled her nose and she got out of bed. Garrett, her three-year-old mastiff, was, at this point, the love of her life. He always started his evening out with the girls in their room, but inevitably somewhere in the deep part of every night, he would find his way into Megan's king bed, and she would wake with the big warm feel of him stretched out beside her. Garrett was too big for even the biggest dog door, so she let him out the back door into the fenced-in yard every morning. Megan didn't like the idea of a dog door anyway, as it was always an invitation for someone to break in. Her retired neighbor Shelly came over every day around noon and took Garrett for a long walk around the neighborhood. It was a specifically symbiotic relationship in that Shelly was an older woman alone out for a long walk, Garrett needed a midday walk, and no one was going to hassle an older woman alone who was walking a 145-pound mastiff! Funnily, Garrett was a major social butterfly in the neighborhood, but he still struck an imposing picture for anyone who might interfere with Shelly, and so they were fast friends. Shelly would be by to walk Garrett later today. Kendra also really liked that Shelly had the keys to the house and was kind of a grandmother figure to her girls. There was always some nice baked stuff being left on the counter on random mid-week days.

After dropping Kendall off a few blocks away at the Goldman's, she left Chase off at her school. Both girls attended Oaks Christian School, which was a private school that Gary was nice enough to pay for. Gary loved Kendall as if she was his own, and without his help, Megan would never be able to pay for such a great school. Neither Gary nor Megan was particularly Christian, but the school was great, and Gary said, "No one can have too many moral compass lessons." Megan found this funny coming from a guy who could not keep his moral compass in his pants, but it was working for her girls.

Her work day actually sped by. Three meetings and a working luncheon with her boss kept her from checking her emails all day, but at least Friday was mostly over, and the weekend was about to begin. As usual every Friday she would water her plants, turn off her office lights, and glance out over the freeway through her window to see what traffic looked like. The freeway was buried and almost at a standstill as usual. It was Friday afternoon, she knew her route home, she knew the two hours she would drive, she knew what podcasts she would listen to to pass the time, and she knew exactly where every traffic jam and accident would be, just like every other Friday. Suddenly, it occurred to her to take some other way home. Just don't do the same thing, just take some other route home? The habitual part of her conscious mind suddenly kicked into gear. What if it took her longer? What if she broke down and no one knew which route she had taken home? She actually felt some kind of weird fear about making this one small change. She thought she could take back roads out past Marr Ranch Open Space and just see and do something different. The need in her to take a new route home warred with some weird fear in her belly. "What if the cell reception was bad out there?" She realized suddenly that she was talking out loud to herself. Smiling, she decided. She was going to take a fully different route home tonight. She would let Garrett out when she got home, and it would just be something different.

Pulling out of the parking lot, for the first time in 10 years, she turned right toward the open space instead of left toward the freeway. Plugging her smartphone into the port, she quickly scrolled and punched in her favorite angry political podcast and then said out loud, "Nope, not today!" Scrolling again, she stopped at a music mix of unknown indie artists and turned up her stereo. Parker Millsap's "Pining" came on and she smiled a broad lovely smile. It occurred to Megan that she had not smiled that freely or broadly, maybe since before Sam had died. She actually thought to herself, man, Sam would love this guy. With both hands on the wheel, she began the slow crawl up and around the Open Space. Megan rolled down the windows and let in the air. She didn't care if her hair was getting messed up. She realized that she just didn't care, and it felt so Goddamned good to just not give one shit about anything. She was headed home on a road she had never driven on, and it was all different. When she got to the top of the first vista, she swerved into the dirt pull-off, and sat looking out over the Simi Valley below. It was beautiful and beginning to be a mixture of sunset orange and reds with the first twinkling illuminations of the lighting of the city. She left the car running, door open, music playing, got out, and walked to the fenced-in edge of the precipice. She pulled a very deep breath into her lungs, and let it out slowly. Inhaling again, she felt some tears welling up far, far inside of her. The tears slid down her cheeks as she looked out over the beautiful horizon. The sun was beginning to set in earnest, and it occurred to her that she was just so tired. Megan was just so friggin tired. Tired of being alone, tired of working and living in the same place, the same actions over and over. She was startled as the first of her phone calls started coming in from her friends. She had turned down all of the various invitations for this weekend, but knew the pleading calls of invitation were forthcoming. Smiling, she said out loud "Nope!" Turning off the ringer, she spun and walked back to her car.

The song playing when she slid back into the driver's seat was Esperanza Spaulding's "Sunny Side of the Street," and as beautiful as that was, it did not stop Megan from screaming and diving right back out of the car at the sight of the passenger who had joined her. She stood there in complete disbelief to be looking into the big golden eyes of the largest yellow lab she had ever seen. The lab sat in her passenger seat smiling at her and panting very happily. She tentatively moved back to the door and said, "Come, get out!" The dog sat and looked at her with absolutely no worry and by no means was it planning to get out of the car. She extended her hand to the dog, and in return got a lot of licking and more smiling. The dog did not move from the passenger seat. Well, shit, what now? She got into the car, and shut the door. It was getting to dusk, and she didn't know what to do. After patting the dog and checking him quickly for injuries, she found that he had a tag in the shape of Gardenia flower on his collar. The name on the tag said "Justice" and had a Simi Valley cell phone number. On the back it just said, "I'm friendly, call home." She laughed out loud and patted Justice's head. Justice just smiled, panted, and relaxed back into the seat. Jesus, well good, at least she could do something with him. Sitting there, she thought to herself how just the one little decision to turn right out her work parking lot rather than her well-trodden path to the freeway had led her to this beautiful overlook at sunset, but also led her to access her long-buried pain over Sam's death and as a bonus, she was now at this romantic and scenic outpost on a date with a handsome dog named Justice. Again, she laughed out loud. Patting the dog again, she said, "OK, Justice, let's get you home" and dialed the number on his tags.

After just two rings, a male voice answered the phone, "This is Zach, how can I help you?" "Well, Zach, my name is Megan, and I am having a romantic look over the city with Justice here." Zach laughed out loud. "Oh man, thank you so much for calling. I was getting worried when he didn't come in for dinner. That dog, he runs this place, and he likes to wander. Are you up at the base lookout spot?" "I think so, I don't know this area well, but it was a beautiful sunset for sure." "Yeah, that's the spot. We are about three miles down the hill to the North. If you pull out of that spot and go north down the hill, we are at the bottom of the hill just before the sharp turn. You will see the sign, 'The Flower Bowl.'" "OK," she said, "Justice and I are on the way." "Man, thank you so much! I don't know what we'd do without Justice!"

Megan hung up the phone and pulled out onto the now dark road, headed north down the hill, and again patted Justice on the head. He just smiled back and sighed with happy relief, she thought, that he was getting a ride home and would not have to walk all the way to dinner. At the bottom of the hill, just as Zach had said, she could see the large carved and lighted sign: The Flower Bowl. Under the carved Gardenia were the words "specialty gardenias." She could see a brightly lit medium-sized Craftsman-style home with a large wraparound front porch, which she thought had been added later because it was more in the styles of the Victorian homes she had seen back east in New England. It was a really warm and inviting looking place. Behind it, in the deepening darkness, she could see the dark bulk of green houses, but could not make out just how many.

As she pulled in, Justice started to whine and jumped to get out, so she reached out and pushed the passenger door open for him. He spun, stopped, and looked at her to see if she was going to follow. Megan heard the front door open, and Zach came out across the porch and down the steps towards her. She was suddenly struck with the insane sense of what she was doing. She was in the boonies, at a stranger's home, no one knew where she was exactly, and she was pretty sure this is how every murder mystery on the Lifetime Network ever started. It was too late though; Zach was leaning in to shake her hand and thank her. At the same time, Justice had come around the car and was in the process of acting as is he had not seen Zach in two years.

For the first time in her life, she looked at a person who was a total stranger and somehow, she felt like she knew him. Zach was just a bit taller than her. It was hard to tell in the light of the driveway, but she thought he had dark short hair, was probably her age, and was well built and fit. The other thing she kept looking at was how impossibly gentle and loving he was with Justice. His eyes were brown, she thought, and his smile was just a bit crooked but big and easy. At that moment, a teenage boy came bounding out the door and off the porch. He smiled at her, threw out his hand, and said, "I'm Travis. Where did you find this criminal?" He grabbed Justice around the neck. Everyone laughed and Travis ran back into the house followed by Justice. Megan smiled, and turned to go. Zach said, "Hey, do you like gardenias?" "Well, yes, actually I do." "Here, let me give you my card, we are having a show here starting tomorrow morning, you could walk through the greenhouses and see what we do here. If you have a green thumb at all, you might really like it." Kendall took the card he hastily offered her and they both smiled again, and she was back in her car. Zach again said, "Thank you so much for bringing Justice home. I hope to see you tomorrow." He smiled, and walked back up on to the porch, turning once to look back at her as she started the car.

Megan pulled back onto the road and toward home. When she got home, Garrett was waiting for her and she was surprised to see that she was only 20 minutes later than normal. She swung the back door of the house open to the yard and watched Garrett as he inspected his domain. She stretched, put on some music, and poured a glass of wine. Megan pulled the card out of her pocket where she had jammed it, and looked at it. Taking another slow sip of the wine, she thought, I am going to go to that show. I am going to go on my own. She texted each of her friends and let them know she was not accepting the many offers they had made.

Megan went to the gardenia show the next day at Zach's farm. Zach gave Megan a tour of his operation, which she loved. She and Zach had many, many things in common. Megan agreed to do some independent marketing work for Zach in trade for classes on gardenia genetics. As time went on, Zach and Meagan dated, fell deeply in love, mixed their families, got married, rented out Megan's house, expanded the gardenia business together, became exceptional philanthropists in the care of animals, and were very happy together. They lived their lives together by choice. They chose what to put their banded energy towards and they told the story for the rest of their lives about how "Justice brought Megan home."

Aralamb

This example points out how many decisions you make every day which will keep you away from, or possibly moving toward, what your highest goals and good are. This example gives you a picture of different moments Megan could have ignored her TMR, and thus would have missed a really powerful life path possibility that she had set up for herself.

Let me be clear, the experiences that you have throughout a lifetime are all valid no matter whether you see the validity for growth or not, but the TMR moment or moments are specially placed opportunities by your own soul to give you the chance to make sweeping changes for the positive. In this example, Megan, for no other reason than that she was just sick of her same routine, decided in just a few minutes to "turn right out of her office parking lot instead of her well-worn path to the left." That one change in direction, that one (Three-Minute Period of Time) where she trusted her intuition, put her upon a path of a complete and positive life change. In the same way but from another perspective, if Megan had not chosen to leave her work by way of a new route, Justice, Zack, Travis, her girls, none of those lives would have been positively affected either. Megan would not have met Zach and all of that future would cease to exist as a possibility. The TMR is a tool that you should remember most certainly because if you are sitting at some "choice point," and even if the choice you need to make seems small, inconsequential, or not important, IF you have any kind of compelling feeling in your gut to make a certain choice, you need to understand that this is most likely a TMR point in your lifetime, and you need to listen to it. Small, simple decisions, when partnered with true intuitive faith, are very powerful tools for you and everyone around you. Keep this in mind as you put all of the information from this book together in your mind and spirit. Your TMR point, or points, that you have set up for yourself are a true gift. The gift is in the exponential growth and joy that it can bring.

CHAPTER 19
Life Paths

Aralamb

Individual life paths will have been chosen before the soul initiates a new lifetime of incarnation. Each soul will come into a lifetime with multiple life path options as well as points of juncture within the lifetime by which those different life paths may be actuated and employed.

Choosing life paths

Before the soul is initiated into the coming lifetime, that soul will meet with its guides, teachers, loved ones as well as the souls who have agreed to exist within the lifetime. Choosing life path decisions is almost always a group event as you will have three to four generations of family souls determining what their options will be within a lifetime of learning together. I mean this literally. Fifteen souls may meet in The Lobby before the lifetimes begin to determine which places each will hold within the lifetime, who they will be in that lifetime, and how those roles will work together in order to employ the lesson needs of the group in the best way.

Incarnation is not unlike a physical family tree, except that these groupings would have been predetermined in order for the lessons of all the participants to be worked out within the lifetime. There is **no** random selection in the process. If you and three other souls in your soul pod determine that you all want to be children of an alcoholic, you would all agree to the roles you would play, and then agree with another of your soul pod to be in the place as said alcoholic parent. This would be agreed upon prior to your birth into that lifetime. You all would agree to this in order to have the challenges, and hopefully overcome said challenges, in the best ways possible for soul growth. There is a larger network/hierarchy of overlapping soul pods by which your pod comes into contact with other family soul pods. There is also the ability to move within other pod groupings should you require it for your own growth. Again, this is all agreed upon by each soul pod prior to birth.

Prior to your lifetime, you would all have agreed to who your own parents would be, who your siblings would be, and your extended family to some degree. You would have agreed to mating, or lack thereof. You would have agreed to whom the souls were going to be inhabiting your closest relationships and they to you. These close relationships will be both joyful and challenging as the lessons you chose would require. It is at this point that each soul's life path options would be laid in place.

Life path options are always within the free will law, and a soul may decide to completely ignore the life path options that they laid out for themselves prior to incarnating. The highest aspirations for the soul within a lifetime would obviously be to experience life path options in order to learn and grow, but it is not a given that this will happen. Usually a soul will, within a given lifetime, choose about half of the lifetime options which were pre-determined as options in order to learn lessons. This is why most souls return to The Lobby having integrated and released new learning challenges positively for their growth. There are very few times when a complete lack of learning is accomplished within a lifetime.

Life path decision points and junctures

Within each lifetime, a soul will place decision points and junctures that will present possible directions at that point in the lifetime. These juncture points can be very simple in nature, such as "do I take the bus or walk to the library today?' As simple as this sounds, you could be meeting two different people on your journey, one will be on the bus, one will be at the sidewalk coffee shop. Your seemingly simple decision on that day will determine the next path your life will/can take for years to come. There is no right or wrong decision; it is simply the lesson path you choose at that time. It may be that no real thought is given to the decision on that day, but you go about your business as usual and either take the bus or walk. However, if you learn to listen to your intuition, learn to hear your soul, it may be that your decision to walk or ride the bus that day came with a whisper of inclination from your soul, your higher knowing. Here are two life path scenarios which would be the difference between the bus ride and the walk on that day. Again, within these two options there is no *correct choice*; it is simply a matter of which lifetime manifests from within that decision.

The bus/Life plan option 1

On that day, you decide to take the bus to the library. You are living in Portsmouth, New Hampshire, and the bus route is a bit longer, but it takes you three miles along the coast. The ocean calls to you and even though the bus ride takes you 10 miles around the circuit on what could be a one-mile walk, seeing the ocean and breathing in the air is like a balm to your soul. Living on the coast is what you dream of. It's out of your reach right now, but some day you will live on the coast and go to sleep at night hearing the waves crash on the rocks just steps from your doorway.

As the bus moves away from the stop, you take a seat next to an old woman who is trying hard to keep her small dog and her shopping bags on her seat. Smiling, you offer your hand, sit down next to her, and pull some of her bags onto your own lap. "Oh, thank you, I don't think I could have held those and Sherm here for the whole way home." Sherm is a soft black mix of Australian Sheppard and what must have been Chihuahua, as he is as round as a neck pillow and only three inches tall. "I'm Beth, what's your name?" "I'm Ken." I give Sherm a pet and he smiles at me too. "Where are you headed?" I tell her that I am headed to the library. She laughs and says, "Well, Ken, I'm sure glad you got on this bus for my sake, but you are about four miles out of your way for the library!" I smile back and explain that I love the ocean so much and that is why I like to ride the bus sometimes out around the loop when I have the time. I realize at this point that my hand is falling asleep a bit from gripping her grocery bags and loosen my grip. Beth and I talk for the next few miles as the smell of the ocean gets stronger and stronger. I tell Beth how I have been working as a chef at a restaurant in downtown Portsmouth. She smiles and listens. I had graduated from the Culinary School of New York two years before. Beth smiled and listened to my general history of travel, trying to figure out what I wanted to do with my life, other than live by the coast. Sherm was fully asleep and snoring on Beth's lap when we pulled up at her stop, which was just outside of the front deck of Bistro Sea Shell on one of the small inlets near Portsmouth Harbor. She smiled at me and said, "I wonder if I could bother you just a bit more, Ken. Could you help Sherm and I off the bus with our bags? I don't think I can manage it all off the bus." I thought, what the heck, it's my day off, why not? "Sure," I said, and smiled again. The bus doors opened wide and Beth pushed Sherm's leash into my hand. Sherm looked up at me, obviously decided I was good to go, and jumped down from Beth's lap. Now I had Sherm on a leash, four of Beth's bags, and her left hand in my right as she stood up to get off the bus. We disembarked in a bumble of arms, legs, bags, dog, and leash, laughing loudly at the bus driver's face.

As Beth stepped up onto the curb, a pretty dark-haired woman of about 28 stepped out of the restaurant toward Beth, grabbing her arm, and looking up at me with a wide smile and flour smears on her chin and apron. Beth turned to me, "Ken, this is Stella, my granddaughter. Stella, this is Ken. He is a big chef downtown. Sherm and he took a liking to each other on the bus, and he is strong, carried all our groceries for me." Beth smiled up at me with such a deep knowing her eyes that I felt like I was looking at someone I had known for ever.

I looked back at Stella, and it was all over, said and done. I will always remember that day. I will never forget it because that is the day that we became Ken and Stella. It's 25 years later, Gramma Beth died two years after our meeting, but she was present at our wedding and always loved to tell anyone who would listen that "Sherm and I picked Ken up on the bus and brought him home to Stella." Stella and I have owned four restaurants together, two in France, one in Florida, and the one we have now and will hand over to our son Michael when we retire, which is in the original restaurant Beth left to us here in Portsmouth. We have always lived on a coastline. We have three mostly grown children and have lived through good times and bad times together. We are living our life and loving each other. When I thank God or whoever is out there looking over us, I always remember how grateful I am that I decided to get on the bus but that day and met Beth, Sherm, and Stella. I will always be so happy I got on that bus and helped an old woman and her dog. That bus ride was the beginning of my life and everything I have.

The Walk/ Life plan option 2

The day was sunny and so beautiful. I looked toward the bus stop, and figured, hmm, bus or walk? Well, the coast will still be there tomorrow, and it's sunny and the walk will be nice. I was working as a chef at a place in downtown Portsmouth and today was my one day a week where I had 24 hours fully off. I loved reading and loved the Portsmouth Library because it was in a really old building and the architecture spoke to me. I love old buildings as much as I loved the ocean. Spring was finally arriving in New Hampshire and the apple and cherry trees along the street were starting to flower. The smell was amazing. Walking fast, my toe caught on a torn-up sidewalk stone and I tripped a bit as I passed a coffee shop. I was able to catch the railing of the coffee shop deck as I was falling and did not go fully down. I did, however, knock my sunglasses off, manage to throw my cell phone, and watched them skid away down the sidewalk unceremoniously. Righting myself quickly, I scanned to see if anyone was watching, like we all do when we do something stupid in public, and heard a giggle to my left coming from one of the small tables on the deck. The table was in full sunlight, and I did not have my glasses, obviously, so I shaded my eyes to see who was laughing at me almost dying in a fall, well, not dying, but I was embarrassed.

The woman looking back at me reminded me of one of those photos from the 1960s of the peace-loving hippies from the Woodstock era. Long wild reddish blonde hair, brown eyes, and kind of a too big mouth but with a pretty kind face. She was laughing at me. I was so embarrassed and so mad somehow. Who does that? Laugh at a total stranger when they are at their worst? Who does that? I scooped up my iPhone and glasses, quickly moving away down the sidewalk, happy to be out of her sight.

I was not great with women, and I hated being laughed at. Jesus, could I just never look cool, ever! Nope, not to be. As I turned the corner and headed up the steps of the old library building, the smell of aging paper hit me in the face. I loved that smell. Books, books, and more books, along with the smell of old finely polished wood and floor wax everywhere. The floors, interior architecture, and moldings were a couple of hundred years old and polished to a fine patina of Murphy's Oil Soap and Pledge. It was heaven for me. I found my way to the section on cooking and a couple of photo books from turn-of-the-century Europe. This book had mostly photos of all of the old medieval cathedrals, which were my favorite. I was kind of a secretly pining architect who had gone to Culinary Arts School because I just did not feel like I was good enough to be an architect. I knew it was me just being scared of possible failure, but shit, I was doing pretty well as a chef after all. Sitting at one of the long tables, I spread out my books, unpacked my knapsack for my bottle of water, and settled in for a few hours of quiet enjoyment.

After about an hour, I had to go to the bathroom and motioned for the librarian to watch my stuff till I got back. She gave me a small nod and went back to her book. I loved the tiles in the old place. The bathroom still had the 100-year-old subway tiles on the walls and floor, which had been an upgrade in around 1910. They were a shade of green that made you think of India or maybe Kat Mando. Just deep and beautiful. They were practically perfect. I stood looking at them while I washed my hands, thinking how much I loved this building.

Upon returning to my table, I noticed on the far wall the same red-haired woman who had laughed at me when I had tripped on the street. Oh man. I felt a hot blush rise up into my cheeks. I did not want to leave, but I also didn't want to be seen by her again. Of course, at that very moment, she turned in her chair, saw me, and crossed over to where I sat with not so much as a hitch in stride. She stuck out her hand to shake mine and smiled. I hesitated and she said, "OK, I should not have laughed at you. It was just funny, that's all. I'm Amanda, what's your name?" I looked into her face and realized that she was sincere and that I had not seen a face more open and real in a long time. "I'm Ken," I said. She grabbed my hand and looked down at the architecture photo books I had. "Architect then?" she asked, continuing to smile. I didn't think I had ever seen anyone smile as much as this person. I said, "No, no, I just love architecture." "So, if you love architecture, then why aren't you doing architecture?" I was getting uncomfortable because this stranger was suddenly asking me questions that were in my mind private. "I just don't think I am probably good enough to actually be an architect," I said.

She sat down across the table from me and said, "Well, if you don't try, how will you know?" I laughed at this as I did not have a good answer. She looked at me again and said, "Do you have any drawings?" I did have a few in my ever-present backpack. "I do, but they are just scrawling, you know, nothing special." She asked if she could see. I slowly unfurled the rumpled mess of my drawings. They consisted mostly of sketches of buildings I had seen and liked. Some were imaginary places I would like to build some day. She smiled and held them out, flattening them one at a time onto the big table. "Well, Ken, some of these are beautiful, you really have an eye for this." It felt good to have someone like my drawings and somehow it was easier to show them to this stranger than to show them to someone who really knew me.

Amanda reached into her pocket and handed me a card. The card read Sisson and Mathews Architects, 1134 Rockdale Road, New York, New York, 00985. The card had the name of Cristi Mathews on the front. I raised my eyebrows and looked at her. She smiled again and said, "Cristi is a great person and if you ever want to look into the architect gig, call her." She stood, took my hand again, said, "Ken, I like your face, sorry again about laughing at you." She turned, grabbed up her bag, and walked away and out of the library in a swirl of skirts and red hair without looking back. I suddenly became aware that the card she had handed me smelled strongly of some kind of patchouli or other kind of essential oil. It smelled like earth, plants, and sunshine all mixed together with some kind of flower. It was a really nice smell. I jammed the card in the front pocket of my knapsack as my phone started blowing up. I was going to meet the guys for drinks down at the wharf bar for the game.

Three weeks later, I got laid off. It kind of pissed me off because I had put good time in at that restaurant and I was head chef. I had paid my rent for the month of June, but had no real reason to stay on Portsmouth. I had a bit of savings, and a reference for a good position in Chicago, but I didn't know what I wanted to do. I knew I was going to be moving to Chicago or somewhere. My parents were in Arizona, but I was not headed there. We were very close, but I was a wanderer, and they were good with that. I decided that one thing I was going to do was to get rid of a bunch of my useless shit. I was dragging along too much crap! I started going through my clothes first, then my shoes and finally my 25 extra backpacks and gear. I grabbed the one I used most and dumped it out on my bed. I was listening to classical music, which was not always my first choice, but it always helped me to think. It was calm. I started looking through the receipts, coins, general crap I threw in, and then I smelled patchouli and picked up that business card that chick Amanda had given me. I flipped it over and over in my hand. Mmm. I sat down hard on the edge of my bed and wondered what to do. I grabbed my phone and dialed the number. I hung up. Why did I do that? I'm such a dick! I dialed again and a very business-like voice answered, "Thank you for calling Sisson & Mathews, how may I direct your call?" I asked for Cristi and was directed to her voicemail. Well, that would be easier than I thought. I didn't know what to say. Hello, I got your card from a hippie chick, and I like architecture? Stupid, oh man, panicking, I have to say something at the beep. "Hello, my name is Ken, and I was given your card by Amanda. She saw some of my drawings and said that I should call you if I was going to be in New York. I would like to talk with you about your firm. Thanks so much, again, my name is Ken, 809-876-3261."

I hung up, shit, shit, I would like to talk to you about your firm? What? So dumb…. What am I? A goddamned carpet salesman? Jesus, too late now, first impression gone and blown. I jammed the card back into my backpack and threw away two more old pair of running shoes in frustration. Okay, so Chicago it was. I called the prospective new restaurant and left a message for the general manager.

July found me trying to settle in to the new restaurant. The general manager was a total nightmare; I just didn't want any more people in my life who made a career of being an asshole to everyone. I was just three weeks into my probation and training as head chef. The money was great, but Chicago was expensive and although it was summer in Chicago, I felt really landlocked away from the coast. I was subletting a tiny place in a large, renovated home that was just a half a mile walk from the restaurant. It was late, and I was finally done for the night. Entering my apartment, I pulled my phone out of my pocket and sat down to stare at Instagram for a few minutes before I passed out. It was 2:45 a.m., and I was tired. My mom had texted me; I had a few texts from my old general manager in New Hampshire. I also had a voice message alert from what was likely the last vulture of a credit company to buy my student loan debt. I went to erase it, but stopped and threw the phone on the coffee table and hit my bed.

I came awake at 9:30 a.m. to the sound of my phone beeping with new messages. I decided to go ahead and listen to the old message first. I figured I should at least save the information in my phone for the new credit company. I put in my password and listened. "Hello, my name is Cristi. I got your message last month, but Amanda, my sister, as you know, was sick and she passed away the week after you left your message. I would like to talk with you about the firm as well as your friendship with Amanda. I can meet you tomorrow at our offices at 3:00. Thanks for calling. I am sure you loved Amanda the way I did, and if Amanda was your friend, then I need to talk with you for sure."

I stared at the phone incredulous and a bit unbelieving. I called in sick and took an Uber to the airport and spent my savings on a flight to New York. For the first time in my life, I was hit with a compelling and strong knowledge that I needed to move towards my future. Twenty-four hours later, I was looking into the face of Cristi Mathews, the woman who would become one of my best friends, mentors, and business partner. She also later introduced me to my wife. I am an architect doing what I was born to do. I thank God, the stars, every day that I decided to walk to the library the day I met Amanda. That walk changed everything.

Aralamb

Either or both of the two decision options for a life path were valid to Ken. There is no right or wrong about the life paths chosen that day. The two options were there waiting to see what Ken would choose. In these two options, Beth and Amanda were both incorporating a Three-Minute Rule as well. Beth was elderly and met Sam in order to use her Three-Minute Rule, so that she might put him together with Stella, thus moving both Ken and Stella forward within a life path. Amanda was using a Three-Minute Rule point in order to bring ken and Cristi together to forward their life paths. Amanda knew that she was at the end of her life path, and used a TMR point to help herself as well as Ken and Cristi.

Ken could have also decided not to go to the library at all that day. As he himself would have built these two life path options into his experience possibility arc, that would have been his decision. The point I make here is that there is always a good reason to *feel into* the decisions you make every day. If you feel strongly that you should take the bus on the long route for the love of the ocean on a certain day, then you probably should. Transversely, if you feel like you should walk to the library on a certain day, you probably should. As a soul, you will have built in many possibility arcs and life paths. Most of them will have some common elements so that you are able to learn and experience your chosen lessons. The idea here is not to overthink every decision you make but to become more in touch with your instinctual intuitions in your daily life.

Melissa's Life Path Stories
Charlie

Some stories in your life you tell over and over. Some stories are held inside; maybe because they are painful or maybe because they would be too hard to hear when spoken out loud. Some stories in your life you just lock down in a place where you never have to look at them much. Well, this is a life path story that has lived on my inside for a really long time, and I don't want to hold this story anymore on the inside, I want it to live outside, so there is room for less painful, more flowering stories on my insides. I also want to tell this story because I recently told a dear friend that you cannot "drag around tons of baggage your whole life and expect to be able to get up off your knees and march into your future. You have to put that baggage down." I have put down a lot of "loaded up baggage," but I am still looking every day for stories that I need to bring from my insides to the outside. This is one of those life path stories.

On New Year's Day, 1993, my first husband and our blended families were living at the old Douglas Dairy Farm down on the Turnpike Road. Ted and I had combined our families and Ted was managing the farm. We were having a great time, working hard, playing hard, trying to enjoy life, and being the best people we knew how to be. Farming is one of the most beautiful, hard, glorious, and brutal ways to make a living. It is truly a calling, and we were doing our best to be dairy farmers.

We were living in the old, small cottage, which sat, and still sits, on the mound of land wedged between the railroad tracks and the barnyard. That house was literally sitting on the bank, 15 yards from the train tracks on the turnpike side, and eight feet from the barnyard on the other. The train would come by four times a day, and it would rattle the windows and pictures off the walls.

My dad Charlie was on heart medication. He started drinking in high school, and had pretty much since that time nonstop. All of that "party" had really taken a toll on his heart, and he was having really scary cardiac issues. He and I sat for a doctor's appointment just weeks before the New Year in 1992, and had been told, "You cannot drink and take this heart medication, Charlie. It will kill you for sure. You cannot do both." Dad understood that. He also knew that he had started drinking again.

My mom would often tell the story of how they went to Maine after they got married for a long weekend honeymoon in 1963. Mom had just turned 16 and my dad was just 18 when they got married. My mom was pregnant with me at the time, thus the wedding. Anyway, Vermont in those days had a drinking age of 18, but in Maine you had to be 21. I guess my dad had packed a few bottles for the three-day trip, but ran out early and decided to cut the trip short to get back to Vermont and his ability to buy alcohol. The gravity of that hits me when I think that they were just children themselves, and my dad was already dealing with an alcohol addiction.

On January 3, 1993, dad had been drinking and staying at the farm with us for a few days after the New Year's Eve party. He was not feeling well, and I could see that. I told him that we needed to go to the hospital. He and I, we would go. We needed to get him squared away again. I just kept prompting him to please let me get him to the hospital at least to get his medications looked at. He refused. Again, and again, he refused. "Melissa, I can get dried out, you want me to, and I will, but I am not going to go through any of that rehab again. I am not going to do it. I'm tired. I won't go through that again."

So, we went around about it a bit more and for the first time in my life I did something I had never done with him. I got mad, I just was mad and afraid, and he was not going to do what I wanted, needed him to do. He was not going to do it…. He was going to drink and take those fucking heart meds and I was scared and so Goddamned pissed off at him. He was 47 years old. Not old! I could not get him to go with me. He uncharacteristically dug in his heels, and so did I.

I should say that Charlie Gates was not a "drunk" in the most regular sort of way. He was funny, rarely angry, and usually just drinking and crying and laughing, and making jokes. He was always clean and well kept. He always had a job as a builder. That made it especially hard, I think, to be angry with him. He was like this lovable drinker who was "literally" killing himself with alcohol. He had so many amazing qualities, yet he could not just embrace them and stop drinking. He just could not. He loved every one of us in his life so much, but alcohol just won, it just did.

He told me on that afternoon, as the final word, that he was not going to get help. He just refused to go and get any help. I did something then that I have thought about so many times since. I have thought of this moment, this time, this place. This *life path* choice…. I said, "Dad, I love you, BUT you can't stay here if you are not going to get help. I am not going to wake up tomorrow and find you dead in the guest room." I just said it like that. I said it because I wanted him to do what I needed him to do. I said it because I was scared of what might happen to him. I gave him that ultimatum because I needed him to get help and I threw down the gauntlet. I drew a line in the sand right then and there.

I know now, having lived some time longer, that you should never follow the words "I love you" with the word "BUT." You see, the word "BUT" after the words "I love you" makes the "I love you" *conditional*. I don't do that anymore. I loved him unconditionally, but on that day, for whatever reason, for the first time ever, I made it conditional. You go to the hospital now, or you leave…. He walked out of my living room.

The house there on the bank of the farm had big front windows that looked out over the cornfield and the south trailing dirt road of the turn-pike and out of site over the Williams River to Rt. 103. Dad left through the front door, and I stood there watching his blue pickup truck drive away down the turnpike and over the Williams River Bridge to 103 and out of sight. I stood there and cried and cried. We never fought like that ever in my life, and something in me knew right then that I had chosen a life path, although I would not have called it that then, and I just sobbed.

I knew he would call me later that night. I was so scared for him, but I knew that he would call and agree to go to the inpatient place at the hospital. He would call and agree to go get help. I knew it, he would do it. I even left my jacket and purse on the table when I went to bed, so that I could go pick him up when he called.

Dad was living in Londonderry then. He was living at and taking care of a house for an elderly woman who lived there also. Dad had a room there and basically was like a son to her, and took care of things around her home. Dad did not call me that evening, and I was worried, but mostly I was sorry for the harsh words I had given him before he left that day. I hoped he would get some sleep and call me in the morning.

We woke up early the next day on that dairy farm (every day, 4:30 a.m. for me). The cows there were milked in shifts, so there was never a time when the milking parlor was not running. You could hear the milking parlor droning away 24/7. January 4, 1993, was a Monday, and at 5:00 a.m.

I was up and in the kitchen, making lunches and breakfast for everyone, as there was always someone up doing the milking and needing food before school, or the shift change in the barn. Our place was like the break room. I was standing in that kitchen at 5:43 a.m. when the big, old-school, yellow wall phone started ringing.

Science is beginning to understand that "time" and its passing and moving, and workings are not what we once thought. "Time," it seems, can stretch and move and slow down and speed up, all seemingly of its own desire, or maybe the desire of the observer. When that phone started ringing, I can remember that "time" suddenly slowed down. It was like each ring of that damn phone was slower and slower and I did not want to answer it. No good call ever comes at 5:43 a.m., everyone knows that. Then, all of a sudden, everything was "fast," My hand shot out and I was saying "hello."

On the other end, a very gentle man's voice said, "Melissa?" "Yes, that's me." "Melissa, I am Dr. Fox, I am here at your father's home. We received a 911 call from his elderly house owner, Helen, about an hour ago. She went to wake him, and he was unresponsive. The Londonderry EMS has been trying to resuscitate your father for 48 minutes to no avail. They have been doing manual breathing for him for that whole time. He was unresponsive when we arrived. I need you to understand that I do not want to transport him to the hospital. He has been unresponsive for a very long time. I would like you to give me permission to let him go."

I remember saying "no" to him over and over for a long time. I don't know how many times I said "no," but it was at least 20 or so times. I know I sat down on the cold floor with the phone in my hand. I asked all the right questions more than a few times. "Can you save him?" "Can he survive?" "Why can't you?" "What happened?" I asked all of the right questions. He said, "I could most likely artificially keep him alive to the hospital, put him on life support, and then you and the family would need to unplug him in two hours' time. He will not survive. I need your permission to let him go here and now."

"Let him go." He said it to me four or five times and then, just like that, I heard, felt, dad right there saying. "Please, Melissa, I'm tired, let me go." So, the words came out of my mouth. "Okay, let him go.... Yes, I understand, let him go." Dad was just 47.

I hung up the phone. I could not unsay those words. I knew there were no other words to say now that would undo those words. Dr. Fox had been very kind, very sure, but I could not unsay the words. I had said them. With the saying of those words, dad had left. He was really gone. I waited for an hour before I started calling the family. If no one knew, then it might not be real.

I have only told a very few people that story. I have kept this story inside. Every year on the anniversary of dad's death, my early morning thoughts have been on the fact that I said those words. "Let him go." I told Dr. Fox to "let go" of Patty and Gordon Gates's baby. I said those words for Christian and Amy's father and for brothers and sisters, wives, lovers, and so many other people who loved Charlie Gates. I was 29 then, and to this day, having been the person to say "let him go" has been a story that I have held inside. It has been a painful story to hold inside. Some of the most "right" decisions we ever have to make, I have learned, are the most painful.

I have felt guilt, anger, deep remorse, even though I know that "let him go" was the only decision to be made on that day. I still wish I was not the person to have to say it out loud. I think dad knew that those words were going to fall to me. I don't know how, but I think he knew it. I think he knew that when someone was going to have to say those words for him, I would do it out of love for him. It didn't make it easier to say.

So, I guess this story that I have been holding inside is now on the outside. I would like to say that from this painful experience, I learned a couple of things.

1. Never follow the words "I love you" with the word "but" because if you love someone then there is not really any condition that eclipses that, even if you think there is. You may not even stay in a person's life, but if "I love you" is part of the equation just let it be that with no conditions.

2. Always leave people knowing exactly how you feel about them. I know it can sound clichéd, but from my personal experience, I can tell you it is a real and solid life law. You absolutely cannot go back and fix or add more words or sentiments after one of you is gone.

3. You can love the hell out of a person, but you cannot "make them do anything that is not on their souls' path." In the end, for better or worse, people choose, and it often has nothing to do with how much they did or did not love you. It's really not about "you."

This life path choice had not only my choice but also my father's. On that day, had we both known that he only had 12 hours left to live, we would have chosen to remain together. Alas, the life path lessons learned are not always those of least resistance, or the least painful, but they are made, and the lessons are in how you learn and use the challenges to help yourself and others. We chose before birth to hold to this choice for and with each other.

Hunter

My dad Charlie was 19 when I was born. He was a kid, but he was a wonderful soul and I loved him. By his own account, at 19 he was already battling what would become a lifelong drinking problem. My mother was 16 when I was born. They were children, really just kids. They got married, and when I was two they got divorced, and my mother and I were back living with my grandparents while my mom graduated high school.

When I was 19, I had been living in California for a year. In California, I had fallen in love with a young guy named Tanner. Tanner and I smoked a ton of weed, worked very little, and he was making money by selling cocaine. Tanner had a brilliant smile, a fast sense of humor, and a massive chip on his shoulder from a missing father he never knew. We had a ton of love and crazy between us.

Before leaving New England at 18, I had gotten myself a full ride vocal scholarship to Emerson in Boston. My initial plan was to have a good time in California for the summer, then attend college back in Boston in the fall of that year. When it came time to go to school, Tanner had started dating someone else and I got on the plane back to New England, feeling heartbroken to a degree that I could not remember. I can remember from the time the plane took off from LAX feeling like I was losing something so important, maybe the most important thing ever, and I assumed that thing was Tanner. Tanner and I had more fun, more fighting, and more pain between us than two people approaching 20 should even know about. I look back at that time now and wonder how I survived it at all.

At that time, I was estranged from my mother, so dad had paid for me to come home, and I was staying with him until school started in Boston in two weeks. The nagging painful feeling of leaving something behind in California stayed with me, and finally, after two weeks' time, and knowing that I had a college scholarship waiting, I sat in my father's office at the big house up on Gates Hill and cried. When I say that I cried, I mean sobbing, shaking, and heaving is a better description of what I was doing. I will never forget that afternoon.

Dad was probably the kindest man I have ever known. Not perfect, but just a beautiful soul. He struggled his whole life with addiction, the same that finally took him at 47, but even through that his soul was bright and good. I cried, and cried, and told him I had to go back to California. I sat on the floor of his office and just wept. I told him that I was making a mistake. I told him that I would get one more extension from the college for next fall, and that I just had to go back to California.

He listened; he cried a little too. He said, "If I buy you a ticket back to CA, your mother is going to kill me." He did not like Tanner from what he had heard about him, and he thought that I was just lovesick for Tanner, I think. He asked me why I felt like I had to go back. I told him, "Because, in my heart, I know if I don't go back, I will be leaving behind something important. I can't tell you what it is, but it's important, dad, I have to go back. I know it seems crazy, but I just have to go back." He hugged me and we both cried some more.

My dad was a hugger and a crier, and if he loved YOU, there was no doubt you knew it. So, after a good long talk, he said. "Melissa, I trust your heart pretty much above any other thing and if you think you have to go, then you do."

He really said that to me. He went to the kitchen and got us both a beer and said, "Your mother is going to kill me."" We laughed and hugged, and I went back to California four days later to no one meeting me at the airport. I took a cab back to my cousin's house and eventually met back up with Tanner. My relationship with Tanner was never going to be great or last long-term, but from that union, from that decision to go back to California came Hunter, my son.

The first time my dad held my son, his grandson, Hunter, he said, "Well, I guess your heart was right, you needed to go back to California and get this little guy." I loved him so much for that. For just telling me to follow my gut, my heart, and every time I look at Hunter I think of dad. On an even greater level, I think of what Aralamb calls life path decisions. Granted, going back to California was not what anyone would have called the easiest life path to choose, but I would not have changed that life path decision for anything. That instinct to go back and get on the life path to Hunter was the most amazing thing I did in my young life. I am blessed by that life path choice every day. I would not change my decision to trust my "gut" for anything, even though at the time it seemed like the very last thing I should do.

Sally

My mother was a really beautiful little girl. She was precocious as a child, I am told, and loved to dress up and would often stand at the end of her driveway and wave at cars, in red high heels as if she was the Queen of England when she was nine. I often think of this now because it would just be six years later that she would be giving birth to me as a 16-year-old. This is at least what I was told of her later by my grandmother at family gatherings, as if this one fact made her an obvious pain in the ass even at a very young age. Our family was pretty rife with divorce, and two years later when my mother was 11, she and a friend rode their bikes out a forest path which they often frequented and came upon my grandmother in some kind of sexual situation with one of my grandfather's best friends. After that time, my grandmother basically asked my mother to keep quiet about what she had seen. My mother told me later that her guilt about lying to her father as this 11-year-old, and "pretending things were all perfect at home" made her feel dirty and guilty. My grandmother did not stop the affair, and would, nine years later, divorce my grandfather and marry the friend.

During the time that my mother was reaching puberty, she told me that she started to have wild emotional swings and could not stand to be at her home or around her mother because she knew that the affair was still going on. Her father was "oblivious" in my mom's words and she could not take the lying. She said that her mother finally just let her come and go as she pleased by the time she was 14 because then there would be no reason for Sally to tell her father about the affair she knew was going on. So, she "got her way," and fought horribly with her mother because of the knowledge of the affair that she had. I can remember my grandfather saying years later, even after his divorce from my grandmother, "I don't know, Sally was just a wonderful little girl and then at about age 11 she went wild, and we could never make her happy after that." I can remember being about 30 at a family gathering and looking at my mother when he said something like that in jest to the crowd. The look on my mother's face was not anger but pain and guilt. At the time I didn't quite know what to make of it, but years later as she lay dying of cancer, she relived with me one more time the day she found her mother in that sexual liaison, and how it changed her life. It strikes me now that, unwittingly, my grandmother had made a life path choice then, which forever changed my mother as well.

When my mother was drinking or drugging a lot, which was daily, even when I was a young child, she would talk about this "knowing and guilt" she had about her father. She would say she knew it was not her fault, but that it had hurt her so badly because she believed the lies that they pretended to have this perfect life. She said it sickened her even a little girl. Looking back now, I can understand the complete lack of feeling that seemed to live between my grandmother and my mother. The story was that my grandmother was this perfect poor victim to her daughter's crazy behavior, but in all actuality, my mother was just another abused little girl and I suppose my grandmother always felt some kind of guilt for that day when my mom's childhood ended as well. From that experience, my mother decided to raise my sister and I in "full truth" about "how the world is." What this meant from my mother's perspective was that the world is a dirty, get down, drug-filled, sex-filled kind of communal experience where you take what you want, and you see things that are too much for your young mind way before your time. I can speak for myself and perhaps my younger sister and say that this was a terrifying and painful way to grow up. Life path choices come into this scenario in a big way.

During her 13th summer, my mother became friends with the young lady who would become my aunt and met my father. They were all very young, but my father's family was a much more fun-loving. Sally would often tell me that she was just attracted by the love and laughter that they all had together. My mother was 12 when she met Charlie who was 15. In the next couple of years, they dated, and my mother became pregnant with me in her 10th grade year of high school.

As soon as both sets of parents became aware of the impending pregnancy, in my mother's words, a meeting was had. My mother's grandparents had money, and it was decided that Sally would be sent to a private girl's school in France, have an abortion, and finish school there. Then on to college. My mother would often tell me this story when she was drinking, and cry and cry. She would say, "I ran away a couple of times because I was not going to France to have an abortion. I knew if I just stayed away from home, they would fight and it wouldn't happen." She would cry, drink, smoke, and say, "I gave up my whole life for you. I wanted to be a writer; I could have been anything I wanted to. You need to understand, I could have gone to France, and I didn't. I gave up my whole life for you." She looked back on her life path choice at that time, which was obviously a good thing for me, and had regrets about what she had missed in life. My mother became pregnant with my sister at 19, and she would often cry and tell us both how she gave up her whole life to have us, this was a mantra for her. She had chosen her life path and was going to just sort of "bare it," and she wanted us to know what she gave up.

When I was a little girl, I was at once terrified and in awe of Sally. She was, I believe now, probably bipolar and emotionally abused. She used alcohol and drugs as medication, and she never knew an adult moment from the time she was 15 without children. She never gave up her anger or pain in this lifetime, and she took it with her when she crossed back over to The Lobby. Through Aralamb, I have learned about how to see the blessings even in the most difficult life path choices, and grow from those choices. My mother stumbled before she really understood that all the blessings are to be found often in the most challenging life path choices. I am so grateful to have been given the challenges that I was with her being my mother. I loved her as a child, I love her still, and understand that learning to work through this lifetime in a different way than she is the biggest gift she gave me. I am also thankful for her every day that she felt so strongly about her life path choice then at 15 because if she had not, I would not be sitting here writing this.

Aralamb

Through these true and novel examples, I want you to begin to trust your inner knowledge. Your intuition and soul will always lead you to the places you need to be and go through your life path options if you will just trust them. You are here in this lifetime to live, grow, and become more of what your soul truly is embodied within your lifetime. Your soul and connection to The Creator/God is not just energetic but also lands itself in science and emotion. You are in your life to live it fully while beginning to understand your part in the workings of your directions, and not just as a leaf blowing through a field. Place your intention and attention on your life and it will respond in beautiful ways. Even through challenging or painful transitions, you have the power and ability to decide how you will respond to every turn of your life path.

CHAPTER 20

Your Guide

Aralamb

Every soul born into every lifetime will have a guide. This guide will be in the role of general overseer, if you like, of that lifetime. A guide will not become active in any way within that soul's chosen lifetime unless the soul directly requests such guidance, or the soul is in danger of accidentally ending a lifetime in which the safety net of intercedence by one's guide, would have been placed by that soul.

Upon the decision of a soul to incarnate to the Earth plane or any other planet for lesson work, a guide will be chosen by that soul to be in partnership throughout that lifetime. A guide is never forced to be in partnership throughout a lifetime. The guide will be requested by that soul, and the choice is made by the guide. In Melissa's case, for instance, and as I have explained in some degree in earlier chapters, she was a soul who had joined my soul pod and shared lives with me. Due to this, when Melissa was choosing to come into this lifetime as an artist, musician, and channel, she requested that I be her teacher/guide for this work. As I am in the Communications Group already, the match for this lifetime was also lauded by those souls above me in The Creation as a good one.

As I did with Melissa, your guide will meet with you prior to your birth and determine what the lifetime possibility arcs will be, who your family will be, what your challenges and gifts will be. You and your guide will look at who within your present soul pod is presently residing within the lifetime you wish to enter. You and your guide will meet with and communicate with any souls in your pod who are currently in The Lobby. In this way, you will be able to build into your lifetime experience arc, hopefully, many experiences with the other souls in your pod that will most help everyone to experience and learn. There are times when you would be going into a new life specifically to bring a new soul into your group, or to have a last lifetime with a soul that you have travelled with for many lifetimes.

At the point when all agreements have been made about your entry point, or birth, who you will be born to, and what your possible lesson curves will be, your guide accompanies you to the Rest Point. The Rest Point is that area of The Lobby where all souls will rest in wait for their re-entry, if you will, to the Earth plane. The Rest Point is an adjacent area of The Lobby to the arrival area that souls enter at the death of the human body. It is truly a sort of arrival and departure area for souls.

Your guide will accompany you to the Rest Point, where other guides will assist you in compressing or distilling your soul into a small, restful, and completely forgetful point of light. It is as if your whole soul resides in a space that would be of the size of a lemon. Your guide will oversee this process and begin to watch over and follow the mother that you have chosen. Each soul who is incarnating will have chosen a mother. At approximately four months into the organic body's gestation of the new fetus, the soul will enter. From the time of the soul entering the Rest Point to the entry into the mother's body, the guide will have been watching over the process.

In the case of miscarriage, stillbirth, abortion, or death of the mother prior to birth, the soul within the newly growing vessel will return immediately to the Rest Point until such time the soul's guide acquires a new mother. Often, up to three mothers will have been chosen who would have agreed to be within the lifetime of that newly incoming soul.

Upon the arrival of a new soul into a four-month-old vessel which is not yet fully born from the mother's body, that new soul seats itself fully over the remaining five months. As the new soul grows within the mother's body, its guide is monitoring and watching for any event in which that soul would have full memory of The Lobby or its past lifetime. There have been souls in the past of your Earth and many more now who come through having or being allowed glimpses of where they "came from," and that is because your whole species is being evolved at this time. The general rule, however, is that a soul should not remember to have the full potential of the lesson plan.

Your guide, once you are born, cannot intervene in your decision-making process at all unless, as I stated above, you specifically ask for that contact and connection. Melissa asked specifically for The Creator/ God to send her word, to give her a sign, to let somebody tell her what she was supposed to be doing. Because of her direct employment of the rule, I was able to begin to contact her, which led to being able to speak directly with her, which led to her writing this book with me, which was one of her main possibility arcs for this lifetime.

Your guide will be there also in order to facilitate you doing, learning, and incorporating all the knowledge and experience that you came into your lifetime wishing to have. These experiences will encompass all the emotional values. Joy, pain, love, suffering, and every other human emotion are but extensions of how YOU BELIEVE life is. You can laugh and feel joy while suffering, and you can be worried and in pain while feeling Joy. You can decide that a broken heart is the best experience you ever had, or you can decide that the gifts you have are worthless, and that nothing ever works out for you. Your guide will stand and take notes for you on all the ways that you decide to feel.

It is your guide's job to keep a record of your entire life, every moment, in order for you to fully and completely go over it all when you leave your organic body, die, and return to The Lobby. Your guide will see you at your best and at your worst. Your guide will know who you loved, envied, raged against, held close, abused, and sacrificed for. Your guide is the constant, if you will, when you get back to The Lobby and engage in your life review.

Your guide is not concerned with watching you in the shower. Your guide is not staring at you all the time or judging you if you drink too much. Your guide is not concerned that you weigh 256 pounds and are about to finish off that Sarah Lee cake by yourself while watching another round of dancing animals on YouTube. Your guide is not watching you try to have sex alone or with someone else. Your guide is not judging you. Your guide sees everything, and says nothing because it is your lifetime. You will stand alone next to your guide and relive, with the "do unto others" rule running, your lifetime in its full glory.

Your guide will, however, to different degrees, always try to give you a clue, message, or direction if you are asking for help from the heart. Your guide will never profess to be a god, The God, The Creator, or in any way all-knowing. Your guide will never tell you to do anything negative or be manipulative of others. If you, from the paradigm of any religious doctrine on Earth, pray to God in any form, your guide will step aside, bow his or her head, and defer to The Creator/God while your prayers ascend through the energetic levels to The Creator/God.

When your soul's time to leave the lifetime comes, your guide and many members of your soul pod in The Lobby will draw close and begin to open the areas of your soul's energy which will lead you back home. This basic process from pre-birth to death happens with every soul-incarnating period. There are uncountable situations that can be set up by the soul and the surrounding souls in order to experience the lifetime, but the guide's responsibilities remain generally the same.

When Melissa became much more aware of my presence for her in this lifetime, her possibility arc came to her slowly as she remembered it. I was never given leave to force any information upon her, as is the law. A guide is just that. A teacher, a guide, a companion but not a controller, manipulator or decision maker. Melissa could have chosen to go a very different way with her life, and I would have no say or power in that process. When she died, she would simply look at the lifetime and understand fully what she had missed and what she had chosen.

As a guide, I am literally in a position of a scribe and hopefully a spiritual counsel to the lifetime. I take it all down and keep it for Melissa, so that she can know what her life was about this time. How she experiences the life is fully between her and The Creator/God.

As you sit and read this or listen to my words, your own guide is standing by for you. I am in no way insinuating that every human will have the same connection with their guide as Melissa does. I do want you to understand, however, that you have at your access a fully loving and willing guide and counsel to go to in all of your life. If you ask, intervention and help can come to you in the form of feelings, inspirations, intuitions, visions, instincts, knowledge, sounds, songs, vibrations, and words that will assist you in your lifetime. All of you have a guide and can have access to that guide's knowledge if you choose to.

Guides and Angels

Often, humans determine that guides and angels are the same entities. In all actuality, angels and guides are at two different levels of existence. But many guides have been, over the eons. transitioned by The Creator/God to angelic levels. An angel is a being who has full access to the direct energy body of The Creator/God. An angel is a kind of ambassador, if you like, of the full Creation energy. Angels are fully capable of creating and destroying whole planets at the behest of The Creator/God and work directly for and in the stead of The Creation. Angels have fully evolved past the need for physical bodies, incarnate lessons, or any sort of understanding of the ability to "be" anything but a full extension of The Creator/God.

Angels are fully light beings who, at some times, will show a façade of some kind of form in order to become visible to creatures and species much further below them on the spiritual energy spectrum. In this way they are able to literally be or look like anything they wish. Angels rarely move beneath the lower 20 levels of energy from The Creator/God in our Universe. As Melissa would say, "Angels are not called in unless the really big guns are needed!" This would, in theory, be true. Because our whole Universe is shifting upward currently, the angels are working in realms where new arrivals at higher vibrations need guidance. The Earth plane is rising in a very controlled way and, so far, has not needed to be marshaled by angelic intervention.

There are no fallen angels, as one of your religious texts would indicate. The fallen angels in the Bible are and were simply off-Earth organic species who set themselves up as "gods," and then had a fractious war amongst themselves. The fallen angels were the ones who stayed upon the Earth. Angels have never come from any levels of The Creation. Angels are also a group of beings who are energetically, mentally, spiritually, and psychically bound to The Creator/God and each other, so any of them "falling" out of the group is and has always been impossible. Angels are a sort of energetic perfection.

Guides are counselor teachers whose souls no longer need to incarnate into organic bodies in order to learn. There are many levels of guides, novice guides, practicing, teaching and service guides who reside at the entry level of The Lobby all the way up to the lower/lowest levels of The Creation. As a guide works with more and more souls through lifetimes, they also are learning and progressing through the ever-winding levels back towards The Creator/God. As a guide, I am in the middle of the entry level and The Creation levels. If you wanted to look at my level of existence through an Earthly lens, I would be likened to a highly decorated college professor with many doctorates on my wall. As I move through the many lifetimes with souls facilitating their growth, I will rise through the levels as well.

There is a point at which a guide or councilor moves close enough to The Creation levels to be raised into the Angelic realms. This does not mean that that a guide becomes an Angel, just that the guide would be able to work within the Angelic realms. This is just the next step in the whole Universal evolution in the journey back to The Creator/God. All guides are within this structure. During different growth times for Melissa, groups of guides from levels above me have visited her to see how she is progressing, and how I am progressing as her guide. All of this is done in a completely non-judgmental way, but in order to keep all of the most powerful and positive energy moving forward through The Creation.

As a guide, I also have the right to "call in" assistance from other guide groups to help further Melissa along if I think it's necessary and she agrees. That is called free will. I have sometimes called in guides to assist Melissa in releasing fear or releasing old hurts that still color her reactions, though they are long gone and should not be in her view presently. This ability is one of the best reasons for you to at least give your guide permission to assist and help you in this lifetime.

In closing this chapter, I would like to say that I am not telling you what to believe. I would only ask that you consider that you have some essential support in your guide, who can really assist you in this lifetime if you would just ask.

CHAPTER 21
Childhood Stories and The Cowboy Hat

**(The Black Cowboy Hat and his or her negative
voice in your head)**

Aralamb

"You're born, you work, you pay taxes, and you die." "He will never amount to anything, he's just like his father, a loser." "Alcoholism runs in our family, it's no surprise she is a drinker." "No one in our family ever lived past 50, we're just heavy people with bad hearts and unhealthy." "He's not good with money, his parents weren't either, they both died broke." "Depression runs in our family, suicide too, it's so sad." "My parents were from broken homes, they were divorced when I was a baby, I can't seem to stay in a marriage." "Life stays the same, struggle, sacrifice, and then it's over." "There is no God, no heaven, a soul is just something made up by scared people." "Science has to prove everything for it to be real, everyone knows that." "My doctor always knows the best medicine for me to take, any other way is quackery, everyone knows that." "People don't really change, it's impossible. Eventually they will show their true colors." "You can't do that, you're not strong enough." "Only beautiful people get breaks, you're not one of those."

This is just a small taste of the infinite number of so-called certainties that your subconscious mind, through your inner talk, will spew at you daily. The issue that is difficult with this kind of negative self-talk is that it was planted there in your mind either purposefully or casually through some of your earliest childhood and even infant memories.

Those negative "statements of truth" become lodged in your subconscious *as the truth* and work against you for the rest of your lifetime if you do not truly see them, hear them, and learn to eradicate them by choice. In this chapter we will look at just how to remove this kind of insidious background voice, so that you can grow and learn within the lifetime that you inhabit. First though, some examples of just how this issue can impact our lives negatively.

Melissa

In the summer of 2015, I set up a really great gig for my band. The gig was an outdoor festival about one-and-a-half hours East of Denver in a cool little plains' town called Fort Morgan. The festival, Bob Stock, was a cool mix of farm, music, beer, and various carnival kind of events. I went out of my way to use money from a bonus at my day job to pay for the rental of a big travel van, so that everyone could just relax and enjoy the festival that I had gotten us booked at. It was a brilliant day, summer in Colorado, and nothing should have been amiss for anyone. I am using this true story to illustrate how the "cowboy hat" became the name for that voice in your head that never has your best interest at heart. From this festival forward, for Aralamb, myself, and anyone I could talk to about it that voice became "the cowboy hat guy." That negative and destructive voice that does nothing but spew fear and self-loathing on you, thereby blocking you from having amazing experiences and growth.

From the beginning of this festival day, one of my bandmates was out of sorts. Jeff kept on finding every possible negative thing he could about the real and imagined negative outcomes of the trip that day. Please know that I love Jeff like family, and he wasn't trying to be an ass, he was just being fully controlled by his negative inner voice. I was disappointed from the start because I knew that Jeff almost always listened to his inner negative voice and framed his whole life within that filter. Honestly, it was pissing me off because I had gone so far out of my way to make the trip super easy for everyone. I had picked this festival and worked hard to get us placed in it because it was the perfect distance from Denver, and just a great spot with great people running it. We had free food and drink passes for the festival, we had a great big stage to play on, and lots of help setting up. The people of Fort Morgan were thrilled we were there, and everyone was very, very nice. When we arrived in town, they were playing our music on the radio for frig sake! I had done a radio interview for the festival a few weeks before which went well. I mean, if you are a struggling musician, it was the best kind of experience. All you had to do was show up, relax, enjoy, and be shuffled along through the day like a rock star! The best!

As soon as we arrived at the festival, Jeff began a long, and frankly difficult to listen to, stream of complaints. Food wasn't good enough, too hot, too big, too small, too whatever, etc. Okay, so you get the picture. At one point we entered the "green room tent," which is kind of a cool deal at a festival. Now these green room tents can be elaborate, or they can be simple with just lots of free snacks, drinks, and water. Either way, they are a free hospitality item for the artistes. Well, Jeff was not happy with the free snacks, drinks, and accommodations, and proceeded to sit and eat, drink and complain loudly about the nice ladies who were working the hospitality tent, right in front of them. I was really getting pissed at this point and we had not even gone on or set up our gear yet. At the time, I could not figure out what the hell was going on with him, but I was embarrassed by his behavior. Again, I reiterate here that Jeff is like family to me, and I now know much more clearly what his true problem was on that day. It's one that a lot of us wrestle with.

It was like I had taken a really spoiled child to Disneyland and they were just being horrible. As the time came to set up, there were approximately 900–1,000 people in a beautiful clearing surrounded by concession beer and food booths, with a second stage adjacent to ours. When we began to set up, Jeff was whining about his placement on stage, just being a total pain in the ass, AND, all 900 or so people, cued by us as the next band, turned all their lawn chairs toward us and waited quietly for us to set up and get going. The sound man for the festival at one point came up and got surly with me because Jeff was not listening to him and was not setting up quickly. I was pretty mortified at this point and could not figure out what was going on. This gig was one of the best that we were ever invited to, and Jeff and at least one other member were both acting crazy. I can remember thinking that I just wanted to get through the show. Once we started playing, all of the 900 or so people really loved us! That was so great! It was easily one of the largest crowds we had played live for up to that point, and everyone in that crowd really, really enjoyed us. There were a few stragglers way out by the concession stands who moved in and out of the crowd, but for the most part we had 900 or so festivalgoers completely in our grip. It was just amazing. At one point, I can remember seeing two or three cowboys come by at the back, lean in, and keep moving toward the rodeo arena. After our set, we cleared the stage and went to get a couple of cold beers and listen to the next act who was a talented blues guy in his teens. He was kind of a child prodigy.

While relaxing and drinking those free beers, Jeff started commenting on how the crowd really liked this kid better than us, and that he was blowing us out of the water. Just about the time I had really had enough of the "ruin this great day talk," a huge thunderstorm rolled in, and we all ran back to the vans. Festival over. All the way back to Denver in the van, Jeff complained about the food, the hospitality, the other bands, the sound guy's attitude, the rainstorm, the uncomfortable chairs, the heat, blah, blah,

blah, just everything. I don't think I had been so pissed off at anyone, who was like family to me, in a long time. At one point, I turned in my seat and said, "Man, that was an awesome time, the crowd loved us!" Glaring back at me, he said, **"Yeah, well, there was a guy back in the concession area with a black cowboy hat, leaning on a post glaring at me. He hated us. He ruined my play."**

That is the point in my life when the negative inner voice that we all carry got its name. Sitting in that van, I came face to face with the negative voice of Jeff and how it had colored and infused his whole experience that day with negativity. Not only that, but it was also a huge wake-up call to me about allowing someone else's "cowboy hat voice" to impact my life, thoughts, and feelings.

Here was the reality that struck me full force that day. Jeff's inner negative voice, using fear and self-doubt, led him to ignore every great thing about the experience—the day, the 900-plus crowd, the venue, his friends—and concentrate instead on one man wearing a black cowboy hat and sunglasses, 100 yards away, who he *imagined* personally didn't like him or his playing? What!?!?!? And here is the kicker, we ALL do it. Some of us infrequently, but some of us daily, until we truly see what's happening and stop it. The Black Cowboy Hat Voice was born.

Jeff was completely at the mercy on that amazing day of his inner negative voice. He let that negative self-talk shine a dark, unreal, and frankly, wrong light on his whole experience. In reality, that dude, whoever he was, had no idea of what was going on in Jeff's head that day. As a matter of fact, when you see a stranger and they seem to ignore you, look past you, or any other manner of affront you feel, you were not even on their radar 99 per cent of the time. It's a complete waste of your time to use strangers as your barometer of your own self-worth.

After that day, "the cowboy hat guy" would come up for us in conversation as the moniker for that inner voice that never gives you constructive talk or ideas about yourself or the world. That Black Cowboy Hat Voice will tear you down, tell you the truth about how shitty, horrible, incompetent, stupid, ugly, fat, afraid you are. Add in the negative self-talk, and the cowboy hat will throw it at you.

Ultimately, this story is not about how Jeff ruined a great day, it's about how much we might be missing in our own lives because of this inner filter cowboy hat voice. As for me, on that day, I started to really pick Aralamb's brain on just how to combat this, where this comes from, and how to tell the Cowboy Hat Guy to just go fuck off already! I don't want this inner voice making my life less joyful and harder! Please.

I have become a personal warrior against the Black Cowboy Hat Voice for everyone I meet or do sessions with if I can get them to a place where they can really hear what I am saying. As of the writing of this book, I will be known to literally ask people who are close to me when they come to me with some worry, inadequacy, or fear, "Is this just the Black Cowboy Hat Voice coming at you, or is this real?" The truth is that if you are not consciously telling your inner negative Black Cowboy Hat Voice to fuck off and go away (which you totally can), then you will be at its mercy. There is not much middle ground, either that negative self-talk has the microphone in your head, or it does not, and frankly YOU TOTALLY CHOOSE! That is the great news here. You decide. It's as if you have a massively shitty friend who always brings you down and never lifts you up, you can tell that bummer dude or chickee to just leave the room. Thank you!

Aralamb

First, I would like to extrapolate for you the difference, and there is one, between the instinct which you have for survival and the Black Cowboy Hat Voice (as Melissa refers to it), in case you might try to see them as the same functioning entity within your subconscious.

Instinctive Survival Mechanism

Your inner mind and soul's need to protect you from physical, emotional, and psychological harm is an integral part of your energetic and physical body. This instinct is the part of you which keeps *you* from lighting your own clothes on fire or drinking poison. This is the same instinct that keeps you from jumping out of a moving car or makes you consider before running headlong into traffic. This is also the instinct that you carry which may make you avoid certain persons or situations that you sense may be harmful for you. This system has been in place within your limbic body since the inception of human life upon your planet and was heightened as an ability for your survival at the seeding phase as well. This is one of your natural survival mechanisms. Simply, this instinct, intuition keeps you alive and moving forward on your lifetime of learning and experiencing the lifetime you are within. This system is very simple in design. This system will never extrapolate on the "why you should avoid an activity or opportunity." This system merely points out the very obvious dangers to be avoided. There is never any emotional blackmail, no wheedling, no flowery speeches on the why of things, it just IS. In this way you will be able to begin learning and differentiating your true survival instinct from what Melissa so aptly calls the Black Cowboy Hat Voice.

The Black Cowboy Hat Voice
(Bill, Example 1)

Please imagine a man named Bill. Bill has a nice wife he loves, three grown children, a job as an accountant, and a mortgage. Bill is reasonably happy but spends hours every weekend on the couch watching the YouTube channel of old football game footage from the '80s and '90s. Bill dreamed of being an NFL coach for most of his 20s and was his team's assistant coach all four years of college. But life, "the right thing," and family prompted him to get a real job and support his family. One Friday morning during his local news broadcast, he hears a story of a local high school needing a coach for their football team. Instinctively, Bill feels drawn to apply, he thinks about the fact that his kids are grown, his wife would love for him to get off the couch on weekends, and for the first time in a long time he feels a bit lit up from the inside. Bill asks his wife what she thinks, and she thinks it's a great idea.

As he jumps in his car on Monday morning heading for work, he thinks, "I'm going to call them today and find out how to apply." Before Bill is even out of his driveway, in comes the Back Cowboy Hat Voice in his head. "Bill, you don't have time for that." "Man, your day has come and gone." "Your back hurts most days, how are you going to stand up for hours during practice time and games?" "What happens if you are asked to work overtime and can't get to practice?" "You could lose your job, and you know at your age, 56, jobs aren't easy to come by." "I can't believe you would be thinking about this again! This boat sailed. You don't get to change course now; your life is your life." "They probably need someone with more experience than you have anyway." "Who do you think you are anyway?" "You made your bed, now you just have to lay in it." "You are so stupid to be hanging on to this ridiculous dream." "Isn't it time for you to grow up?"

These are just some of the ways that the Black Cowboy Hat Voice will try to deter Bill from something that may very well change his life for the better, AND more importantly be a built-in part of his soul's growth path. This decision may well be a three-minute rule decision. What if Bill is supposed to apply for the position because it will allow him to further several other young souls along their paths? What if he chooses not to apply, and misses these opportunities?

Chelsea

Chelsea is a barista; she loves being a barista. The constant contact with people coming and going makes her feel alive and involved in life! Chelsea works at a major coffee house chain near her college. She is studying to be a preschool teacher like her mother was. Chelsea is also a talented artist. Painting is her passion, but she knows she must support herself in some sane way. "Artists don't make money." Chelsea's mom, Sandra, was a single mom and had raised her and her brother pretty much alone with the help of her grandmother, Tina. They lived altogether outside of Boston in Newton, Mass. Both Tina and Sandra worked full-time to support her and her brother, Tina as a cleaning woman in some of the bigger homes in the Beacon Hill area of Boston and her mom as a preschool teacher in Newton. They worked hard to be sure that both Chelsea and her brother could attend college.

Chelsea had a large extended family, and in the summer, they would have big BBQs and gatherings at her Aunt Michelle's house on the old family farm outside of Newton. All the cousins would sit up at a big picnic table and do paintings on paper plates while they ate dripping popsicles in the sun. This was the best part for Chelsea. Even at 10 or 11 she loved to paint and draw, and she was already gifted at it. The family would comment on how she was a little artist, and her mother would always smile in that certain way, and say, "No, Chelsea is going to be a teacher. Artists are starving, and we aren't going to have any of that for Chelsea." This was the main thought as Chelsea grew up. Chelsea always excelled in her art classes, even to the point during her senior year when she won a statewide student art show with a watercolor she did, which depicted one of those sunny afternoons at the farm from her childhood, melting popsicles included. Her art teacher, Mrs. Heinston, gave her the ribbon at the school's final graduation ceremony and then called her mother. Mrs. Heinston urged her mother to allow Chelsea to minor in art while she got her teaching degree, but her mother had politely told her that her daughter was not going to be a starving artist. She told her that she had starved as a young mother, and her daughter would not ever relive that nightmare. The conversation ended and four months later Chelsea found herself in her freshman year of at the University of Massachusetts gaining a pre-K teaching degree. She was working as a barista to help offset her loans, and secretly buy painting supplies. Her mother had told her that she could not help her with painting supplies and if she wanted to keep on pursuing that expensive hobby, she would need to pay for it herself.

On that Wednesday morning, a woman from the college came into the coffee shop, ordered a coffee, and asked Chelsea if she could hang up a flyer for a program starting at the college. Chelsea smiled and agreed, giving the woman a roll of tape to hang it in the window.

After her shift, Chelsea walked past the new flyer the woman had hung earlier and stopped dead in her tracks. The flyer was for a competition whereby the three top finalists would be given a sizable scholarship and working internship position within the art department of the college. The deadline for submitting the artwork and essay was in three weeks. Before she knew what she was doing consciously, Chelsea's hand had reached out and ripped the whole flyer off the door and into her bag. Two blocks away as she moved up the sidewalk toward her dorm room, thunder rumbled, and rain started lightly to hit her face. Chelsea didn't feel the rain on her face as her inner Black Cowboy Hat Voice started running in her head. "Artists are starving." "Art is not a real profession." "You are not good enough." "Also, this would kill your mother." "After everything she has done for you, you would do this behind her back." "You are not going to starve because you are strong and artists are weak and broke, everyone knows this." "It's not a real profession."

As Chelsea slowed in front of her dorm building, she realized that hot tears were streaming down her cheeks and mingling with the rain. She reached into her bag, looked at the flyer, crumpled it in her hand and threw it into the rain-filled gutter. She turned away and decided to look for an intern position at the pre-K program. Being a barista was a dead end, and so was the painting. She would concentrate on being a teacher and stop letting her "head be in the clouds," as her mom would say. As Chelsea wiped the rain and tears from her face, she ran up the steps and into her dorm. The Black Cowboy Hat voice had won, she was fully engrained and invested once again within the negative self-talk loop that had been pro-grammed into her since her early childhood.

Now, when Chelsea threw that flyer into the gutter, a few things were put into place. Firstly, she was most likely instituting a life path choice, she probably passed up a three-minute rule option, and she also gave herself over fully to the Black Cowboy Hat Voice, thus making that inner negative voice even stronger. Repeatedly listening to and keeping within the action loop of that negative inner self-talk only works to cement the habit of the negative loop. I do not intend to insinuate that Chelsea is now ruined on her life path, only that she may have made it much harder to deviate from the path she had chosen.

Chelsea will most likely have built into her lifetime other critical points of decision around her soul's innermost talents and yearnings, but each time she allows the negative Black Cowboy Hat Voice to have power over her decision-making process, the harder it becomes to understand the reality that YOU have all of the power to eradicate that voice.

Samuel

Samuel is 34 years old and lives in Oklahoma. Samuel always wanted to be a pilot. Samuel has always worked on his family's farm. There was not enough money to go to college, and cities are full of "wicked people and sin." Everyone knew this about big cities, and his family's pastor had always preached that being "close to God means keeping close to home." Samuel's dad had left the farm when he was a little boy to drill rigs just south in Texas. He had been killed on those same rigs in an accident when Sam was nine. Sam and his mother had been able to keep the farm with the help of his grandfather and uncle. They milked a herd of dairy cows, which numbered about 400. Twenty-four hours a day the milk parlor was oper-ating with 180 heifers rotating in and out every 12 hours, with feeding and cleanup in between. It was a living and Sam loved the animals, but this had been his father's dream and not his own.

Sam's cell phone rang, Tim, his cousin calling. Tim was Sam's age and just graduating with a degree in agriculture from Iowa State. Tim was always talking to Sam about going into a partnership to convert the dairy into an all-organic operation which Sam and he could run, or, Tim could run it with Sam as a silent partner while Sam went and got his aviation training and license. Either way, Sam's mom and family would have help on the farm, and Tim and he would both be able to do what lit them up.

He looked out over the corn field, let the phone vibrate in his pocket, and waited for the voicemail to beep. The sun was warm and beautiful on his face. Something in him just felt like a ship getting ready to sail. A warm, glow inside like his life might just be getting ready to turn. Then, just like a sign from above, overhead a Piper Cub glided over the horizon, disappearing into the sun and out of sight to the west. Sam smiled, looked up and said, "Okay, I get it."

Tim's message said that he would be at the farm by the weekend with paperwork and that he had met a man in Bakersfield, California, who owned a small airstrip and would love to talk with Sam about lodging and internship in order to offset flight school and the training it included. Sam's knowledge of crops would also come in handy because crop dusting would be his first job there, once he was certified. Sam turned off the phone and looked back toward the barns a mile away. He started the tractor and headed towards home. In the first two minutes of that one-mile ride back to the barnyard, the Black Cowboy Hat Voice started in. "You are too old to start new like that." "You can't move to California, people there are crazy." "You can't leave your mother, just like your father did." "You are a farmer, that's what your people do." "You are so selfish to be thinking about leaving the bag in Tim's hands." "This is your life; you can't just decide and leave it." "You need to stay here and find a nice girl to start a family with, you are running out of time." "You're not smart enough for college." "The farm will go under if you aren't here."

Aralamb
The truth about the Black Cowboy Hat Voice

At this point, I think that you have enough examples of how this negative voice in your head works to keep you where you are on your life path, even if where you need to be is somewhere unknown, untried, and full of learning. If you take nothing else from my explanation of this, know these two things. The Black Cowboy Hat Voice is about keeping you in FEAR and keeping you from growing by using that FEAR.

The negative self-talk that seems to have your best interest always at heart is a lie. That negative self-talk voice is a lie. Everything that your inner Black Cowboy Hat Voice tells you about your life, the why you can, can't, should, could, couldn't or wouldn't be able to do is a lie.

If you are literally 350 pounds and are getting ready to eat a gallon of ice cream, the Black Cowboy Hat Voice will or may tell you the following: "You can't control the urge to eat it" "You're fine, it's just ice cream and it makes you happy." "You're just big, your whole family is big." "You're great just the way you are." "You don't need anyone in your life." These are all lies. I am simply telling you that your inner negative self-talk will often, just like an addiction, pose as your best friend and protector when in reality, it is just the opposite.

The idea here is to bring that Black Cowboy Hat Voice to your attention, so that YOU can just stop listening to it. You have all the power to manually tell that negative self-talk to be quiet, turn away, go sit in the corner, and stop talking. I don't care if that voice comes in the form of your parents, your teacher, your siblings, kids who bullied you, strangers, ex. It does not matter what form or memory those voices take, if the information is not positive and helpful to you for your betterment, IT NEEDS TO GO. You have the power to eradicate that voice.

First, you must recognize it when it begins to influence your decision-making process and stop it over and over. After some practice at this, you will begin to immediately notice when you are hearing that negative

Black Cowboy Hat Voice speaking. Whenever you are presented with any kind of choice to react, experience, and learn, you can begin to ignore and eradicate that voice, so that you can stop filtering your life path through this destructive and unnecessary filter.

You have the power to do that. Once you understand that presence of the Black Cowboy Hat Voice in your daily life, you will begin to make the choice to silence it and be balanced in your decision-making processes as well as your emotional responses to life.

In the beginning when Melissa would recognize the negative Black Cowboy Hat Voice (her own negative self-talk,) she would imagine herself making the Black Cowboy Hat turn and face the corner with duct tape on his mouth. In this way, it was a physical manifestation of silencing that old habit. Now, much later, in sessions she will describe it as if her angry, drunk uncle is in the back bedroom and if he decides to start yelling at her, she just yells back to "shut it up!" and closes that door. This is a great way of visualizing the banishment from her conscious mind the bad habit of letting the Black Cowboy hat Voice run her life.

In order for you as a soul on your growth path to learn and expand in the ways that you would have aspired to in this lifetime, you need to banish this inner negative self-talk to grow fully. You can do this, and just being aware of the insidious power of this inner voice will begin to free you. If you had a neighbor who was sneaking in and filling your refrigerator with rotten food each night while you slept, just the act of becoming aware of what was going on would immediately give you the tools to lock your front door and take action against their negative intrusion into your life.

This is the same truth with the Black Cowboy Hat Voice. Just pointing out the existence of such a voice immediately shines light on its presence and takes away its power in your growth process. Also, keep in mind that whenever you are about to make a really amazing life/soul decision, the louder the Black Cowboy Hat Voice will scream and accuse you. If that happens, feel joy because it means you are on the right track.

CHAPTER 22
The Fabric-Time Travel

Aralamb

In past chapters you have heard me often refer to the DMF, or Dark Matter Fabric, of the Universe in which we live. I have spoken about how gravity, intention, frequency, and your soul can come together to manipulate the DMF in order to create that which you would create from the very "stuff" of the Universe. Time, the DMF, and travel are all linked to this operation of frequency as well.

Einstein said that time was relative to the observer and where that observer was located within a physical plane. He was correct, except that the idea that a person's body must be in a specific place in order to experience time as relative was not quite correct.

The missing piece in his extrapolation was that there is also the aspect of "where" in time that person was resonating. The frequency of any soul's consciousness can be resonant to a specific "place" as well as a specific "timeline." Because of this fact of our Universe, many species that are much more evolved than Earth humans can shift whole groups of themselves from one time/frequency/place to another. Often this is done within an inter-time-traveling ship or vessel of some kind. I tell you this only so that you can understand that time is truly only a measured and experienced situation upon planetary species that are very young to the Universe.

If you can envision the idea that once a species is able to move through time/place/frequency shifts, that same species is much, much less likely to engage in violent, destructive, or non-productive activity, and often only shift timelines in order to learn lessons from their very distant past. Earthlings, should you survive into your next millennia, which I believe you will by branching out into your solar system and the next closest to you, will also begin to understand the gift of frequency-shifting time travel through the DMF, and use it to your advantage.

Remote Viewing and Astral Travel are two very simple techniques that humans are already able to perform with some proficiency, which are the beginnings of frequency, DMF-based Time Travel. Remote Viewing and Astral Travel are the first steps in a human learning to see, feel, and know the difference between his or her body, consciousness, faith tether, and soul. Once that human being can differentiate between those parts of him or herself, the consciousness while attached to the energy of the soul can literally leave the organic body and travel outside of the known limits of "time" as it is known on Earth. Once out of the timeline, that person's conscious energy resonates with a place/time that is not where their organic body is sitting or lying. Simply said, your body is in one place and your fully engaged consciousness is in another place/time.

The reason that you are not able to open a door or knock over a plant while in this kind of time/place/frequency travel is that you have not resonated your frequency highly enough to actually move your organic body along with your consciousness to the new time/place/frequency. There are species in the Universe who have evolved to this method of travel.

The level of Remote Viewing and Astral Travel that humans are evolving today upon your planet is the fully conscious/soul type of time/place travel. Within this early system of "seeing," you will have the ability to "see" details from wherever you are traveling to but are not able to interact with the place/time that you view. The piece that is missing for your scientists is that not only can you move laterally to other points in space and upon your planet, but you also have the unknown ability to travel forward and backward in timelines within the same techniques.

Moving forward and backward in time is not so much about actual linear movement, but more specifically, time is a massive circular energy force moving outward from every sentient being within the Universe at all levels and strata all the way up to creation. The idea that the timelines move only backward or forward is a very young adaptation of any species. Time, which is linked completely with the DMF, has a fully evolving nature in every possible way. Every second of your lifetime is constantly being manifested in front of your eyes by your attention to the infinite possible timelines which will not manifest until you place your attention upon them. Because of this, it is completely within your power to visit a potential timeline in your future or your past to determine what could or should happen within your lifetime for you to grow as a soul. The truth is that what you place your attention upon becomes your timeline, and what you have experienced is, and can be changed by what you place your attention upon from your perceived past. Time is not a line upon which you walk but is an ocean of energy in which you float. This distinction of description is very, very important to evolving your understanding of time.

If you, like Melissa, had a difficult childhood and that is what you place all your attention upon, you will stay within the victimhood of that timeline. Should you place your attention upon the lessons learned, you will overcome that timeline and your "future" timeline is changed because of that decision.

I will also pose to you that should you, within a meditative state, Remote View or Astral Travel outward to a time in your perceived past, you can "see" exactly what happened and release that or relive some joy around that specific place/time. This is a real ability.

The energy link between frequency, gravity, and the DMF is similar to a radio wave which can be tuned to a specific time/space in order to travel to that time. On your planet the belief is that if one could visit a time in the past and murder one's own grandfather, you would certainly be killing yourself in the future timeline. This is wholly untrue because if you murdered your grandfather in a past timeline, your soul would just adjust and incarnate within its chosen timeline. In this way, the integrity of each species and soul's timelines are protected. As romantic as it seems, going back to right some wrong in a timeline is not within the scope of the Universal or energetic laws because that would open the upper levels of the Universal Strata to species that were not ready or evolved to the point of overcoming war, rage, and control of others. There is a safeguard in place which does not allow young species to inadvertently travel within time in such ways, as it would alter another's timeline. I say this because I want you to begin to understand how time truly works and want you to understand that you can begin to study this for yourself without the fear of accidentally harming a past timeline or loved one.

What you can do with this ability is to begin to feel into time differently. It is wholly possible, for example, to plant 100 seedling pine trees in a field, go into a meditative state, and travel outward from your body at the correct frequency and find yourself standing 150 years out into time when the seedlings are 100 feet tall, and the field is now a forest. You could smell the pines and hear the birds chirping. Humans at this time can only send their consciousness and soul energy in this way. You can see, smell, feel all the forest in the future timeline, but your body will remain in the empty field of pine seedlings. There are species right now in the Universe who can not only send their consciousness and soul energy forward to those 150-year-old trees but also their organic bodies. They simply move by means of frequency and gravity along the DMF to that time/place.

There are also species that travel from galaxy to galaxy in this way within vessels. The vessel itself shifts frequency to the allotted time/place and they appear in the time/place without having changed or aged at all, much the way that Einstein explained the difference in time experience if you are standing along train tracks, as the man inside the train is experiencing the frequency of time differently as it passed you. In this way, the vessel can visit a time/place/frequency without the reality that when they return to the time/place/frequency from which they came, everyone would be 1,000 years dead and gone. Since the vessel is instantly shifting from time/place/frequency to time/place/frequency and back, the ratio of "time" slippage is no more than you might have flying in an airplane from Boston to Chicago and back even over eons and eons of perceived time. This system of time movement has no connection to what your scientists would refer to as light years, so there is no need to involve space travel within the actual light year calculations. Within this system of time/place/frequency travel, you would never be gone or in transit for years, months, or even days. Explorers will often travel to time/place/frequencies to study possible futures and multiple pasts for the sake of moving their civilizations and species into positive-outcome time/place/frequency timelines.

Begin to think of time/space frequency as moving out from your organic body in every direction. If you are in a sea of "time," then you have control of where you are going within that sea of time/space/frequency. Think of the healing that you might do for yourself if you really grasp the idea that you have the power to influence your sphere of time and your experience of it.

The DMF

The Dark Matter Fabric is quite literally the substance of the Universe that makes the time/place/frequency work within the infinite timeline possibilities. The ability for species to travel and explore in this way is fully a function of the DMF.

The DMF is, as we spoke earlier, the energetic substance that makes up everything that has not yet been manifested into "something." DMF is the unilaterally available energetic substance which is, at its smallest parts, able to be intended into any form that any sentient being needs or wants in order to experience itself. When any sentient being intends, imagines, incorporates emotional attachment to either specifically or unintentionally upon the DMF, the frequency of that intention is transmitted to the gravity field which accompanies every energetic particle of the DMF and begins, with enough attention, to coalesce itself into that manifestation or vision of matter. Time travel and time/place/frequency travel is the correct and specific frequency and intention placed upon the DMF and gravity in such a way that a "tuning" happens which coalesces and transports the "intender" to the intended time/place/frequency.

When a species becomes very advanced in its ability to "tune" either organically or technologically its frequency to specific time/place frequencies, they will be able to travel easily within the ocean of time, and without the difficulties that light year travel exposes a human being too.

CHAPTER 23
Life Cycle of the Soul

Aralamb

Prior to your birth, you were an all-encompassing soul. You lived fully within in The Creation. The Creation is the energetic realm of **The Creator/ God** from which all souls leave to live reincarnated lives on Earth and many different planets, in many millions of galaxies in your Universe. The energetic mass upon which your Universe is built is the Fabric. The "fabric" is the term I have used to describe for you the unseen level of energy which is the simple tool by which ALL things are manifested by you, through and by The Creator/God. The "fabric" is the all-powerful way in which every last bit of your Universe finds itself into being. Interestingly, scientists in your timeline are trying to find the "absolute *physical* mechanics" of this fabric, but the energetic fabric responds directly to the energy sound/light waves made up by souls and intention at its most basic level. It is truly and physically what you might call "the genie in the bottle." All incarnated souls have the "actual and physical" ability to create realities by way of the fabric. The fabric is an unknown mixture of "dark matter" and "gravity" which, upon inspection, intention, or attention from a sentient being attached to a soul, will bring itself together in the reality by which there is consensus either by the individual or groups of souls.

Souls are completely unique and remain unique throughout the hundreds and sometimes thousands of lives which are lived in order to raise soul vibration and grow back toward the initial level of The Creation. The Universe in which you are living was created when two much older Universes collided by the movement of The Creator/God. The Creator/God has created an unknown number of Universal fabrics, which would look like a water-filled balloon to you. All of the unknown number of Universes float side by side in *an unending creation field*. At my incarnation level, I am not able to understand exactly what the scope and scale would be of *an unending creation field*. However, the life cycle of Universes is vast and incomparable by way of calculation, and when it is deemed necessary by The Creator/God, two Universes will be touched together, thus creating what you would know as the "big bang." It will create a wholly new, clean, clear expanse of energy which, with the slightest touches of The Creator/God, will evolve a wholly new fabric of time and space. Should your scientists try to determine what happened in the time/space just prior to this "big bang," they will find an endless void of energy which is simply the moment when The Creator/God was combing the two previous Universes and the distilled energy of each. Pure reintegrated energy still holding every particle of atomic, subatomic, and ultra-atomic information from each prior Universe. This is akin to a dried seed holding all the information of the tomato until such time as it is watered and germinated into a new plant.

When it is deemed necessary by The Creation to bring two older Universes together to create a brand new one, all the base particulate and energy of each are blended together to make a completely new environment. A great new expansive canvas as it were.

The seeds of every soul which will reside in a Universe at its conception are numbered. There are a very specific number of souls who will inhabit the teaching arena of a new Universe. Any sentient soul beings that inhabited a Universe upon the moment of its combination with another Universe will, by nature of The Creation, be brought forward to the newly created Universe. No more, or less are ever added as far as I/we have seen. Each new seed of a soul will return hundreds of times to many different corners of that created Universe. From the very start of a new Universe, which can last eons of billions of years in human time, all souls are in a sleeping state until that new Universe evolves to be able to support bodies/ beings which can be a vehicle for a learning soul. Earth humans are not the only beings which harbor souls and there is a good likelihood that you, the reader, have inhabited other being/bodies in your journey forward. When/ if a new Universe is created by putting two together, all the souls from each Universe are then reverted to their "seedling" state and incorporated even- tually into that new Universe. It is taught, by much higher energy levels than mine, that The Creator/God will sometimes blend two Universes, in which one Universe would seed the other with higher, more evolutionary promise. The Creation is constantly trying to upgrade/enhance/better the energetic meaning of what is created. So, if one Universe was full of species that were only nominally self-aware, and the other was a very old and long- lived Universe with many old and traveled souls, combining the two would press each of the soul groups to learn new lessons from each other. Earth sits in one such Universe. The Universe in which you live was created by combining two much older Universes. One of them was approximately two times the size of the present one, and filled with mostly very young spe- cies of plants, geological-based matter, and a large and spread-out colony of species that were mostly non-sentient in the way that humanity would recognize. The second Universe was smaller but very old, and the beings had progressed long past the need for organic bodies, organic substances, or manual material existence. They were mostly light beings to whom exis- tence had become non-material. The decision was made to combine the two, so that the souls from the latter may go back again to re-experience the corporal, material existence they once had. Thus, the present Universe was born with the souls, matter, and energy of both. This also explains why your present Universe is full of such a wide expanse of beings/souls, both sentient, corporal and non-corporal, and light/energy based.

The Creation for our study is approximately 2,200 full levels higher and lower than the Earth plane. I, Aralamb, reside for now on what you might call 89th level. Earth's energetic plane, as well as the Milky Way Galaxy, resides at approximately the 58th level. It should be noted that at this time, which I touched upon in in a previous chapter, the Earth is, along with the whole of the Milky Way Galaxy, in the process of a natural "shift" to the 71st level of energetic expansion. Your scientists would call Earth a three-dimensional reality, when in fact, there are all of the other dimensions/levels that I speak of. It is, however, a great forward movement that string theorists are beginning to embrace the idea that there are many other dimensions. It is interesting that they do believe that dimensions or levels reside in a side-by-side formation lying upon one another, when in actuality the "Jacob's Ladder" mythology is much more accurate in that dimensions/levels do reside somewhat above and below each other. Thus, also true is the old Earth adage of As above/So below.

The 89th level, which Melissa refers to as The Lobby, is where I am residing currently. This is the level of Creation where all souls coming/going, being born/dying, moving to and from Earth will travel to. No matter what level your personal soul resides upon, if you are going to be born onto Earth or any other planet in the Milky Way Galaxy, or you have been a soul living any kind of corporal life upon Earth or any other planet in the Milky Way Galaxy, you will, when your "body" dies, travel back to the 89th level, The Lobby again. Melissa's connection to me, although very spiritual and cerebral in this lifetime for her, has its energetic roots/connection at the same place on the 89th level that her soul will return to when her life on Earth is complete this time. Every human soul has a connection to The Creation, whether that human soul can remember or believe it in their lifetime.

Before you were born, there would have been a kind of meeting at The Lobby. You will have had a meeting with the other "important" souls that you were going to share this life with. When I use the word "important," I do not intend to insinuate that some souls have more worth than others. I use the word "important" to delineate those persons with whom you are agreeing to spend a lifetime of lessons with. The word "agreeing" is **VERY** important here, as you would have agreed *before your birth* who your parents would be, siblings, major relationship interests, children, difficult relationships, people who would be in your life to challenge you, people who would be your supports, people who would love you and assist your growth. Every human in your life who has, had, or will have an effect on you negatively or positively will have made an agreement with you to do/be those things, *and you for them*. **In this way, every human on Earth is supposed to be learning how to grow, change, and always be rising their soul vibration**. At this point, you might say, "But there are horrible people doing horrible things all over the place. What possible good could come from any of that?" That is where the secret lies. Every soul who reincarnates has the one true gift of free will. Free will is given to every soul to give each one the complete freedom to learn and move forward from difficulties and joys, or if they so choose, use many, many lifetimes to keep wrestling spiritually, emotionally, and sometimes physically with the same issues, which are often negative in nature. From lifetime to lifetime over different planets and places, a soul has complete control and responsibility for his/her/its own growth. Understand me when I say **complete responsibility**. The Creator has no interest in controlling a soul's growth but is willing to allow every soul as long as it requires to grow and hopefully keep ascending up to higher and higher levels of incarnation. Again, I am in no way making some "judgment" delineation between the levels of souls. There is no better, higher, smarter soul. The simple truth is that the higher frequency you keep your thoughts and emotions while incarnate, the more you forgive, the more you give, the more you support the growth of other souls, the more open your own soul is for abundance on all levels. It is that simple.

So, after you and the other significant souls all agree on exactly what roles you will play in each other's lives, you will each begin to incarnate at the correct times for that to unroll upon Earth. It is truly as if you have all agreed to be in a living movie together to learn lessons. The other important issue to know about this is that once you reincarnate back to Earth, neither you nor anyone else will remember fully what the lessons, roles, and issues you all agreed to work on when you left The Lobby. By this mechanism, you always have the ability to "give your *movie* a better, higher, plotline, and outcome in the end."

When I suggest that you would have all agreed upon what lessons you would work out together, I am speaking of emotional life lessons. For example, Melissa had a mother and father who both suffered from alcohol and drug addiction, as well as undiagnosed bipolar issues. They birthed her into this life at the ages of 18 and 16. They both had broken marriages, broken relationships. They both struggled with health issues, and both died quite young. Melissa's father was 47 when he died and while he had many, many talents and abilities, he struggled with alcoholism and died very early. Melissa's mother was 16 when she was born. She struggled with broken mental health issues, anxiety, fear, alcoholism, undiagnosed mental health issues, and much religious fear. Melissa's mother was also funny, artistic, had a huge ability to show love, and could be totally selfless. I describe them in this way to describe the idea that no soul is born completely "good" or completely "bad," to use language that humans would understand. Every soul born has the seeds of all things/experiences/realities as possible. What each soul decides to do with his/her seeds is totally and *fully up to them*.

Every soul brings with it a full version of all the information and learning from each successive incarnation (lifetime). Very simply put, all the hard lessons which a soul learns from and responds positively to will be brought forward to the next lifetime, thereby adding new tools each time to overcome many obstacles. For example, if you are a soul who has been a substance abuser or really any kind of addiction that imparts negative situations in a lifetime, you will deal with this in as many lifetimes as it takes until you have lived every possible piece of that issue/reality. In one life, you may be the "abuser" in order to let the souls around you (hopefully) learn the lessons of acceptance and letting go in love. You may be teaching them conviction and commitment lessons. You may be in the position to acquire the skills of self-love. It may take you several lifetimes of difficulty before you make different choices in a lifetime. You may be mated with an addict in several lifetimes and then spend a life as the "addict" in order to fully understand what that "feels" like emotionally. In the subsequent lifetime, you may feel that you have fully learned that lesson and "addiction" becomes a lesson learned and no longer is necessary in any future lifetime you decide to engage in.

As each soul has these multiple experiences, the goal is to "literally walk a mile in the shoes of all of the sides of a challenging issue," and hopefully come to terms with forgiveness of self and others and find no need to re-visit the issues at all. It is not uncommon for the soul within a family group who is the "difficult" one to actually be the most highly ascended of the group, who agreed to participate as the "problem" in a lifetime in order to allow the fellow souls to learn from the experience. This soul would have already learned, say, the lesson of "addiction" from all sides and agreed to go in one more time, to literally "be" the addict in order for the fellow family souls to hopefully grow in the situation. The soul always has completely free will to make a change in its own beliefs and reactions at any time, any second, any moment of the day. Along the same vein, often a disabled person/soul would have chosen to come into that life for the sole purpose of being the teaching instrument to the soul family.

You might ask, "Why would any person/soul choose to be born with all kinds of difficult issues? And why would any person choose parents with difficult issues when you could pick really great, easy parents?" Well, therein lays the whole crux of the way The Creator/God set it up. Souls who choose to come in with all the deck stacked against them, in the form of hard life issues, are choosing that to hopefully learn to overcome all of those challenges and learn a new way, a new level of being. To learn NOT to keep repeating the same reactions to the negative circumstances, and instead *choose* to deal with adversity in the most loving, forgiving, and growth-oriented way. Some souls choose over and over to experience pain and suffering lifetime after lifetime and finally learn new ways to react to adversity, which immediately changes the outcome. There are always an infinite number of possibilities floating in the fabric, waiting for the next reaction/decision of the incarnate soul. Each and every time a decision/reaction is made, an outcome is chosen. Free will then makes it possible for a soul, even in the most seemingly dire circumstances, to create and steer the most positive outcome.

Victimhood is one of the most prevalent emotional crutches that humanity is leaning on at this time. Pretending that you are powerless, even in the most challenging situations, is truly an illusion. Pretending that you "came from a hard place," so now you need to have power over others, is also an illusion. Choice is always choice and choosing the path of positive growth is often the most difficult and frightening step for incarnate souls on Earth right now. To respond to a difficult situation with grace, love, and respect, and choose to take other directions can be very frightening. Within this kind of vulnerability is the strongest attribute of all. The ability to let go of difficult situations and move forward in love is very, very powerful for all souls involved in the challenging situation.

Upon your decision to incarnate into a body on Earth, you will have chosen a physical mother and father. Between the approximately 12th and 16th week of the female human body's gestation of the new vessel for your soul, you will enter it. Contrary to the belief of various religious systems on Earth, the new soul enters during this time, and not at the moment of the organic conception. Although the conception is a "miracle" in and of itself as far as The Creator/God is concerned, it is not yet connected with the soul of the possibly incoming child. Within these 12 to 16 weeks, many organic malfunctions can and often do go wrong, as well as the free will element that would be within the mother's soul's path to end the pregnancy. The soul of the new life will often be close by the gestation field of the mother but will not enter until both souls have decided and the organic body of the vessel is complete and accepted by the mother. This is not to infer that the soul awaits a "perfect" body to inhabit, as some souls are choosing disability as a journey/life lesson, and thus the entry of the soul to the new body within the mother is totally about the agreement between those two souls. Very often, the new body does not take hold, or is ended, and the new soul will simply await the next new start with the same mother and father. To explain in more detail, if a mother-to-be miscarries or ends a pregnancy, the soul of the incoming child may wait for the next pregnancy to happen with this chosen mother. This is sometimes part of the pre-lifetime agreement as well. It is possible that the "mother" soul needs to have the experience of loss of the pregnancy as part of her life lessons. As an aside, in Melissa's work with communicating with souls, she has, on occasions, dealt with the circumstance of a miscarriage where the soul waiting to be born to a specific mother and father simply waits for the next pregnancy to commence and then is born with no complications after nine months of Earth's timeline for human organisms. A perfect example of a soul awaiting birth to the specific pair of human parents that was chosen prior to the lifetime.

At the moment that the soul of the new human enters the human embryo, between the 12th and 16th weeks of gestation, all/most of the memory of The Lobby, the past lives, and the "mission" for which the soul has chosen for learning specific lessons is 80 percent forgotten. In past eons, human children have quickly thereafter suppressed all memory and knowledge of the upper realms of The Creator/God, but since the Earth year of approximately 1961, the planet began its traverse upward in frequency, and with it, new souls born onto the planet have slowly been growing in their ability to "remember" or sense The Lobby and The Creation.

This is energetic evolution in its perfect form. With this realization comes much more responsibility of the single soul reincarnating, as well as the responsibility of the whole. With knowledge comes responsibility.

At the point of your birth into a new body, and on the Earth, you will begin the "incarnate schooling again." For souls, which are fully "energetic" in nature and purely parts of The Creator/God, it is unnecessary to have lifetimes in corporal bodies. There are so many reasons for this. Within the realm of creation there is *full knowledge*. Souls have full knowledge of the true nature of The Creator/God, and of every aspect of emotion, time, love, birth, death, and the workings of those attitudes. When a soul is not incarnating to Earth or some other planet/living platform, the soul is residing at home, within the 89th or higher level of creation. Each soul will be directing its own curriculum of learning. After a lifetime incarnate in a vessel/body is completed upon Earth, that soul, upon its body's death, will immediately traverse back to The Lobby. The soul will be met by other souls within its home pod for catching up, assessing the last lifetime lived, and a sort of "self-grading" of the lifetime just exited. The self-grading process is always facilitated with guides, key soul family members, and sometimes guides or souls who would be interested in meeting and evaluating for future lesson plans the soul recently arrived back home. To be very clear, with a soul's return to The Lobby, once again *full knowledge* is attained. To have this *full knowledge* is to truly feel, understand, and be fully able to judge one's OWN actions in the previous lifetime.

When a soul has *full knowledge*, there is no reason at all for The Creator/God to judge or punish. When you as a soul remember and re-embrace your full knowledge in the The Creation, any "sins" that you have engaged upon others, or yourself within the lifetime, will be felt, experienced, and seen in full scope as every individual saw, felt, or experienced your action, word, or deed. Oftentimes, thoughts or intentions will play into this *full knowledge* as well.

For example, if you spent your life as a raging victimizer of those around you, you will upon your arrival back at The Lobby, and at your own insistence, relive all of the ramifications that your actions in that lifetime had on those around you. I do not mean that you will necessarily spend eons of time in a self-imposed hell in the sense of the Christian doctrine, but you will certainly have whatever allotment of space that you need to feel, sense, know what your actions were to those around you in real time. So, if you spent many years belittling your younger brother to your family and those around him, all the while holding nothing but contempt, secret jealousy, and hatred toward him, you will, without questions, spend time when you return from the lifetime feeling every last emotion and sensation that he felt from your actions and negative thoughts. You will also be shown "how" your actions, words, and thoughts changed the trajectory of his life for the negative. You will also be shown how, with your love and encouragement, his life trajectory could have been so much better for him and you.

If you spent your whole life being afraid and not following your dreams and inclinations as your intuition would have had you do, for example, become a teacher of the Spanish language and live in Spain with a large family and circle of friends instead of staying in your town of birth and working at a job which you hate, and quietly allowing a lifetime of excuses to pass you by in misery and self-loathing, you will be shown how that lack of faith in yourself robbed you of a whole possible life of joy.

Again, I want to stress that none of this is about judgment by others. A soul judges itself upon return to The Lobby after every lifetime lived. There are no reproaches or harsh outcomes other than the ones the "you," the returning soul, must examine from your exited lifetime.

This examination process is as long or short as you need to truly have full knowledge of the imprint that you left with your lifetime for other souls around you. Did you do a lot of uplifting, creating, growing, helping, loving, laughing, enjoying, or did you spend a lifetime worrying, being angry, running, avoiding, medicating, hating, taking advantage of, cheating, etc.?

The simple system set up by The Creator/God is one in which lifetime after lifetime the goal is to continue to tip the actions of your lifetimes to the positive side of the influence in each lifetime. Simply put, each lifetime is meant to get you to fully embrace and grasp the DO MORE GOOD THAN HARM each and every time you incarnate. This is not about perfection while incarnating into lives. This is truly about healing, doing better, and understanding that you always have a choice in HOW you react in any lifetime.

Every soul incarnates from whatever level they are on at the time to whatever planet they choose with the one concrete purpose of doing better each time. Doing better has no boundaries, no limitations, and no one path. You can literally be, achieve, create, invent, live any life you choose as long as you are on the path of "doing better" each time your soul chooses to incarnate.

As always, I stress that free will trumps every other rule set out by The Creator/God. So, if a soul chooses, it can continue to live lives in complete stagnation and just never "do better." This situation is very, very rare, however, because the joy that is created by the return of a soul to The Lobby who has done even a "bit better" in the last lifetime feels so intensely joyful to The Creator/God, the soul's family pod, and the soul itself that an exponential rise up in frequency happens automatically. It could be likened to a small child who learns that to touch a flame with the hand is painful and causes a burn and possible worse ramifications. Once that child has learned that from experience, it never needs to be re-visited and is fully incorporated into the full knowledge of the person. No one need ever worry about that child repeating the painful and unnecessary action. It is also true with most souls on the learning track through incarnations.

A soul may revisit certain emotional or physiological challenges through multiple lifetimes to investigate and experience that challenge from many sides, that is, the perpetrator, the victim, the outlying player's guilt, but once all sides have been experienced, those lessons will not need to be repeated. The truly joyful news is that upon your soul's return to The Lobby, you also get to have *full knowledge* of, and relive every moment of happiness, love, triumph, blessing, joy, creativity, and GOOD that you experienced in that lifetime. So, I would implore you, if you do nothing else in this life, enjoy and feel love whenever and wherever you can choose to find it. Bask in love, joy, and gratitude for everything. You have the ability to choose these experiences and spread them around. You will not regret that when you get back for your next meeting in The Lobby.

CHAPTER 24
Companion Animals

When sentient beings "die" on your Earth plain and drop their bodies, they cross (over-upward) vibrational levels, to a level that might be called "Heaven" in many of your religious teachings. Melissa calls it The Lobby. If a human on Earth had animals as companions, those animals will very often be waiting on the next level to meet the human soul when it arrives. Most animals on Earth have a kind of soul, and that "soul" passes to the next level prior to their humans. Often all the companion animals wait in one central area for the human soul they have bonded with to return to The Creation plane.

Particularly, Earth mammals tend to return again and again with the same human souls to Earth. It is also noted that if a human were to have "saved" or "rescued" an animal on the Earth plane during a lifetime, that companion animal will bring other mammal souls to assist that human in the next lifetime endeavor. A human lifetime that is spent in the service of animals will be added to a "list," so to speak, within The Lobby that would mark that soul as one who specifically enjoys working with the soul energy of animals on their journey of growth.

I use the term "mammal" here, as the bulk of human souls will attach themselves to mammals during their lifetime. Other animal beings may also accompany souls, but usually do not reside in the same energy plane as humans upon crossing over due to their level of sentiency. For example, although a fish on Earth is seen as no lesser or greater or of value in the sense of The Creator/God, a goldfish will and does have a very different "sentience" than a "dog, horse, parrot, cat," for example. Again, I stress that the value is not lesser or greater, but The Creator/God allows all species to excel and grow at their own pace as it concerns reincarnation, sentience and understanding. So, a goldfish would have a very difficult time understanding the soul level of a human, compared to a dog, cat, or horse. That is the reason that these particular species, as well as the species that humans farm for food, are of a much higher sentience.

So, in order to understand the connection between human and companion animal souls, it is important to understand the levels at which they reside on the continuous ladder of education and reincarnation of the souls of those humans and companion animals. It is often that a companion animal, such as the domesticated cat, dog, horse, will await the re-arrival of a specific human soul and reincarnate back into that human's life upon re-entry. It is also common for, as an example, a dog to die, drop its body, cross over, and reincarnate into the next animal that the human decides to have. This is only in the case of a newly born individual animal and not an already adult animal. It is more common, however, for the animal to "literally" wait out the human lifetime and meet that soul upon arrival back at The Creation.

The other interesting point to be made here is that as humans are evolving on Earth and preparing for a shift in energy levels in the universe in which you reside, animals on Earth are also shifting up in energy and sentience levels. Currently on your planet, dogs, cats, horses, cows, pigs, goats, sheep, whales, dolphins, birds, and all mammals are also shifting up approximately 7.349 levels of energetic frequency. What this means is that on the Earth plane, all of these species are growing more and more sentient. By using the word "sentient," I mean to say that they are growing in emotional, understanding, language ability, learning, and reasoning as well as actual "feelings" of "visceral knowing," which has always been the arena of humanity and some highly evolved primates on the planet. This being said, it will come to some as a surprise that humans are in the process of stopping all *consumption* of what would be determined to be "sentient species."

The initial hunter/gatherer human is quickly evolving away from animal protein sources. At this time, the only "animal" products that humans should be consuming are the eggs of fowl, fish from waters that are not contaminated, and a very few bird species. Humanity is being prompted by The Creation to move away from consuming "sentient species" as food when it is totally unnecessary to do so. As in all things, free will is always at the forefront of The Creation plan, so humanity may well take some time to make this change. There is no judgment; there is just an actual evolution in place, whereby Earth species will not continue to consume each other for sustenance.

Another change in the energetic blueprint of animals is that their "extra sensory perception" skills which have always been stronger than humans is ramping up very quickly. If you notice that your companion animals are more and more attuned to you and your thoughts, that is because this is exactly what is happening at this time. In approximately 1928 on your Earth plane, all sentient animal beings began to shift up. This shift has taken place in every third generation of all animal species on the planet since then. With this extraordinary energetic evolution, Earth animals have become much more attuned to the changes on the planet and the coming geological Earth changes. Your companion animals are no longer "just for your fun and enjoyment." All animals on the planet are moving in a much more sentient direction in preparation for the Earth-wide changes coming.

It is also worth noting here that there was a time in the ancient human history on this planet when humans knew, that in other planetary systems in the Universe, mammals and other families of "animals" had and have evolved to sentience, which is actually intellectually and spiritually "higher" in frequency than Earth humans. This being said, it is only in this epoch of "forgetting" that this truth is again becoming known to humanity. Slowly, the true history of humanity and its place in the galaxy are coming forth. There are many planets out in our Universe in which species that you would call "animal" are more intellectually and spiritually evolved than on Earth.

The animals on this planet currently in your societal history are in transition and due to that fact, many are traveling from life to life with one human. As a guide, I have witnessed one such animal soul which has been traveling with the human of a fellow guide for over 20 lifetimes in this learning session. Animal souls also have a wonderful innocence from which humans have a lot to learn.

On a more difficult portion of the animal/human soul bond, there is the subject of human souls abusing animals. This is a very, very difficult issue. On the Earth plane currently, and due to the ascension of animal souls in frequency, specific abuse by a human upon an animal has dire repercussions to the soul of that human. Should a human in this epoch determine that animals are less than, or simply a life for to be used and abused, that human will be expected, upon return to The Creation level, to go over this mindset and go through the appropriate karmic training. This is to say, as I have said in other sections of this writing, "You will be made to FEEL and experience whatever you propagated upon that animal soul." There is no avoiding this action. It may well be considered when determining how humans deal with, treat, and care for all animals on the planet.

It should be noted as well that in your time, the mere existence of humanity and its choices are impacting animal life on Earth. When souls pass over to The Creation from this time, their actions towards animals will be taken into consideration as well. More simply stated, each soul born from approximately the Earth year 1867 to the current year will, upon return to The Creation, be asked/shown what their personal impact was upon the animal life on the planet. Although this sounds rather harsh, it is a good way for the whole species to begin to understand in a very one-on-one way what it means to have the responsibility of reincarnation and spiritual education.

There are, after all, planets in close galaxies to your own where humanoids live in complete symbiosis with nature. Many of these colonized planets have upon them species entirely more advanced than Earth's. Considering the learning repercussions, treat all animals as you yourself would be treated. With love and care is what, I assume, would be your answer. Be peaceful in knowing that animals that you have loved and cared for will be waiting for you upon return, if it is their wish. Peace, Aralamb

CHAPTER 25

In Closing

Melissa

This is the day that I dreamt of. This is the day I feared, this is the day I hoped for. Thank you for listening to my stories, thank you for reading. Thank you for sharing this time with Aralamb and myself. My truest and highest hope is that you get some healing and growth from sharing this time with us. The future is what you make it. It really is. Go and be a bright, shiny, amazing soul.

Aralamb

I am pleased and honored to have shared this time and information with you. You and your planet are in the most wonderful throes of growth and enlightenment the likes of which you have never seen. These changes while alarming at times, are also the natural order of the Universe and glorious to be a part of. It has been my greatest experience sharing knowledge with you about your soul and the universe that you reside in. May your dreams and travels hail you well. All my best,

Aralamb

Aralamb's suggested reading list and comments. ☺ In no particular order.

Aralamb

The books and writings that I list below are not given to insinuate that they are the "only" texts upon which you may rely on to grow and evolve as a soul upon Earth in these next 100 years. I simply found that these pieces of writing have, upon weight, at least an 80 percent or higher truth value as well as the techniques needed to learn the lessons within. You may find many other sources for growth that will also be valid, and I would encourage you to seek them out as they speak to your own soul. The list below is simply a group which will help you to understand who and where you are in the Universe as it is evolving today.

Penny Peirce:
Frequency and *Leap of Perception*

Both manuscripts are factual and an outline for the necessary steps required to be in touch with their soul, the "faith tether," although Ms. Peirce does not refer to the faith tether. However, read within the order they were written, these books are a veritable primer for an evolving soul to begin to release the fear of the last eon on Earth and move forward to the next shift.

Gay Hendricks:
The Big Leap

Gay Hendricks outlines very specific steps on how to get outside of the structure that humanity is at this very time, struggling to become free in order to evolve. The lessons on "time" and its reality are especially true and important for human souls to understand.

Masaru Emoto:
The Hidden Messages in Water

Water, like the DMF, is a great conductor and giver of life. Water has its own type of sentience and can be used in all forms of matter creation. Water is sentient unto itself and the intent of all other sentient beings in the Universe. This book should be perceived as a textbook of learning and growth.

Dr. Joe Dispenza:
Breaking the Habit of Being Yourself
Becoming Supernatural

Both works are truth. In the coming hundreds of years on your planet, as the reality of the Universe and The Creator/God become more and more known, this information will make your evolution much smoother.

Chris Putnam & Thomas Horn:
Exo-Vaticana

The geopolitical and religious control sectors of your planet through-out history are well presented in this book and much of it is true within your history.

Jen Sincero:
You Are A Badass

In order to take the next steps toward human evolution, both spiritual and mental, humanity must begin to break free from all the programming of your minds to the system that has been put in place for you. This manuscript gives you many tools and specifics on how to break free from the programming and begin to see and feel your connection to The Creator/God and your power within the energetic Universe. For these reasons, I suggest this book as a text to be read and incorporated into your evolution. This book also made Melissa laugh out loud, and laughter is a very good medicine.

David Morhouse, Ph.D.:
Remote Viewing

Remote viewing is a factual ability that all humans will come to realize. I am in no way promoting any political or religious body around the practice of remote viewing; however, this book is a factual primer for that natural ability and how the governments of your planet have subverted this knowledge.

Timothy Freke & Peter Gandy:
Jesus and the Lost Goddess

Earth's ancient mythological history is pulsing with combinations of what I would refer to as "actual historical events" and "combinations of the same historical events re-packaged for new evolutionary timelines." This book outlines the mechanism of this in great detail.

Melody:
Love Is In the Earth

This is the most comprehensive book on your planet for the time being, which begins to attach energetic, crystalline structure to spiritual soul evolution in a factual and correct nature. For this reason, I believe it will open your soul and mind to the true scientific connections between soul, energy, and science.

Peter Tompkins:
The Secret Life of Plants

I include this short book because it is true. The book is an early account of your planet's scientists fully discovering the sentient nature of energy and plant life. There are trillions of plant-based planets in our Universe, and some of those plants are fully sentient. This book will open your mind to the idea that as we talked of in this book, energy has facets that you are only now beginning to understand.

Michael Newton, Ph.D.
Journey of Souls

I recommend this work due to the fact that within its pages The Creator/ God is touched upon in a very valid way. The experiences recounted by humans remembering their past journeys to The Lobby and its subsequent lessons are valid.

Gary Zukav:
The Seat of The Soul
Soul Stories

Gary Zukav in both manuscripts details and gives real-life experiences of The Lobby. The general workings of the comings and goings of souls are delineated in these books very well.

Karla McLaren:
Your Aura and Your Chakras

The human aura and its connected chakra system are real and within the coming shift you will need to become more aware and educated on this matter. I found this book for Melissa and still find it a very good teaching method.

Marsha Sinetar:
Ordinary People As Monks And Mystics

I include this manuscript as a very important tool since it resonates the divinity within humankind and human potential. In order for humanity to raise itself up to the next level of evolution, humanity must begin to grasp the idea that every human is capable of great soul growth. This book is a solid primer to that end.

The Urantia Foundation:
The Urantia Book

I include *The Urantia Book* in my list of reading because in many parts it does sufficiently give history and structure to the upper levels of the energetic Universe in which Earth resides. I am not, however, endorsing every religious specific in this tomb. The specifics were written and channeled over 50 Earth years ago for the beginning of the shift that is happening now. Because of the changes on Earth and the mental, spiritual, and physical evolutions that are now taking place, some of the details will have evolved as well. *The Urantia Book* is, however, a solid tool by which the general structures of the Universe work. It is to be read as you would read any religious or historically spiritual important text which has come from your planet's history.

Graham Handcock:
Magicians Of The Gods

Graham Handcock in his works begins to uncover the idea that humans in many forms have been upon Earth for much, much longer than it is believed today by your species. Graham Handcock will, in the future, be heralded as a groundbreaking human because what he is unearthing is correct.

Michael Tellenger:
Slave Species of the Gods

In this work, the "general" idea of the seeding of the human species upon Earth is correct. Many of the actual named players in this book have been extrapolated from incomplete knowledge from the ancient artifacts. But the book is generally very factual within its premise on the seeding and making of worker humans.

Barbara Brennen:
Hands of Light

Humans are fully capable of running energy and "light" through their bodies and hands in order to heal, manipulate, and create. This book is truth.

Joshua Leeds:
The Power of Sound

Sound frequency, energy, manifestation, healing, and all other creation within this Universe requires some organized frequency. The premise of this work is true and will help you to more fully understand the nature of sound, frequency, and energy.

melissagatesperry@gmail.com